Mounds In The Mist

BOOKS BY HARRY HARRISON KROLL

Riders in the Night
Bluegrass, Belles, and Bourbon
The Cabin in the Cotton
I Was a Share-Cropper
The Keepers of the House
The Ghosts of Slave Driver's Bend
Rogues' Company (A novel of John A. Murrell)
Perilous Journey (*with C. M. Sublette*)
Three Brothers and Seven Daddies
The Mountainy Singer
Return Not Again (*with Annette Heard*)
Fury in the Earth
Darker Grows the Valley
The Rider on the Bronze Horse
Waters over the Dam
Their Ancient Grudge
The Usurper
Lost Homecoming
The Long Quest
Summer Gold
My Heart's in the Hills
For Chloe—With Love
The Smoldering Fire
The Brazen Dream
No Romance, No Moonlight (Play)
Foxfire (Poetry)

Mounds In The Mist

by Mildred Y. Payne and
Harry Harrison Kroll

South Brunswick and New York: A. S. Barnes and Co.
London: Thomas Yoseloff Ltd

© 1969 by A. S. Barnes and Co., Inc.
Library of Congress Catalogue Card Number: 77-81679

A. S. Barnes and Co., Inc.
Cranbury, New Jersey 08512

Thomas Yoseloff Ltd
108 New Bond Street
London W1Y OQX, England

SBN: 498 06900 1
Printed in the United States of America

to
Jim and Marcie
and
to Chris

Contents

	Foreword	9
1	The Name Is Mt. Pinson	13
2	Wild Lands of the Mound Builders	19
3	The Rutherford Expedition	42
4	Ghosts at Key Corner	51
5	Heap Much Romance at Reelfoot	59
6	Land of Unforgotten Sunshine	74
7	The Unlettered and Unremembered	91
8	City of Cisco	101
9	The William E. Meyer Expedition	111
10	Mounds in the Mist	124
11	The Mounds and I	145
12	The Rise of the Great Central Mound	162
13	Squaw Work Never Done	186
14	Mound Builder Erotica	211
15	"People of the Flints"	226
16	Footprints of the Archaeologists	271
17	The Mystery in the Mists	296
18	Through Mists to Reality	304
	Index	309

Foreword

Basically designed for popular rather than for technical or archaeological reading, MOUNDS IN THE MIST is a study of the Pinson Indian Mound Complex. This area, some six square miles of prehistoric Indian towns and outlying settlements, lies 60 miles south of The University of Tennessee at Martin, 10 miles below Jackson, Tennessee, at the village of Pinson on Highway 45, not far from my birthplace, Selmer, Tennessee, in McNairy County.

Though fascinated with Indian lore and legend during my schooldays at the A. B. Hill Grammar School, Memphis Central High School, and Memphis State University, I little dreamed that years later I would write seriously of Indians. In the spring of 1963 while visiting my son and his wife in Memphis, I was their guest at a dinner party where conversation turned to an exhibit of Indian artifacts at Southwestern, a Presbyterian college in Memphis. My interest in Indian life was rekindled, but upon my return to The University of Tennessee at Martin I became so engrossed with teaching, serving as college yearbook adviser, and the myriad other involvements of a college professor I laid aside my idea of making immediate study of these people and their way of life. Some day I would, but I was too busy now!

Not until 1966 while working with Emeritus Professor of English Harry Harrison Kroll on BLUEGRASS, BELLES and BOURBON, his last published book, did I mention that sometime I would write a book on Indians. He was delighted, for he knew there was a wealth of material here that could be incorporated into a book. And I was doubly delighted when he suggested we collaborate on a study of the Pinson Indian Mounds so near us; he had visited the site often and remembered well his first impression of the mounds. I must, he said, go alone to these mounds, give myself entirely to the "feel" of the experience; then if I felt impelled to work with this subject that had thus far been unexplored, we would begin our book.

MOUNDS IN THE MIST is the fruition of our plan. My regret that he did not live to see the task completed is sincere; my promise to finish the book is fulfilled.

Mildred Y. Payne

Mounds In The Mist

1
The Name Is Mt. Pinson

In the spring of 1820 a land surveyor named Joel Pinson was running land lines through the wilderness a few miles south of what is today Jackson, Tennessee, in a region at that time known as the Western Territory. Pinson had two men helping him, Samuel McCorkle and M. H. Howard, with a pair of stout Negro men to carry provisions and axes and long rifles, and make camp nights, chop wood, tote water, and sing songs in the lonely and pathless wilderness. There was game to be had—deer, wild hogs, maybe a bear if anybody hankered for bear steak; and no end of wild turkey, blackbirds, wild ducks, rabbits, and squirrels. Food was no problem but bears and wolves were, and rattlesnakes and copperheads and water moccasins. Land lines often went right through tangled swamps, where the men waded to their thighs with transit and chains, the axemen cutting through the great mats of legumes known as "wild peas." Their garb to a man included heavy leather hip boots, buckskin britches, heavy homespun or doeskin shirts, and leathern jackets. At night they slept on the ground; the next morning they were up at dawn, ready for a hot breakfast of journeybread and rabbit or turkey broiled over a bed of coals by the "cook," and they were at it again.

They were surveying land grants from North Carolina for such early settlers in that country as John Hargrove, Dick and Duncan McIver, John Bradbury, Seth Waddell, Jim Brown, and Bill Doak. In 1820, immigrants from North Carolina were pushing into the district by scores and hundreds, and Joel Pinson and his crew were busy people.

The wilderness was said to be lonely and trackless. But no region could have been less trackless than the one they were in. There were simply millions of tracks of buffalo and deer and wolves and panthers; and as for being lonely, when these weary men lay down at night to sleep, asking nothing but a measure of honest snores, the wolves crept in close, howling at the edge of the firelight. And anybody who has ever heard a hungry panther scream at night when he catches the human scent can testify that there is scant loneliness here. In fact, the men would have welcomed a stretch of loneliness.

The path they had been tracking for some miles—they were now following the lowlands of the South Fork of the Forked Deer River—was remarkably open for Tennessee wild country. A clearly beaten trail came down rather directly from the north. Though oak and gum and poplar and sycamore timber grew large in the bottoms, the undergrowth had all been grazed out by migrating buffalo and deer. The party noted this and appreciated the ease with which they could survey this immediate locality. They were practical fellows, little given to speculation and not at all to an imaginative explanation of conditions about them, and their only remark was made by Joel Pinson.

"Looks like a right smart travel must have come this way sometime."

"Thought the Injuns had all been chased out of these parts," Sam McCorkle said.

"Even when Rutherford and them was running the lines for old Col. Tom Henderson, back 30 year or more, they said they seen no Redskins," Henry Howard commented. "That was before my time," he added.

It was up in the day, on a humid late April morning, when the men crossed the fork of the river at a point that must long ago have been a ford for wild beasts. The trail was fairly open on both banks, and the men made the crossing on a raft of logs hastily chopped and tied together with willow bark. They started climbing up a bank some 20 feet high and covered with briars and bushes and some willows and a smother of cottonwoods—a "towhead." They came out on top of a ridge about ten feet wide that immediately sloped off on the far side—the east side—to a level region that they thought was second bottom to the river, and now pretty much overgrown with young timber. It showed to their experienced eyes that the land hereabouts had once been Indian old fields—those tracts of land the aboriginal inhabitants kept cleared to grow their maize and peas and pumpkins and squash and tobacco. The fact that there were no huge oaks or poplars or gums in sight indicated that it had not been such a long span of years since the region had been populated.

"Good land, good land," Pinson nodded.

One of the Negro men had been scuffing around on top of the ridge or levee and called, "Boss men, they been a fence here sometime."

They began an investigation of the ridge and soon enough concluded it was man-made, and it had been topped by rude timbered palisades. They found some chestnut stobs in very good preservation. Pushing through the brush in both directions, they established the fact that this Redskin fort was a trifle too large for them to figure it exactly on a hot morning like this, and they looked about for a possible spring.

"I want me a cool drink of water," one of them said.

"One thing sure, if Injuns lived here, they'd picked where water was," Joel surmised. "Let's go down there and see what we can see."

They broke through to the flat field land and a more verdant line of growth indicated a water course. They remarked again on the absence of large timber, though when they came to a gurgling spring branch some old oaks and gums followed it. It was no distance up the stream—they waded in their boots—till they found the gushing spring. Wild creatures scurried away at their approach. High in the hot sky some buzzards circled languidly.

"Boys, this sure is one mess of cold spring water," Pinson said, and kicking back through the cane he lay on his stomach and drank his fill, while sweat poured from his dry body and blackened his shirt. The other men followed and drenched their parched throats. Then the Negroes drank. The men relaxed with backs against trees, and took thought of their surroundings. The spot was ideal for a white man's farm and habitation. Good land-clearing would not be difficult; nice spot for a log cabin; plenty of cold spring water—and the early settlers looked first of all for a spring. Without a water supply there was not much of a home. Pinson consulted his boundaries as stated on the grants he carried in his saddlebags. Looking at the indefinite descriptions, he wondered if this land might be preempted by the first man who could squat on it and establish that primitive claim. A cabin here and a family, a patch of ground cleared and a farm boundary blazed, and presto a man had a fine newland farmstead. There was the prong of the Forked Deer to flatboat or raft out his produce, or fetch in his needments from the growing settlement of Jackson some 12 miles to the north, and no end of game.

"Who'd ask for more?"

He said it aloud and his companions, reading his mind, echoed. "Yah—who'd ask for more? Give me the dirt just south of here."

"Gimme the dirt to the north."

"Well," Joel Pinson stirred, "let's see just what this dirt's like we are fixing to prove."

Actually they were jesting, or at least half joking; all of them had homes and families back in North Carolina, and this surveying raw lands for other men was just a job. They had another swig from the spring. They mopped their faces, Joel using some elder leaves for his mouth, which he said kept his false teeth from making his mouth sore, and they pushed on, following the easy going in a more or less easterly direction. The distance to the Indian mound they came upon then was so short that it was a wonder they did not sight it from the embankment. Save for some tall growth it could have been seen readily; and considering its immensity they could not have missed it for long.

They just stood and stared at the massive dirt pile. Its sides and top were green with April verdure. Joel Pinson shivered with a real prickle of his spine.

"Boys, there's spooks around this place! I just felt a Injun step on my grave!"

" 'Tis sort of boogary, ain't it?" the others agreed.

They shivered together, enjoying the uncanny feeling these monstrous earthworks give rise in men. So for a time, in awe, they stood, barely thinking of the toil, sweat, and tears that went into the raising of an Indian mound of this size. Joel Pinson was six feet tall, and the top of the mound was above his head. They estimated it as at least seven feet high. They climbed the sloping bank to the level top. The growth was thin and they could explore the dimensions of the place. McCorkle said, "Joel, you can build your cabin here at the east end. Sixteen-foot square main house, and kitchen 8 foot by 16, and some dirt out back for a garden. Me, I'll take this other end and put me up a house of the same size, with some ground in back and we'll have a big front yard in common. We'll move the ole women down from No'th Ca'lina and start raising cotton in this wild land and in two-three year be big planters, eh?" His big haw-haw chased away loitering spirits and he clapped the boss surveyor on the back.

"Bub," Joel nodded thoughtfully, "there's room on top

of this mound for two houses and ground like you name. The old women might not like the ghosties and wolves and panthers, though. My woman likes the bright lights of the village."

They went through the humorous business of establishing their claims by cutting ragged sleeves off their shirts and tying them to trees with limber bark. "This'n mine, that'n your'n." But time was burning. The day was deepening and they had work to do. They returned by way of the spring, took on a fresh bait of water, and made their way back across the Forked Deer.

"We'll call that there batch of dirt Mount Pinson," said McCorkle.

"We'll be back," Howard said.

Yet none of them had the least idea they would ever return to the scene. All they did when they sent in their report to the land agency was to describe the ridge, spring, and mound, and Joel added, "It's name is Mount Pinson."

2
Wild Lands of the Mound Builders

One can only wish that Joel Pinson, Sam McCorkle, and Henry Howard had made less a jest of their impulse to explore this locality and prove title to farmlands, and had stayed for a day, or two days, maybe even a week to follow up their first discoveries. In that length of time their astonishment would have been tremendous. They would have come upon, some two miles to the south, the two vast mounds which today are the heart of the Pinson Indian Mound complex, and are easily among the most important artifacts of that mysterious and lost race of men known as Mound Builders; they'd have drunk water from a dozen splendid springs, for the enclosure was well watered by ever-flowing streams; they'd have stood in awe and felt the ghosts crawl up their spines from more than a score of smaller mounds within the defenses, and they'd have established the magnitude of this fortress and the splendid city it must have been among these primitive folk.

Joel Pinson might have done a little better by the place than men who followed him did. For when we first saw the Pinson Mounds we passed over the broad mound he had named after himself, and hardly realized an impressive mound had once been there. A century and a half of cotton planting, with white farmers hungry for dirt to make more cotton, had gradually cut the mound down, leaving the earth round in order to make cultivation easier; thus Mount Pinson was just a modest rise above the rest of the acreage. All of it was in cotton, as far as the eye could reach; and Negroes and mules and one-beast plows were moving rhythmically over lands where once

Mound 6 (Twin Mounds), view to Northeast.

Mound 6 (Twin Mounds), view to East.

Mound 6, View to East.

the Indian had his women dig potatoes and shuck nubbins of corn. At least Pinson would have done as well, and being a sensitive man he probably would have been an improvement over the land-starved farmers that followed shortly on his heels, to discover the large mounds, and suppose, from the talk, that the largest was really Mount Pinson. They bestowed the name on it, and thus preserved the old surveyor's fame. His name, too, survives in a village a couple miles west, which we pass through on Highway 45.

But there is no record that Joel Pinson ever came back to the spot. If he respected Indian lore and history, he never really knew what he had found.

Mostly the practical dirt farmers that moved in to develop the lands wished the pesky Redskins hadn't gone to so much pains to scrape together that good dirt into piles

Mound 6, View to Northeast.

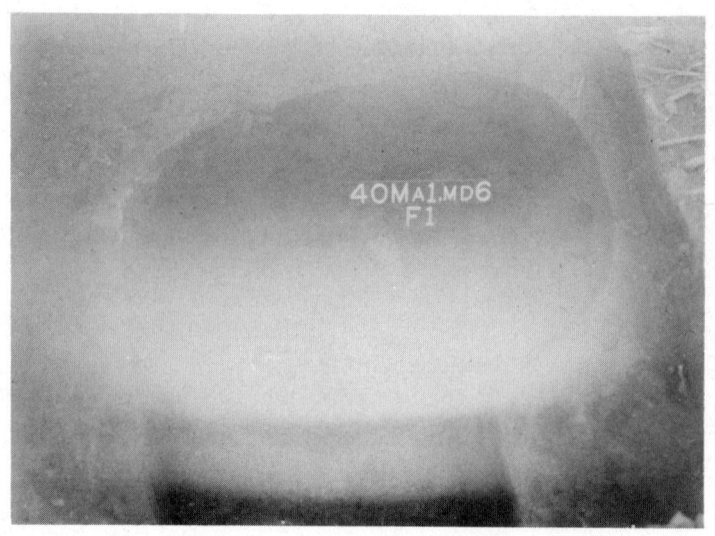

T.P. 3–F 1 (Twin Mounds), view to North.

Wild Lands of the Mound Builders 23

T.P. 2 (Twin Mounds), view to Southeast.

T.P. 1 (Twin Mounds), view to South.

Mound 5, View to South.

too steep to plow and too tall to cut down, and thus cheat them of prime cotton land.

It remained for another man absorbed in Indian lore to come into the region almost a hundred years later to a day to explore the mounds and fortress, to journey all the way around it on the already badly eroded outer breastwork, and maybe to find a few charred fragments of chestnut palisades that once had protected the city. About all he got was the tales of old settlers who had seen less ravages of time, and had heard tales from their fathers and grandfathers of what things had been like. He was W. E. Meyer, a Tennessean whose passion was archaeology,

Mound 12, View to South.

with particular reference to Tennessee where a great many relics of this primitive culture still remain. He led an expedition in 1916, and spent some months in the vicinity. He measured the mounds, searched out all that he could find, charted the outer palisades, and accurately mapped the entire complex. He offered possible explanations of the folk who erected the Mounds and the motives that led them to such enormous activity. He noted the trails that Pinson observed without trying to explain them beyond wild beast migrations; and withal did a job that hasn't been added to since. We'll come to more details on this in a later chapter, but now we drop back to answer a

Mound 9, View to East.

Mound 9, View to East.

Wild Lands of the Mound Builders 27

question that always rises: What was the white man doing here anyhow?

His land-hunger pressures were a long time building up. When at last the bars to the fabulous Western District lands were let down, the flood started, and the work of Joel Pinson and his companions was but a drop in the bucket of land grabbing.

The earliest surveys in the wild region were begun in June, 1785. This was some 35 years before Pinson found the mounds. The Revolutionary War was over. A lot of good North Carolina men—mountain men—had been involved in one of the crucial battles of that war for independence—the Battle of King's Mountain. The "Long

Mound 9, View to South.

Mound 9, View to East.

Hunters" and their Long Rifles had made this decisive victory possible. We remember visiting the battle field and going carefully over the cone-topped low Carolina mountain; and the Park Authorities who have preserved it went to pains to dramatize the fight. The British general, General Ferguson, was a capable warrior and he had under him a stout, seasoned army of British regulars—the professional soldiers mostly used in the war against the colonies. They were armed with the latest English rifles; they were provisioned with a splendid train of wagons and mules and supplies; and their mountain fort was regarded as simply impregnable. King's Mountain was high enough and steep enough to be difficult of assault save from one approach, and this avenue was strongly guarded by Brit-

Mound 9, View to Northeast.

Mound 31, T.P. 1, View to East.

(Ducks Nest—T.P. 1), View to Northeast.

(Ducks Nest—T.P. 1), View to Southeast.

(Ducks Nest—T.P. 1 and Ext.), View to Northeast.

ish cannon of heavy calibre. General Ferguson had taken his headquarters in a special wagon, something like a modern trailer for that day, and he was comfortably domiciled behind cover of a huge granite boulder, with a comely Indian woman to cook for him and serve him. Spies had gone out and he sorted reports and readied for the attack. He did not know when it might come; but he was prepared. We have no record that he doubted victory for his arms.

Nevertheless the Carolina men managed a fair surprise attack at dawn on October 7, 1780. Before good daylight they formed a ring completely around the base of the mountain. They were not strong enough in numbers to withstand a stout counter attack, but as they advanced from tree to tree in the heavily timbered area, they aimed their long rifles at any red coat showing itself, and be-

(Twin Mounds—T.P. 3 & 4), View to Northeast.

Mound 14, T.P. 1, F–10, 11, 12 & 13, View to Northeast.

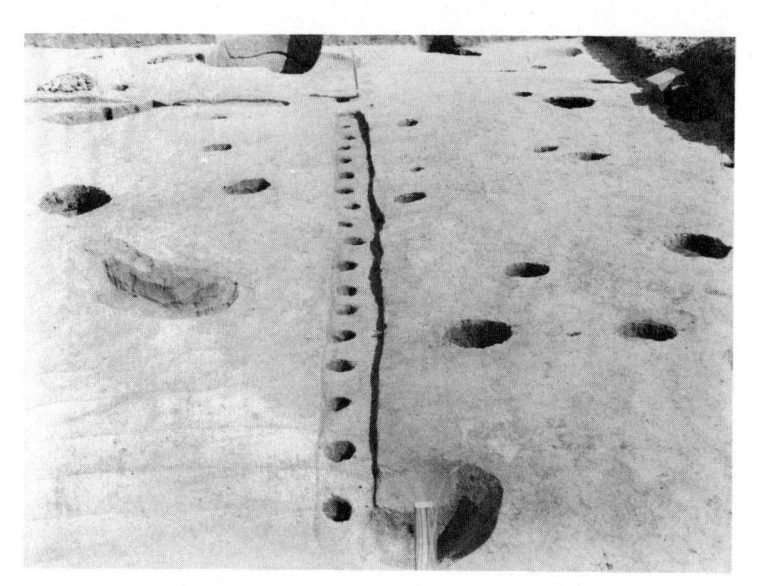

Mound 14, T.P. 1, View to Southeast.

Mound 14, T.P. 1, F 44, 45, 47, View to Northeast.

Mounds in the Mist 34

Mound 14, T.P. 1, View to Northwest.

cause their home-bored guns would carry a slug a mile with force enough to kill a man, while the splendid English rifles would hold up at somewhat more than half of that distance, they picked off Britishers one by one by one, darting from cover to cover Indian fashion, until toward the middle of the day, without suffering too heavy casualties themselves, they had killed almost a thousand of the enemy, including General Ferguson. At last it dawned on the survivors that they faced complete annihilation at the hands of these uncouth frontiersmen unless they negotiated a cease-fire to save their hides; and by late afternoon they had surrendered. The victors got the booty, buried the fallen chieftain on top of the mountain, dispersed the British army, and turned the tide of war in favor of the Colonies.

It may seem a far cry from land surveys in the Western

Wild Lands of the Mound Builders 35

District. Not so. These mountain men had fought on their own, organizing and provisioning their own backland army, and they'd got the fat out of the fire for a parcel of landed men back along the Carolina coast. Now they demanded what today would be called a "bonus." North Carolina had spent herself into bankruptcy carrying on the war.

"We have no money," the authorities told the veterans. "We appreciate your noble services and love you as brothers, but we're dead broke. How can you get blood out of a turnip?"

The mountaineers said, "We'll take the turnip."

"Tell you what," the authorities said, "for compensation we'll give you grants of this fine land we hear tell is in the Western District."

"That's fair enough," the mountaineers agreed. "But we hear tell that country is full of Indians. They'd kill a

Mound 14, T.P. 1, View to Northwest.

man. Who wants to go out there and get himself scalped?"

"Get enough settlers in that country and they will chase the Redskins out."

The mountaineers shrugged. "Somebody's going to get hurt in that deal."

"The ones that hang on will have hundreds and thousands of acres of the finest land the sun ever shone on."

For men who scratched a living out of little mountain farms this thought made their mouths water. They agreed to accept land script in lieu of a bonus. North Carolina then began issuing land grants by the bushel. It didn't matter that the territory was claimed by the French, Spanish, British, English, and such formidable Indian tribes as the Choctaws, Chickasaws, and Cherokees. Carolina got the veterans off its neck. While dumping these fellows in the comfort station they also took on a bunch of free loaders in the form of once well-to-do Carolina

Mound 14, T.P. 1, View to Northwest.

Mound 14, T.P. 1, View to Northeast.

Mound 14. T.P. 1, View to Northeast.

Mound 29, View to Southwest-South.

Mound 29, View to Southwest-South.

Mound 29, T.P. 1–0–4.5', View to East.

Mound 30, T.P. 4, View to North.

Mound 29, T.P. 3, View to South.

landed proprietors and bald-faced speculators who were out to turn a fast dollar. These gentry ranged all the way from honest men to rascals. The word "speculator" itself took on a disreputable meaning when grand rascals like the famous outlaw John A. Murrell denominated himself a "speculator," to cover his horse-thieving, slave-stealing, and murdering.

In 1784 the North Carolina legislature appointed William Tyrell Lewis as surveyor of the Western District. Lewis betook himself to Nashville for headquarters. He knew well enough about the Chickasaw claim to the region, and he also knew these pesky Redskins would fight like red wasps. They'd licked the French who tried to get a foothold in their lands; and they lambasted the Spanish; and they were ready at any time, after helping the British, to scalp any other intruders on their property. Nevertheless Lewis went about the business of organizing his survey parties.

Among his deputies were Colonel James Robertson, of the Cumberland Settlements (in East Tennessee); Henry Rutherford, Edward Harris, a North Carolina master surveyor; and Isaac Roberts, who became a brigadier-general of militia. These men met in Nashville and organized a surveying expedition to map raw lands in the Western District, which became in time West Tennessee. They were going into the wild lands of the Mound Builders, though they had no idea of such a mission.

3
The Rutherford Expedition

In June, 1785, three surveyors and two helpers for chain-bearers got ready in Nashville—Fort Nashboro—to survey lands in the district. Henry Rutherford was head man, a well-to-do gentleman of some book learning and knowledge of land surveying, from North Carolina of course; James Robertson, a stalwart mountain man from the Watanga settlements in what became upper East Tennessee, who had used a long rifle effectively at King's Mountain (he now had it with him for this wilderness junket); he, too, hailed from North Carolina and had been illiterate until he married a wife who taught him to read and write; and another North Carolina semi-gentleman by the name of Edward Harris. Not much seems known about him at this remove, save that he had a personal interest in the enterprise, holding a grant of some thousands of acres of wild land, that might be stones, rocks, snakes, swamps, miasma, or worst of all savage Indians.

Rutherford and Harris were speculators, or in the employ of the larger speculators. Robertson held two claims for land—1000 acres in one grant, 1500 in a second; and it is interesting to note that in time his 2500 acres would be sold for taxes, so little value did he appear to attach to his grant for services. In a way it was unfortunate that the small veteran claims had the least attention; they were deserved awards. But the cannon-fodder warriors were not organized and the influential speculators were; and at least they had resources and energy to push the first surveys.

Of the two helpers one was a Negro man, the other a Cherokee Indian whose mother was pure Cherokee and his father a white "long hunter." His name was Two Horses. He'd come down to Fort Nashboro with Robertson, and was one of the refugees from the Sycamore Shoals treaty where the Cherokee chiefs had ceded the claim to Kentucky and Tennessee to Judge Richard Henderson's huge land-grab syndicate, the Transylvania Company. Through various stages Two Horses became Charley Horse and finally Charlie. He was a stout churl, under 30, and said he spoke several Indian tongues—Chickasaw, among them; and Rutherford and Robertson thought in an emergency they might use him as interpreter. Robertson did not trust him very far, but he was muscular enough to chop paths through western jungle and drag a surveyor's chain. The colored man was general cook and bottle-washer, and useful any place he was put.

In the early part of June a flatboat of logs topped by a shack for shelter against the heavy spring rains that had a habit of drenching everything was launched at the bank of the Cumberland River. Two canoes were attached. The expedition was provisioned for some eight weeks. The preserved foods were the old reliable smoked buffalo rounds, heavily salted hams and bacon, and a bread known as journey-bread. This was a rocklike substance of wheat flour, corn meal, lard cracklings, powdered dried beef, and rancid butter. It would keep for weeks and stick to the ribs. But they also included a barrel of flour and bags of meal, and the makings of fresh biscuits and cornpone. For fresh meat they would depend on wild game—deer and turkey. And they could fish.

All sorts of reports of the abundance of these needments had filtered in to the adventurers. The sky was darkened at times by pigeons. All one had to do was knock them out of the sky with a club. Their wild flavor was beyond compare, save the breast of the turkey, almost as plentiful. As for fish, when they saw a man peering down at them with a husky appetite they'd leap ten feet out of the water into a hunter's frying pan and nestle down for marvelous provender. It is to be remembered this was an era of the tall tale, and the bigger the lie the heartier the howl of laughter. The surveying party took this with a large grain of salt, but the head men were sure they would not perish in the wilderness.

Along with these hunters' fables were disquieting rumors that gave Rutherford and Robertson some sleepless nights. These had to do with Indians. One report had it that the region was claimed by the Chickasaws, who were a fierce and warlike people that would defend their lands to the death. Their success in defeating the French who had tried taking away their country was common knowledge—primitive men against the trained and disciplined French soldiers, and they'd licked the boots off the French and sent them scurrying. They had manhandled some of the English, too. It sounded ominous, if true. But neutralizing this report was another that the Western District, as it was known, was common hunting ground for the tribes to the north, and the Chickasaws and Choctaws to the south. And except for meeting while hunting buffalo, they met hardly at all. By this time the buffalo had been almost exterminated by the rapacious slaughter of French traders, who shot the beasts for pleasure. If they did shoot for food they removed only the tongues. It was something for hungry Indians to remember and the recollection was not going to endear them to some trespassers who came in bearing transits and chains. The bones of the first expedition might whiten in the wilderness, minus the hair.

They frankly doubted if Charlie with his alleged linguistic talents could talk them out of this trap if they got hung in it; but their land hunger drove them on, and they set forth down the river in due time, drifting, poling, paddling in the humid days, as often as not stolidly sitting out the sharp rains that now and then churned the river and threatened to flounder their craft. They came out of the Cumberland into the Ohio and hit the long blue river as June turned into humid summer.

They saw no signs of Indians. But when they came within the vicinity of the junction with the Mississippi, they discerned an Indian village on the right-hand bank, and some sinister characters standing and waving and gesturing and shouting at them in strange jargon.

"We'd better keep going," Rutherford said.

"They friends," said Charlie. "They say come get food. Come rest."

Robertson said, "Ah, that's what they're telling us, eh?" He was dubious.

Charlie was sure they were friendly, and probably had had contact with the English traders who had mostly toted fair with them. It was a chance, but greater chances might be waiting, and they were tired and hungry for vegetables; Rutherford gave the order to steer in and they stepped ashore. They were met by Indians who carried a pipe of peace. They all sat on the ground in a ring and had a puff around, and afterward Charlie translated enough of the conversation to say they wanted to trade; they were friends; and nearby were great mounds of earth, like mountains, where they did homage to the Great Spirit. The women fetched food—meat and vegetables—and the vitamin-starved surveyors gobbled squash, roasted green corn, and green beans. The men noted how comely were the women; and the virgins were often beautiful. In the moonlight afterward the young chiefs led the party through the thickets to the great mountain they had named, and Rutherford and Robertson had their first sight of one of the impressive relics of the prehistoric race of Mound Builders. The Indians denied any part in erecting the mound, and none knew the ancestors who had toted earth and mud to build a hill some 40 feet by 30, and 20 feet tall, flat on top. They only knew that a long time ago—an endless time ago—red men had dwelt here on the bank of the river and toiled to make this monument. Some trees and bushes grew on its summit, but the local folk had kept the spot fairly clear, and when the men climbed the used path to the look-out, they stared in genuine awe at the mysterious forest in the opal moonlight. It would have been pleasant to visit a while, and they were offered squaws; but Rutherford said they must be on their way, and the following morning the outfit resumed the voyage, after sharing drafts of whisky with the chiefs as a token of their good will.

About all the information of any value they secured was the name of the river up which they expected to start the surveys—"Okeena." They could not spell it. Nobody knew whether there were Indians on the Okeena or no. Maybe so, maybe no. "Very enlightening," Robertson muttered.

On a hot June morning shortly after sunrise they shoved off into the Ohio and drifted southward. A few miles below they entered the Mississippi River, which swept in from a northwesterly direction. The two rivers now were wide and deep and murky, the pretty blue of the Ohio losing its sweetness with the silty current of the Mississippi. The weather was very hot. Spring floods had subsided but the timber along the banks still wore skirts of caked mud. There was everywhere a vague fishy smell, mostly from the back waters that had been trapped in the sloughs on the east shores. There were still no Indian signs save a cliff—bald and yellow—which rose against the morning sun some one hundred feet above the waterline, where evidently there had been a long time village. There may also have been extensive burial grounds here, high above floods. The Indians liked high dry ground for their dead. Some fragments suspiciously like stakes and poles of habitations, with rags of what appeared to be decayed leather, indicated Indian houses, or shelters.

They were not wigwams, after the manner of northern tribes. If a village, it now was deserted.

"Us stay a spell," Charlie suggested. He was becoming interested in his remoter kin folks.

Rutherford shook his head. "Charlie, you've got squaws on your mind. We've got land on ours."

"Some squaws nice to have around," Charlie said.

The cook said, "They put poison in your bread, they will."

"That's because you got black hide," Charlie said.

"You all tend those oars and shut up," Rutherford ordered.

Rutherford now kept a close watch for Indian signs as the day increased and the distance to their destination decreased. Probably for the first time he began to develop more than just a passing interest in the savages. At Mounds he had found them a hospitable and friendly people. Their folkways, such as he had taken time to observe, fascinated him. He was a close observer—frontiersmen necessarily must be if they would survive in a primitive and hostile land—and he'd seen more than he had been quite aware of. For one thing, that food amazed him. The great dish was succotash, made mostly of corn and beans, and flavored with herbs and peppers, with a large fish in the center of the pot—an iron pot. At the time Rutherford was so hungry for this food that he paid no attention to the cooking utensil; but now it occurred to him no Indian had ever made an iron pot himself; these people had got the pot from traders. Lazing in the shadow of the tent flap in the drifting boat, he turned the thought in his mind. "Interesting," he half murmured. But it was remembrance of the savory food that lingered in his mind. Maybe squaws were nice to have around, but you also needed beans, corn, squash and herbs.

The river rolled along at about four miles an hour. Toward late afternoon they passed the mouth of a small river flowing in from the east.

"That," Harris said, consulting his crude map, "must be the Obion."

"Obion, Obion," Rutherford muttered, "Injun name, I reckon."

Charlie said, "Means River of Many Forks."

"Yes? Where'd you pick that up?"

"Squaws," the Negro sneered. They all laughed and Rutherford said practically, "We want the Okeena. What did that mean, Charlie—did the squaws tell you that?" Insulted, Charlie shrugged. They did not tie up for supper, but ate journeybread and the last of the food supplied by the Mounds Indians. The moon came up big and yellow above the dense forests on the eastern river banks, and they determined to navigate until they reached the mouth of the Okeena, which could not be too far below the mouth of the Obion. Toward midnight they sighted such an opening in the timber and steered in, reasonably sure this was the end of their journey. They tied the flatboat to trees at a low bank and got ready to make camp, if a reconnaissance of the locality should reassure them of its safety.

The region under the trees was fairly open, though the oaks and gums and cypress trees were very large. They found buffalo chips.

"Beasties have been here clearing the land," Harris said.

Guns at ready, they scouted the surroundings, finding nothing but millions of mosquitoes. Bad as these pesky insects were, it was better than Redskins. They returned to the landing and got ready to make camp. The cook said the mosquitoes were "gallon-nippers." "Get a gallon of blood every time they bite you." They bit with the viciousness of wasps. Rutherford growled, "If you swung a bucket over your head twice you'd catch it full!" Everybody was soon scratching madly. "My heavens, who can sleep like this? We'll be bloodless as turnips by morning!"

The Negro and Indian demonstrated their primitive skills by building smudge smokes on the windward side of the camp, and though the smoke choked the men, it was far better than being devoured blood-raw by insects.

The night itself was beautiful. If they had not been apprehensive in spite of finding no enemy, they would have luxuriated in the soft air moving in from the river, and the moonlight that gave added mystery to the strange night sounds on every hand: insects, noctural birds drawn by the campfire, maybe creatures such as polecats, opossums, raccoons, and deeper in the forest perhaps a panther or wild cat or even wolf—the midnight life of this deep wilderness. Maybe when one got used to it the beauty and the mystery would creep in to give him pleasure. Mostly now the men lay on the ground in their blankets and hardly slept. When the wind veered, the mosquitoes zoomed in by the thousands. If they wrapped in blankets to defeat those needle-like bills, they almost smothered. Once Rutherford muttered in his mind—not aloud—"If it's going to be like this all summer, I'd as soon have stayed back in civilization. No land as full of bugs and brutes as this is worth surveying, let alone own." Morning found them swollen of flesh, bruised of bone, and bleary-eyed from lack of sleep.

Then the buffalo gnats hit them.

"Buffalo gnats!" Rutherford groaned, swatting and waving. "What are they?"

James Robertson said, "They come with the buffalo each spring."

"Don't they leave with the buffalo?"

"They stay."

Harris at last cried, "Boys, I'm fed to the gills this time. Let's roll up our little ball of knitting and get out of this while the getting's good!"

The Negro walled his eyes. "Buffalo gnats cause swamp fever. Mosquitoes make malaria. Then there's water moccasins and rattlesnakes and copperheads . . ."

"And panthers and wolves and bears," put in Charlie with a dirty grin. "My ancestors the Cherokee ate snakes, made pie out of mosquitoes and gnats, and we'd rassle wildcats and bears single handed." He flexed his muscles. "The wilderness and I are brothers."

"Boy, you've had some bad kin folks," Rutherford remarked dryly. There was no further word of turning back.

The cook made up a camp fire for cooking breakfast, and with a brisk breeze blowing in off the river the mosquitoes were somewhat dispersed. They were too fragile to stand up under wind, and the party was to find that after a stormy, windy season the insect population was apt to be decimated until a fresh generation emerged. After breakfast and hot black coffee stout enough, James Robertson said, "to float an iron wedge," the men began to feel as if they could face the day with fortitude. A look about camp convinced Rutherford this was no spot to start the surveys, however. While they were discussing this business, a buck came through the woods to drink at the river. James Robertson was a fast man with a long rifle. He up with his gun and shot the beast before it caught the men's scent. A fine fat animal he was, too. This was going to spell a supply of fresh venison for as long as the meat could be kept from spoiling. They would save their preserved rations and feast on venison till they devoured it or spoilage set in. This would not be long in the humid almost suffocating bottoms.

The deer had strangely shaped horns. They followed no pattern the hunters were familiar with. Deer antlers are a complicated system of prongs and forks. But the horns of this buck forked into a peculiar twist, so odd as to engage their profound interest. But Rutherford, glancing from the head to the murky river flowing through the jungle, had an idea.

"We'll name the river Forked Deer."

4
Ghosts at Key Corner

Two Horses skinned the buck, using a primitive man's secret skill with a hunting knife. With the Negro helping, they quartered the carcass, sliced steaks for immediate broiling, and wrapped the rest of the meat in mats of green leaves, heavy with mint that they discovered along a nearby spring course. In addition to gnats and mosquitoes they had green flies by the myriads to contend with. They built smudge smokes and worked in choking clouds. The job taught them a secret. The crushed mint on hands and face served as a repellent for the mosquitoes. The pesky critters were not wholly dispersed but their bites were far fewer.

The Indian took the hide, scraped it carefully, washed it in the muddy river, and lacking salt to preserve it, he dug with his hands a blue clay from the river bank and smeared it over the blood-side of the skin.

"Help keep it fresh," he said.

Rutherford watched all this with mingled interest and impatience. That red man had a cunning he'd never known he had, or needed. But he wanted to get up the river. When the hide was thrown in a bundle on the flatboat and the venison carefully packed in the large provision box where the other foods were locked, they ate breakfast, the meat being none too well cooked over the smoky fire, and Rutherford gave the order to break camp.

"Boys, let's ride from these parts."

They started up the river, poling, paddling, warping where pole or paddle was not adequate. But the Forked Deer was fairly full; there had been rains high up at the head waters, and navigation was easy enough for stout men. Mostly the banks were low, alternately open and sunny and densely wooded and smothered with a vine they called "wild peas." This was a coarse legume that climbed dead snags, draping them in grotesque raiment, or crawling over the ground in tangled carpets of dark leaves and vines; and now and then hanging from over-bending trees to catch their heads. The channel was open for the most part though now and then a fallen tree across the stream would prevent their progress until Two Horses and the Negro had chopped limbs away. By noon they sighted a nice spot and tied up long enough to devour more half-cooked, half-smoked venison. It took stout teeth to masticate this rugged food, and iron stomachs to dissolve the sinews. They muttered, "Good! Good!"

All through the morning hours Rutherford had kept alert eyes for Indians. At the noon rest Two Horses scouted the surrounding forest.

"Not a sign," he reported. "No footprints. No paths. Don't smell a Injun." He twitted his nose. "Smell Injun a mile."

"How they smell?" James Robertson grinned.

Two Horses did not crack a smile. "You smelled 'em."

James explained to Rutherford, "Indians do have a peculiar body odor. Some is plain Redskin. Some plain filth. Some the paint they use. All of it is one heck of a stink."

"Let's get going before we start smelling 'em," Rutherford said, and they were back in the middle of the river, beating the sluggish current.

As long as they kept moving, and rubbed themselves with the supply of mint they had laid in, they dodged insects pretty well. Now and then there would be a big hungry horse fly they would have to swat, and worse than the horse flies a small yellow fly that hit and bit before they knew he was there, and raised a red and painful swelling. They could see the fish in the river, swimming subsurface, and Rutherford knew the fish stories were not all fiction. They'd have fish and flesh in plenty till the buck spoiled. It was about four in the afternoon when the bank on the south side began to rise above the bottoms level, and while the sun still stood high they came to what looked like a bald bluff of some height above the water. There must have been an acre of open ground on top, and the single tree was an immense beech that cast a shadow down the side of the bluff and on to the quiet water.

They slowed. It looked like the spot Rutherford was hunting for. Two Horses said, "Injun town—maybe." As they stopped poling, Rutherford reached for his gun and nodded to the other men to grab their arms. He peered. There were no habitations, no signs of life. With guns at ready they cautiously edged in against the bank at an easy angle for climbing, and while two of the men kept the craft ready to take off in case of hostile people, Rutherford, James, and the Indian climbed the rise and came out on top of the bluff. If there had ever been an Indian settlement here they discovered no relics of it. The land was fairly sloping away from the river, and an acre or two was a generous estimate of the area. The vegetation was scraggly undergrowth that had been chewed off by roving buffalo early in the spring and now was leafed out but not at all dense, and weeds that grew fast and tall. The white men knew enough about early peoples to realize this was what they knew as "Indian old fields." They were everywhere in the wilderness—great prairies in Kentucky, which the roving Indians burnt over each fall to kill off the unwelcome insects and growth for spring buffalo grazing when the buffalo grass sprang up and the herds migrated; and at Fort Nashboro they were familiar with some beautiful fields that the white settlers immediately broke to the plow and planted in corn. And now and then angry Indians would steal in and kill a farmer between the plow-handles. This, then, they surmised, was some such spot in the deep wilderness.

They scouted a wide circle, investigated the shadows of the encroaching forests, and Two Horses used his craft for signs.

"Nothing here for ages," he reported.

"It's the very place," Rutherford said.

They returned to the tree, and Rutherford stood staring at the beautiful giant, already more than a hundred years old. Standing alone, it was like a monument or sentinel. Hands in his hip pockets palms flat, he lost himself in admiration.

"Men, that's beautiful." They stood silent. "If I ever come out in these wilds to live, I'm going to take in 10,000 acres of this rich land, build a fine mansion right here," he nodded about, "get me a hundred slaves and raise cotton and tobacco and roll in wealth. I'll read in Latin and run for governor and ride blooded horses and when you poor boys meet me in the big road you'll stand to one side and take off your hats." His big laugh filled the clearing.

"Well, holler at 'em to tie up and fetch the camp gear."

They fixed camp, building smudge smokes; they located a spring and brought water for cooking, and fresh mint against the mosquitoes. In the humid afternoon the men had sweated a pasty perspiration, and to keep their armpits and groins from scalding they crammed alder leaves in the vulnerable areas.

Rutherford himself brought the surveying instruments from the lock-box on the scow. He thrust the Jacob's Staff into the silty ground, and set the heavy brass compass on top of the monopod, fastening it with the set-screw. It was the typical instrument of the time, and George Washington in his surveys had made use of the same kind. The magnetic needle picked out the north, and the men established the cardinal points. This would be their point of origin of all the surveys in the Western Territory. Without a knowledge, maybe even much of a suspicion, of the vastness of this territory, they could suppose that the beech tree might well be the center of the universe. Rutherford had a large brass key, in form of a jackknife, which served the lock of the provision box. He opened this key and went to the tree, drawing a pattern of the key with the tip of his hunting knife in the smooth bark. Then he cut the picture of the key deeply into beech bark, where it would be enduring. He'd always heard that no matter how old a beech tree grew, the carvings of lovers' hearts and initials did not grow higher than when originally cut. They would remain there for years, for a century, and always at almost the original level. Under the key device he carved the words: KEY CORNER.

Black Ned, the cook, built up a big campfire, brought the iron pot from the boat, the haunches of venison, and soon had the pot boiling. He cut steaks to broil for supper. This while Two Horses got his buckskin unrolled and washed, and fetching it up to camp squatted on the ground and began kneading the rawhide and working dry sandy topsoil into it. Once he said, "Fine pair buckskin britches, eh?" As long as daylight lasted Rutherford and James Robertson drew a fairly crude map of the country and the Forked Deer River as they so far had explored. Nightfall brought swarms of mosquitoes. There was the business and discomfort of smudge fires. A late moon was rising when supper at last was ready. The men ate hungrily, but Rutherford partook frugally of the deer meat, for he had found that it soured on his stomach. The wilderness was no place for indigestion, or any other ailment, though he expected there would be fevers before the summer's work was done. After food he gave the word for the men to roll in their blankets.

"You'll need your rest. Me too."

He posted guards. The cook was to stand guard the first part of the night; the Indian the second part. Harris said he would try to watch both ends of the night, as he was a light sleeper. Two Horses did not immediately turn in, Rutherford noticed: the red man continued kneading his rawhide, digging soil with his hunting knife. Now and then the blade struck something stony and Two Horses then would wipe off the soil and examine what he had discovered in his shallow excavations. He seemed more intent on this than on sleeping, and in the firelight his coppery face was set and strange. The fellow simply was odd. Rutherford still distrusted him, though why he could not have said. It just was that Two Horses was *strange*. Indians were peculiar enough to the white man who tried at all to understand them; Rutherford did not know the race very well at best. But James had told him in some detail Two Horses's background: the attractive Cherokee mother, the Long Hunter who had drifted into the tribe and married her after the easy ritual of the savages, and later had gone crazy as a loon and either killed himself or the tribe had killed him lest he butcher them. This mixture of blood and feeble wit seemed to make a startling pot of hash in this fellow who patiently kneaded, dug some more, pored over his discoveries, and once or twice, instead of sleeping as ordered, had gone down to the river and washed whatever artifacts he had excavated. Rutherford slept fitfully, that venison doing him wrong, and Harris snored like a buzz saw in a knotty log when he was the man who was to check on the guards. What was worse, the cook went to sleep with the pot of venison bubbling. At hand were the mysterious night sounds, and the rise and fall of the winds in the big timber, and the mosquitoes.

Then, maybe near midnight, Rutherford saw this queer doing of his scout. The moon was very bright. The air at the moment was very still. Two Horses stood erect with the moonlight full upon him, a muscular if not noble figure. If he were doing anything reasonable, he was praying. He had beads made of rawhide and those things he had dug up, and he held his hand over his heart and closed his eyes and seemed to be muttering a silent incantation. Rutherford knew enough about his Redskins to know they were really a very religious people; God to them, so far as he could discover, was Spirit; they had rites and rituals to ward off the Evil Spirits, Demons, and other bothersome creatures—a fair enough imitation of the white man's Satan, except he was kind of watered down with many small Satans; and here was a fellow Rutherford would never have thought of as subscribing to any of this superstition standing as if he were in the Presence of Something. It gave Rutherford a shock.

For a long time—moments on end—Two Horses stood so, in prayer and worship, and Rutherford had not the heart to speak and let his guide know he had been observed in whatever holy action he was engaged in. All at once Two Horses seemed seized by a Demon. He uttered a groan and collapsed on the ground. And the camp came awake to a man with a yell, everybody reaching for his gun. Two Horses got up and stared around him as if to ask, "What's bit you fellows?" He seemed totally unaware of what he had done.

The camp settled back again finally—it was now well past midnight and Two Horses's trick—and Rutherford resumed his fitful sleep. As in a dream he heard Two Horses telling the Negro what had struck him.

"I saw the spirits of all my people."

Black Ned's eyes got white in the firelight. "Spirits—you mean ghosties?"

"Ghosties," the Indian said solemnly. He waved, "Like the leaves of the trees!"

"Jesus save us!" the black man stifled his moan. "This place ha'nted?"

"They're all around us."

"Spooks? You see 'em?"

"Millions of 'em. They been here since the beginning of time."

The cook rose to shaky feet. "I ain't gwine sleep on this ground! I'm gwine sleep down there on the boat." He gathered his blanket, and the pot of venison that now had boiled low, and staggered away into the gloom, disappearing down the bank toward the flatboat.

Rutherford's thought was that this was too much. Men can live without wine and men can live without books, but one thing sure, men could not live without cooks; and here this Injun was scaring the daylight out of his black cook with these mad tales of ghosts, spooks, and haunts. If this kept up, the surveying expedition was doomed from the beginning.

5
Heap Much Romance at Reelfoot

Yet in the morning Rutherford felt somewhat better, for he had slept in spite of his aching bones; and then he saw the string of arrowheads Two Horses had dug up during the night. There were small, long, keen heads, probably used for spearing fish when attached to a cane. Two Horses demonstrated by cutting a four-foot cane and attaching one of the heads to it with thongs of his rawhide, and going down to the river and spearing a catfish, which Ned broiled for Rutherford's breakfast. It was a boon, for the man could digest fish. It promised food when their store-bought provisions began to run low. It did not quite explain Two Horses's trance last night, and Rutherford spoke of this to Robertson.

"He's crazy," James laughed.

"Didn't the Indians have to kill his daddy when he went crazy?"

"So they say."

"Well . . ."

"We'll knock him in the head if he goes crazy and tries to kill us."

"Yas—and what if we're dead? Besides, I'm not sure that fellow saw just ghosts. He might just have seen some live Injuns. You know what I think about Redskins generally—the only good Injun is a dead Injun."

"Didn't you think he was praying?"

"A Redskin with a prayer on his lips is the most dangerous of all. You'd better look to your hair." They laughed, though it wasn't 'specially funny; and Rutherford had James and Harris both scout for Indian signs. Ned was willing enough to do his work by daylight, but he insisted he wasn't going to sleep in the camp. The spot was far too good, however, for such permanent jump-off as they could find to abandon it because of a Negro's superstition.

It must have been at this time that Rutherford—and perhaps Robertson and Harris—found themselves impressed with lost memories of a previous civilization and culture that had existed in the wilderness. They had a certain knowledge of Mound Builders. There was the Indian settlement up the river at the big mound—The Mound. They had a vague general imaginative notion of these strange previous folk from trappers, hunters, adventurers and missionaries who had returned with tales. But such people seemed more remote than the ancient Egyptians. Rutherford and his companions were not easily intrigued by the long past and forgotten races. Their interest was in land. Their job was to survey the fabulous Western Territory. They'd fought in the Revolutionary War and were men of action; they were outdoorsmen, frontiersmen. Yet Rutherford was an educated man as well; and in that day and age learning implied more than just land, chattels, corn, cotton, and slaves: it meant also some knowledge of the arts—architecture was one such art; as were the languages, the skills of war, the techniques of land bounding. George Washington was a master surveyor; Thomas Jefferson was an architect. John Donelson, an ordinary Virginia farmer-gentleman, enjoyed translating the Greek and Hebrew scriptures by hanging his Bible between the plow handles. That Rutherford was destitute of these appreciations cannot be established by the meager references to him as a man of culture.

Yet he was steeped in the prevailing notion that the only good Indian was a dead Indian; and he was in the heartland of the Chickasaw Indians who were reputed to be fierce warriors in the defense of their lands; and there was his distrust of Two Horses that had hounded him. There was his lack of confidence in Richard Henderson's treaty with the Cherokee chiefs—mainly Little Carpenter—at Sycamore Shoals on the Wautauga. Yet here at Key Corner there seemed *ghosts* of a population that in the dim misty long ago had been people: men and women falling in love; women bearing children; men tilling the fields, hunting, fishing, slaughtering one another; and even to this good day they still haunted the land they had once used.

Rutherford did not understand the primitive mind—the Indian's, the Negro's—that seemed to communicate with this lost, timeless, strange past. But he was stirred if not fired in his imagination. He gave Two Horses his hand in digging arrowheads. The white men dug a bit for themselves. Rutherford excavated quite a collection of beautiful artifacts to carry back to show his folks in North Carolina. But wonder grew in him how the earliest Indians had fashioned these flint weapons. Some were long and chisel-like; others were blunt but knife-edged as well. An unanswered question was where the flint came from. Certainly not in this wild land, which was stoneless and alluvial, and had never known flint—so far as he could tell. To be sure, the Cherokee back in East Tennessee used flint arrowheads and it was said they had secret flint mines. Rutherford had heard some such mine was miles out from Fort Nashboro. He'd heard the report absently and it had hardly registered. Certainly the Moundsmen would have had to journey a long distance in either case, and they must have been tradesmen of parts to have got supplies of the gray-blue stone that would chip artfully and hold sharp edges. But how had the Indians fashioned the heads?

He talked of this to Two Horses as they washed the flints and strung them. Two Horses made a comprehending gesture.

"Great Spirit. God."

The Indian used *God* in the sanctimonious tone of the

Baptist and Methodist preachers that were following hard upon the heels of the land-grabbing white men. That it carried any real understanding of the Christian Deity was not apparent in the Indian's manner. Rutherford pressed him for more explanation—"How do you mean, God?"—but Two Horses shrugged. But when Rutherford sought his answer in the arrowheads, in their strange and artful beauty, and marvelous utility, he had a kind of answer for himself. It was the Indian's finest skill and art, which one might call God; and the heads had something that man has always chiseled into his stones, composed into his music, written into his books. He let it pass and God was a good enough answer.

With time pressing, Rutherford's party pushed their surveys eastward with no loss of time to see if an Indian had more "spells" and the Negro hid again from "ghosties." They used Key Corner as camp so long as it was possible to return at night. But the wild legumes grew more dense, and the men had literally to hew their way through the tangled vegetation. Such a wide trail was left that Rutherford was afraid it would betray them to any hostile Indians lurking in the forests. Lest they be set upon in their sleep and butchered, they did not make camp near the lines of survey, but usually sought a likely spot a half mile away. Buffalo gnats and mosquitoes tortured their nights and days. Each day two men worked the raft upstream, tying to trees at night. Their food supply was dwindling. But Two Horses was an expert fisherman—indeed he preferred fishing to trail cutting and chain dragging any time; all manner of game—turkey, rabbit, squirrel, turtle, quail, now and then a deer—was abundant; and soon broiled meat supplemented their dried, salted and preserved rations. The work was hard; they ate ravenously; but they grew lean in their bellies; and their muscles became as tough as rawhide. Strangely enough they remained free of illness. Fevers were plentiful, but the vigorous life seemed to ward them off. Nobody had any idea in that time that malaria, the fever transmitted by a mosquito, must be carried from man to man; and since nobody had malaria germs in him, no mosquito could impregnate another. They grew brown and rugged and happy.

Yet there was always the haunting fear of Indians, and anxiety drew networks of lines about their eyes—the taut expression of men who lived on their guard. Day after day the surveying went on, through buffalo-chewed undergrowth, through swamp and bog, across creeks, backwaters after the heavy summer rains. Storms were often savage, and once they survived a cyclone. What gave them a worse stitch was an *ignis fatuus* sighted one eerie night in a dense bog, rising like a pair of huge eyes and drifting and staring at them. The Negro was frightened into a gibberish of prayer, and he flung himself on the ground moaning and covering his face. Two Horses stood with folded arms merely staring at the phenomenon.

"Great Spirit," he said, when Rutherford suggested it was his ancestors.

Rutherford's party penetrated the jungle to the east till the rivers grew into forks and creeks, and at a point on the Forked Deer which in later times became the landing for flatboats and keelboats and even small steamboats at Jackson, Tennessee, halted to catch their breath, patch their britches, and rest a spell after surveying what probably was not far from a million acres of wilderness. They had seen no more Indian mounds and had sighted not a single Indian. Rutherford made a reasonable map of the Forked Deer basin, which later would be used by early mapmakers to map the bulk of West Tennessee. Curiously enough they were practically sitting on the craters of the great Pinson Indian Mounds, and scores of smaller mounds in the general vicinity. They were indeed in the heartland of the Mound Builders.

Probably it would not have mattered too much at that time. What they had seen and partially measured was a wild and haunted country whose fabulous fertility, when later they reported back in North Carolina, fired men of rib-wracking hunger for good earth to mate their plow shares with. There would be a great stir, like tossing a rabbit carcass into a yellow jacket's nest. The cry would go up, "Lead us to this land!" There was just one small hitch. The Chickasaws claimed the last beauty spot of it, and already Rutherford had lived in fear of even being caught as trespassers. Six weeks of that kind of torture had reduced him to sober respect for what he was doing.

Yet if any of these men felt qualms about "robbing the red man" of his ancestral lands, they did not record it. What they had seen was endless thousands of acres of virgin forest and dirt of boundless fertility. The bottomlands they had measured had plowshare depth as far as they could dig; and the hills' subsoil was reached anywhere from 8 to 12 inches. Compared with the old lands in North Carolina and Virginia where often the top soil had washed and leached completely away, leaving only hard infertile clay or sand, they were left gasping for adjectives. Any small scruples against grabbing had little chance in their Christian folkways. Rutherford shared in the prevailing feeling. The Indians had had thousands of years to make something of their inheritance. Here came the rush and moil and greed of the western white man to snatch all this God-given wealth from bears and wolves and panthers and the less distasteful deer, elk and buffalo, to erect homes, rip out great fields of corn, cotton and tobacco, maybe with slaves and maybe without, and to wax fat and influential. What was the parable of the talents all about, anyhow?

Yet far-off thin voices of dissent were either being raised, or soon would be when the avalanche of settlers moved westward. William Tatum was one of the earliest to raise objections. He protested against land speculators nearly a thousand miles from the scene encroaching upon the province of the Chickasaw Indians "who had so gloriously boasted their friendship for the white people, and who instead of deserving the ingratitude we have shown by trespassing their rights and taking their lands away without their consent, without cause or provocation, have ever shown us an example worthy of our imitation; and a specimen of magnanimity far above our reach." Later when a formal treaty was made with the Chickasaws, known as the Jackson-Shelby Treaty, it fell into the slot of "heart-breaking treaties." James Malone was of the opinion that the treaty of 1818 was understood by the chiefs and head men; but blank paper to the ordinary Indian. There was the tale that the Indians did not understand the meaning of interest. He got hold of a hen, and found somewhere 100 eggs. Then he added six eggs, to illustrate his financial wizardry. The Redskins could see and count the extra eggs, which would be part of their eventual egg crop.

This was, of course, years after the Rutherford party finished surveying the eastern boundaries of the usurped wilderness. They had come into the region in June and this was toward the latter part of July. They loaded their freights and poled and drifted down the Forked Deer to Key Corner. The summer days were hot and humid. Nights were breathless, though, thank heaven, the buffalo gnats had finished their cycle, though mosquitoes put in full 24-hour shifts. The men were tired and lazy. Rutherford saw no more trances on Two Horses's part, and the Negro saw no more ghosts. They'd long ago talked out all the items of conversation and mostly the down-river trip was silent. They rested a few days at Key Corner, allowing time for Rutherford to make corrections in his maps, and to plan his surveys into the north regions, along the Obion River, and up a small river known as Reelfoot.

It was an Indian name of uncertain meaning; any similarity to English sound was mere coincidence. A small tribe of Indians was known to reside in the locality, where the bluffs came down to land a quarter of a mile or so to the bank of the stream. Some of this knowledge Rutherford had from the Mound Indians; some was Two Horses's interpretation of folk tales he'd heard there. At the northern tip of land claims were those of two speculators known afterward as the Caldwell & Doherty surveys for some 40,000 acres in what, a quarter of a century later, became the jumbled, tangled basin of the New Madrid earthquake.

Nothing was to be gained by loitering, and urged on by restlessness the party boated out of the Forked Deer and up the Mississippi to the mouth of the Obion. They still saw no Indian signs. They ran surveys in what later became Dyer, Lake, Obion and Gibson counties. They had less rugged country to measure and in less than a month had pushed the boat up the desolate little stream called Reelfoot. By now they had ceased exclaiming at the beauty and fertility of the land. For miles east of the Mississippi to the base of the Reelfoot cliffs the land was first or second bottom. There were no hills, and almost no rolling terrain. The summer was dry and the scenery restful. So at last they came to the village of Reelfoot and met the chieftain they later called Chief Reelfoot.

There was nothing remarkable about this Indian. There was nothing remarkable about the villagers. The party did see for the first time a lingering remnant of early Indian culture; one could almost have said a ghost of old Mound Builders. Two Horses took to them like the wild ducks to the sluggish waters. He thought they were somewhat smaller in stature than most Indians, and certainly the Cherokee. They were stolid and docile and friendly. The virgins, Rutherford remarked again, were comely and sometimes charming—especially around Two

Horses, who had a way. After the customary pipe of peace Chief Reelfoot offered the strangers squaws, either for their pleasure during their visit or to carry away with them when they should depart. It was easy to note the surplus of females, and Rutherford accounted for the discrepancy by the braves' getting killed off in wars. What did interest him greatly were the mounds.

In an area long cleared of timber, probably cultivated for centuries in corn, squash, beans, and other vegetables—Rutherford's party devoured these foods ravenously, not knowing it was vitamins they craved—running from the base of the cliffs to a line of timber along the small river, were the mounds. They were arranged perhaps in some order of the Trinity—three, as he was to observe in later time when he'd return to check his surveys. The main mound was about the size of a typical log cabin, but rounded of top and grassy of surface. Though at times fires had burnt here, there was no indication these had any ceremonial meaning. The much larger mound, in terms of base, though not more than half as lofty, crowded against the steep rugged bank of the river. If it had any typical use among the Reelfoot folk, it was when they gathered in the open for food, for their dances, and small social activities. South of this flat mound was a smaller one, low, well kept but not in use. Then came the vegetable fields and the village of bark-and-hide huts, varying in size and shape and somehow reflecting the habits of white men. Traders had been in here, and Catholic men had penetrated to convert the natives to Christianity. Such influence showed up in a shack or two, and a more spacious domicile for the chief. They saw no mark of Christian faith as such.

On the whole it was a typical Indian village, and the inhabitants could not have numbered more than 150 or 200, even allowing for men absent on the hunts. There were dogs about, and a bony mule. Rutherford felt it was all a bit sordid and dirty. Yet he was cared for so graciously, and through Two Horses was able to communicate with Reelfoot so well, that he might have lingered long. One night the earth trembled, and he leaped from his shakedown with a grunt of terror; but the quiver passed, leaving him dazed and wondering if he had simply had a bad dream. In the morning the chief explained that these tremors came now and then, and ages ago there had been a terrible shaking of the earth. "Think nothing of it."

In the days immediately following, Rutherford tried to complete his surveys, but Two Horses was succumbing to the Indian's natural laziness and could not be located to drag the chain, and Black Ned sulked and said he was sick, but was really suffering from jealousy that Two Horses had choice of wenches but the Negro was rejected by the females. Chief Reelfoot sent substitutes but they didn't know how to use any of the tools. Yet a boatman took the three white men up the sluggish river and into side streams where again mounds were discovered, in the triangular arrangement of those facing the village. Rutherford managed surveys but doubted their accuracy. He was impressed with the strange beauty of the locality. In a long swamp area the timber was mostly cypress, intermixed with gum. Often the trees were immense. Back in the levels there were oaks—red oak, white, pin; huge gums, occasional elms, hackberry, pawpaw, catalpa, and up the faces of the bluffs giant poplars. The forests were alive with game and at sunset the skies were blotted out with blackbirds. Their chatter filled the twilight hours until they were settled in canebrakes and reeds. Bats and swallows tended to decimate the insect population, except for the flies around the habitations, and back into the woods used by the folk in their natural functions.

Rutherford did take time to inspect the mound formations, and Chief Reelfoot in reply to his question said,

"They were built moons ago as many as the birds of the air and fish of the streams." He shook his head. "Not by my people, but the people who lived here beforetime. I know them not. We do not worship on them as of olden times. Many ages ago they were altars to the Great Spirit, and in times of great floods when the rivers ran backward they were refuges."

Were there great chiefs then? He did not know. Did he have any memory of great men of old? No, the Indian had no such memories. Were there heroes? He shook his head, puzzled by the word; and Two Horses, translating, could not explain. Rutherford's men were left puzzled and troubled at people who had no recollections —legends, or written word—of their past. When Rutherford watched them come and go about their daily tasks, shiftless, lazy, uncrowded by ambition, content with today's food, he was less mystified; for men who remember greatness must know and need and understand it. The red men had no such urges.

In spite of Rutherford's impatience to be off, now that they had accomplished their surveys (they had bounded nearly a million and a half acres), he found a study of the Reelfoot folkways absorbing. There was their food. Fish and game made up the meats. Their garden supplied grain and vegetables. The squaws knew all the strange wild plants that supplied what later man found were vitamins—wild mustard, dandelion, pokeberry, sassafras root, black berries, walnuts, hickorynuts, acorns, chinquapins, ginseng, grapes, roots and plants for medicines. Fish could be had for the bother. Small game had grown scarce and wary. But the young men killed a bear; again, they fetched in a buck. One of the fascinating activities was for a dozen young men and women to go down into the marsh grass and cypress knees with their cedar-wood torches and shatter the birds out of their roosts by lashing wildly with limber limbs. The dazed, fluttering, dying birds were crammed into sacks and baskets and brought to the village to be wrung and defeathered, and thrown into a large metal pot and cooked with green corn not yet dry enough in the shuck to meal. Seasoned with herbs and bear grease, it was a tasty dish. Rutherford's men were not sure they liked the communal business of gobbling this goo in competition with the other diners, but a young, quite attractive woman—it developed she was a niece of the Chief—looked after Rutherford and saved his civilized manners.

Courting and love making fascinated him even more than foods. Two Horses and his companion simply went about together as matter-of-factly as if they were consented in marriage. There was no show of tenderness, no "sparking," no coquetting. All the silly, pretty tokens of young love were absent from their habits. If they hugged and kissed, Rutherford did not observe them; nor did he discover any other young folk engaged in amorous play. Married people were stolid and unemotional. There must have been some love play because the place reeked with naked children of all ages; but none was practiced in public. The beauty and pleasure of sex did not seem indigenous to the Indian nature. Yet Rutherford observed how modest were the women; for the girls soon donned garb, though the boys ran naked two or three years longer than the females. In all the weeks he sojourned at the village he did not see any brazen nudity in the females, young or old. He remembered Captain John Smith's comment on this characteristic. "They (the women) are very shamefaced to be caught nak'd."

He gradually became aware that Reelfoot had three wives—a withered squaw who ran his establishment; a middle-year woman who took orders from Wife number one; and a silent, sullen wench just out of her teens who might as well have been a Negro slave, who fanned the flies while Chief Reelfoot devoured his fish and bear steak

Heap Much Romance at Reelfoot 71

and venison. Rutherford asked Two Horses about this: Was it customary for status Indians to practice polygamy? "There is no tribal law against having many wives. But the senior wife must approve any junior wives." Thus it was apparent that few but the mighty in authority could enjoy variety in concubines; and the younger wives might not share the benefits.

The white men found this situation amusing. But Rutherford was beginning to champ at the bit. Two Horses was the stumbling block. The Cherokee had reverted to the ways of his ancestors and he was in love with this virgin that Rutherford, not understanding Indian dialect, called Pawpaw Bloom, partly because of her shade of red, more because of her velvety skin. Two Horses had a way of disappearing when needed, and to avoid anger Rutherford began to shrug the Cherokee off and enjoy the summer days after the long rugged weeks of surveying. Reelfoot's niece—he named her Taffy because of her lighter coloring—beguiled him, and they were often together though they could understand hardly a word of each other's talk. She took thought of his needs, moving quietly, in a woman's way. Probably she would become his squaw. Indian women would often submit— maybe willingly, because of the scarcity of mates; perhaps because of some secret yearning for a pale-face husband (despite his beard). Pale-faces cooperated with the expedient, occasionally, as in the case of Daniel Boone who had to take a red wife to avoid having his head bashed in. He cohabited some months with the squaw before finding opportunity to escape by night and return to his shack on the Yadkin and legal wife and seven or eight young. The situation was by no means rare, and many a man could thank some more or less comely female for his scalp. When such marriages dissolved, Rutherford found himself wondering how the Indian woman reconciled herself to her widowhood. With this play of idle thoughts, Rutherford watched Taffy. She baffled him. Yet war and the wilderness had taught him continence and he had no desire to return to his family with the feeling of having violated his marriage or his rather stern Christian faith.

One night there was to be a wedding. Rutherford gathered this news by noises, activities, and sounds Taffy made.

"Well, now!" Rutherford said to her. "That will be nice. Who's going to get married?"

She gestured and grimaced secretively and made signs. The gibberish did not inform him. But there was a feast in readiness when the moon rose huge, round, and yellow over the Reelfoot bluffs, and the villagers went down through the beans and corn and pumpkins to the big flat mound. The couple, faces draped, were placed in the center of a ring, and faced by a medicine man who was fiercely disguised in the head of a wolf. Everybody had gourds filled with pebbles or dried peas. The young and middle-aged formed a ring around the couple. They began to dance and to rattle the gourds in ear-wracking discord, circling the bride and groom. Since Rutherford was in for it, and Taffy took his hand, he danced too, finding a gourd in his hand. There was little rhythm or tempo to the rattle or thump of drums. The chant was even less musical. The dance, which had neither grace or unison, ranged from grotesque to absurd to silly. Rutherford had never thought of himself as a society man. But he'd attended his share of formal dances of the time, and could acquit himself with credit at the waltz or minuet. If he had been younger, had had more social practice, he would have loved the prevailing dances. All this raucous noise outraged every aesthetic instinct in him. There was some contact of males and females, but mostly it was accidental; and he found that Taffy made no effort to promote or avoid the touching of persons. She had a certain lithe grace, and so did the other virgins. Beyond that, it might have been a party of the village dogs clattering around a pile of bones to be gnawed.

Yet the night, the moonglow, the dark swamp beyond the wall of timber were beautiful. Here were all the elements of love, romance, marriage, gaiety save the charm and celebration the white man brought to the same ceremony. It grew in Rutherford's understanding that the Indian was not an aesthetic man. What was more, it dawned on him that he was taking part in a ceremonial that might just as well have taken place a thousand years before. The mound they were trampling had probably been hardened by feet twenty centuries before. He was in fact back in the time of the Mound Builders, himself acting the part of a Mound Builder, himself a primitive, a savage. The bang-bong halted, the medicine man began a gibberish of wedding words, and Taffy advanced and removed the masks of the couple.

They were Two Horses and Pawpaw Bloom.

6
Land of Unforgotten Sunshine

The report that Rutherford's party carried back to North Carolina fired land-starved farmers, speculators, and grabbers by the tale of thousands and thousands of acres of fertile, well-watered land to be had for the taking. There were rivers both small and large enough for navigation; beautiful stands of oak, walnut, hickory, beech, maple, gum, cypress, poplar; sites here and there for wonderful homes. They had seen no Indians in all the months of their travels, except a remnant of friendly natives back from the Mississippi, where the traders and the missionaries had made contact with some of them. It was indeed a land flowing with milk and honey. Only one thing stood in the way of a flood of settlers. The Chickasaw Indians, though not hostile to the white man, were not hospitable to his moving into their domain and elbowing them from their territory. They'd have to be traded with.

The threat put a damper on a general exodus into the promised land. Still, intrepid pioneers kept seeping into the Western Territory. Up in Kentucky this flood was a deluge until the Shawnees and Wyandottes squelched Richard Henderson's Transylvania Empire. Except for some of the fiery young chiefs like Dragging Canoe, the Cherokee pretty much respected the treaty made at Sycamore Shoals. Nashboro was a thriving post. White settlers had pushed in by way of the Tennessee and Cumberland rivers in sufficient numbers to stabilize that spot, although now and then some farmer working an outlying field would be set upon and killed and scalped. Those who braved the more western lands were groups of men such as the one that explored and named Stone River. Yet all the tales filtering back confirmed Rutherford's report: wonderful lands lying virgin awaiting the settler. Pretty soon a small group of perhaps three families in wagons took to the old Indian traces, and stopped within the zone of safety where they began building log houses and clearing land. Other families and exploring groups followed, pressing westward. If they had any idea they were following the avenues established in a score of centuries, they made nothing of it. They passed the great Harpeth Mound west of Nashboro and remarked, if at all, that it was an oddly formed cliff looking down on Indian old fields along the churning river. But they were in the footprints of a long and faded history. Mound Builders toted raw flint from the flint mines back from the Cumberland River, going to Pinson, to Reelfoot, to a hundred isolated mound groups along the western rivers. They transported other artifacts, as need grew into a kind of commerce.

By 1810 pressures were building up in Washington for a deal with the Indians. Rutherford returned to Reelfoot country in 1811, to verify after a quarter of a century his surveys. He came with a couple of younger surveyors, finding in the back country a small settlement of white people who had occupied land near what eventually became the village of Hornbeak. The great New Madrid Earthquake caught his party, scattering the squatters, and sending the survey party back along the Forked Deer and Obion rivers before he finally braved his push to Reelfoot. The region was desolate. The gentle bluffside where the village had stood was covered with a landslide. The picturesque little river that had been the haunts of catfish, buffalo, carp, crappie, and perch had sunk into a shambles of cypress and gum, the great trees prostrate, or sticking above the miasmatic swamp and bog at grotesque angles. An area that appeared to be many miles in length and two to three miles in width had become the graveyard of Rutherford's rather pleasurable recollections of his lazy visit here. He had to admit that time had painted the interlude with more glowing colors than it probably had had at the time. What seemed less changed than anything else were the old fields and mounds, which the shakes had not reduced. The rounded mound was actually a nice grassy green, as if pastured by deer and elk. The flat mound where the wedding had been celebrated lifted its flat surface above the weeds and bushes that indicated the ground had been abandoned at least two years. It was apparent, then, that the earthquake had not killed off the Reelfoot folk. They had disappeared no less than two summers before. Did they have a premonition of the impending calamity? He was under the impression that primitives functioned by obscure apprehensions not vouchsafed to white men with more sophisticated sensibilities. He recalled, too, the brief shock that caused Chief Reelfoot to speak of some great calamity that would come in the future.

Where had the Indians gone? Up the rivers to join the Indians at the Mounds? Or down the rivers to join the Chickasaws, of whom they were an obscure tribe? Or had they simply taken to the wilderness? He shrugged. One thing he was certain of. Their reason had been urgent enough to tear them away from a long established home.

Inevitably his memory reverted to his weeks of dalliance at the village. After the wedding, Two Horses and his bride disappeared. To honeymoon in the surrounding forests? To return to the land of the Cherokees? During the wedding festivities Rutherford had eaten too much of that indigestible Redskin fare, and to tear up his stomach still worse he'd imbibed freely of an alcoholic beverage that seemed to be fruit brandy—perhaps blackberry—increased to a syrup by wild honey. Then the unwonted exercise of the dance, perhaps an excitement induced by Taffy, and the alcohol added up to making Rutherford sicker than he had ever been in his life. He managed to stagger back to his outdoor mat at the village before he began to vomit. He crawled away into the brush below the spring and sought relief. It was there Taffy found him heaving. She washed his face, provided him with alder leaves to cleanse himself, this being an Indian remedy for effects of diarrhea. Dogs came to devour the vomit and she thrashed them away. Toward dawn he was empty and exhausted, and did not care very much whether he lived or died. To pack the flatboat and leave now, without his Cherokee and sick as he was, was out of the question. Taffy nursed him devotedly. The nostrums with which she dosed him were of doubtful value, but he swallowed them obediently. His bed was an elevated mat somewhat like a hammock, under which by night smudge smokes could be built to ward off the insects. By day some one fanned away the flies. So for three days he lay ill. Not until the fourth day was he able to take nourishment when Taffy brought him some boiled crappie and a soup with gruel.

Rutherford's sick spell occasioned some amusement among his companions. Harris asked, "What did that Redskin hunk give you to drink none of the rest of us got?" Robertson said, "She was fixing to knock you out and hide you in the swamps till the rest of us hulled out, and then she'd make a good Injun out of you!" Rutherford feebly protested that he'd suffered from his stomach for years, but he began to suspect that his drink had been something special, rather than what the others got; and that Taffy was at the bottom of it.

"Has anybody seen that rascal Two Horses?"

"Nope," Robertson reported. He rid one off at a lope and that Pawpaw Bloom rid the other, and nobody's seen hide nor hair of 'em since."

Rutherford relaxed with a sigh, while Harris shook his head. "These Redskin charmers always get their men. I've heard it all my days." And he kept on shaking his head lugubriously.

It didn't seem expedient to leave without the Cherokee, and Rutherford was still feeling poorly. He lay and watched the desultory life of the village—the old squaws going about silently drudging; the younger wives filling the big iron communal pot and cooking the food three times a day; the children running around naked, spending the livelong day at their aimless games; the dogs barking and fighting and licking the dishes put out by the women after meals. Rutherford wished afterward he had paid closer attention to these utensils, for some of them were of native craft and very old. Others had been acquired from traders that had been going up and down the Mississippi maybe for a century. The iron pot came from this source. He supposed at times the Reelfoot folk had a trading post some five or six miles on the river bank. The men came and went—fishing, hunting small game, smoking their home-cured tobacco. The young men were fine-bodied, alive; the old men aged prematurely and laughter and frolic went out of them. But over the land and the village hung a lazy, indolent lassitude, a feeling of don't-care, a kind of lackadaisical come-day-go-day. Rutherford could understand how many white men found this sort of existence to their taste and, abandoning their own way of life and even their families, took up the carefree ways of the savage.

He had to admit it wasn't for him. He had too much drive and greed, not to mention family obligations. But during his ailment and leisurely convalescence, which Taffy's attentiveness and devoted nursing delayed rather than hastened, he found time to contemplate the life of a white man turned savage. He also noted a marked change in the Indians as his illness identified him with them. At first they wore the mask of the red man. The Indian was the originator of the poker face. He was poker face all over. The Indian women went about silent and stoic. The old squaws in the hot summer weather were bare to their waists, their wrinkled and expressionless faces above their flopping leathery breasts. But the younger women, including Taffy, kept discreetly covered. Taffy wore a brief blouse of woven rabbit thongs, which, one day, she divested herself of to show him how the tender skins were cut to almost thread-like thinness, and then handcrafted over and under to make a lovely garment. Once she had uncovered herself the young women followed suit, and pretty soon the women were going and coming without show of unusual modesty. Rutherford was male enough to note the general shapeliness of the female, especially in their youth or before child-bearing. There was more laughter now, and it was not only the children laughing and even singing in fairly tuneless songs. There was a good deal of general gaiety. It came to him the Redskin really was a gregarious, fun-loving fellow. The young men were affable toward Rutherford. No doubt behind the show of friendliness was guile, for they wanted to trade for guns, and when Rutherford's party had no guns to spare, they at least would bargain for powder. He'd hear them down in the river afternoons yelling and hollering and swimming and wrestling in the deep pools. Now and then the women and children would have communal swims, perhaps in the river above the large wide mound, or farther downstream. There would be fun there, and Taffy would leave him alone to share it. He gave her a small bar of his precious soap, and she was set apart in status. Though she always smelled clean, even without soap.

But those withered squaws warned him where even Taffy's glow and curves would go. It was hard to visualize her soft curves and fresh eagerness disappearing into the mummied carcasses of the old women, for a man finds it difficult to imagine life that still has to be lived. A man wants to think of his relationship with a comely woman as enduring. He knows it isn't. He also knew that he was growing fond of the Indian woman; likewise, time was at hand for him to take up his bed and walk. His companions knew it, and kidded him. But they, too, were falling under the lotus blandishment of the savage. But Rutherford lay around, drank Taffy's potions, and soaked up Redskin ways of life. One night he dreamed that Taffy was the mother of his raft of naked little half-breeds. He woke sitting straight up, and maybe he had groaned. The woman was there by his mat, holding his head and dosing him with something that would make him sleep. His face was against her breast.

"Get the hell up from there!" James Robertson told him the next morning at breakfast of boiled fish and rabbit meat. "Half-assing around here making as if you're sick! I heard you hollering for that 'Taffy' last night!"

"I'm still a sick man," Rutherford mumbled.

His legs really were not too dependable, and he'd watch the women weave baskets in the shade of the trees, squatting, tracing in and out the supple thongs of elm, pawpaw willow and buckeye bark. They wove garments of rabbit skins, knee-skirts, small jackets. When the whole village would have a "rabbit-run" for meat, they would skin the animals and remove the summer fur with wood ashes and plucking, knead the skins into pliable rawhide, and with knives the Indians had traded from the passing white traders cut the leather into long thin thongs. They wove garments from the inner barks of such trees as the pawpaw. They dyed some of these with oak tanbark, which was also used for tanning the hides of big game—deer, elk, bear, buffalo. They used the tanbark liquid to tan the hides of the children, so they could run naked even in winter.

When Rutherford was up and knocking about, he took part in one of the rabbit-runs. The rabbit was one of the readiest meat-providing creatures at hand; rabbits bred rapidly, so fast indeed that it was a common saying, "They breed like rabbits"; and when boiled over an open fire and flavored with wild herbs the flesh was savory and nourishing. To kill the game with bows and arrows was bothersome, and to waste powder and lead on a rabbit was absurd. After a rain when rabbits seemed to be grazing, practically all the folk in the village except the old women would take to the glades and canebrakes, along with the dogs, and set up a beating of the bushes and yelling and howling, till every rabbit in the vicinity was alarmed. Then the young men and women would take their position at the edge of the cliffs with a long net, and limber limbs for slaughtering, and the men and dogs would form a two-thirds moon to run the rabbits out. If the catch was good there would be a few minutes of terrific beating and killing, with 50 or 100 rabbits darting to avoid the clubs or lying and kicking in death throes. The kill was thrown into baskets and hurried back to the village for the women to skin and gut the carcasses. The cleaned game was stretched and hung to branches of trees, and the flesh, always subject to blow-flies, would be covered with wide green leaves, such as oak and poplar. Smudge smokes would be fired, further to run the insects. For a couple days rabbit meat was cooked in the big pot and eaten three times a day. For a time the folk were greedy. But rabbit had a habit of early satiating the appetite. If meat was left after the gorging, it would be smoked and cured, and perhaps dried to make pemmican. The entrails would be used for fish bait or carried downstream and cast into the river for the catfish and turtles. The skins would be processed for clothing, such as the small garments that the young women and girls wore. In summer the fur was worthless, but the hide was good. In winter the far more valuable pelts of raccoon, 'possum, polecat, fox, muskrat, squirrel and even the rabbit again would be made into winter coats. Deer and doeskins would be made into blankets, pants, moccasins, and long-coats. The buffalo was disappearing, but buffalo hides worked into shelters and housing, and bearskins made warm beds. Much of this life Rutherford, of course, did not observe; he only surmised it from old tales and observation of the Indian culture about him.

Articles made from bird and animal bones were endless. Taffy showed him needles, punches, awls, and even toothpicks made of turkey bone. One interesting artifact that caught his attention above the other was a toothpick made of the penis of a raccoon. She showed him how she had used the punch and needle to weave her rabbit-fabric jacket. She had a very precious store of linen thread and a steel eye-needle she had bargained from a passing trader. Once, squatting flat on her behind at a pile of flint waste that must have accumulated for a lifetime, she cleared up the mystery of how arrowheads were fashioned. With a heavy piece of flint in form of a hammer-wedge, she beat carefully on a pig of raw flint until her keen eyes saw the microscopic shaling of the stone along the grain of the flint. Then she painstakingly chipped the shales off. He sat fascinated watching nearby, and once she looked up at him with an apologetic smile and said what he interpreted as, "I'm not so awfully good at this." But after perhaps an hour she had fashioned a reasonably decent projectile point. Again she smiled and spread her hands. "It's a job for those who know how. But you see how it's done." She brushed away the rock waste and he took the arrowhead, rude as it was. "I'll keep this for a souvenir." He could now study the flint waste at their feet and imagine the craftsmen working at this or that size arrowhead, some tiny for birds, some larger for small game, some for powerful crossbows to slaughter deer, bear, buffalo; and long keen killers for warfare. His thought was that up through eons of time the Indian had only these primary requirements: food first, shelter perhaps second; self-defense third, and his habit of warring on other tribes or being warred on occupied the skills and muscle of all the able-bodied men from the time they could tote a spear. Down in the maize the women worked; back in the hills the females of all ages gathered chestnuts, acorns, walnuts and hickorynuts; berries in season and pawpaws in autumn; roots and herbs and barks for cures and clothes; and then generations died and now and then their unremembered bones could be found where old grave-spots had sunk or hillsides had eroded and collapsed. It was a life without any recollections or memories or monuments; and once, even, Rutherford had thought, without love— till this change came in the folk and now he saw sex loveplay in plenty. Of course all these failings in some measure pertained as well to the white man. But it was oblivion that his race struggled against in its gravestones, its books, its religion, its hero tales, its very hopes and dreams and schemes. If he did not form these ideas as he watched the Indian woman, the stuff they were eventually fashioned from did seed in those days at Reelfoot.

The life he saw here now had changed to include some of the good and bad things of the white man—instead of the stone tomahawk for killing, the Indian now could brain and scalp his enemy with a hatchet of English steel which he had traded from the hucksters going up and down the rivers; instead of the spear and arrow he had the musket and powder and lead. But his squaw could skin the willow and pawpaw with the hatchet, too; and the red man could shoot the rare buffalo that loitered in the land after the ravages of the Frenchmen.

Now the white man was pushing in, taking over the earth, measuring it in huge chunks for easy riches; and at least he was willing to bargain for it instead of forming midnight attacks and dawn scalping parties to seize it. In either case, it looked as if Taffy and her people would emerge losers.

Would Taffy and her comely sisters find paleface husbands in the riffle? Perhaps—a few. Would the red men find paleface wives? Not even a few. A white wife had bother enough keeping a white husband at work and prospering; while a red husband didn't know his ABC's about domesticated toil. When he wasn't hunting, fishing, killing, he was sleeping in the sun; and these talents had scant use on a newground farm. In time something would have to give and it probably would be the Indian. He couldn't help thinking, sentimentally, that Taffy deserved something better than what he could envision for her.

He sighed and went with her another day up into the deep hill woods to gather. He didn't know what they would find to put in her basket. It was too early in the fall for nuts; the wild fruits were gone; persimmons would not ripen fit to eat till frost; wild grapes must wait till October; maybe there might be on some sunny hillside a ripening pawpaw. But Taffy took the basket, perhaps as pretense for their quitting the village together. So up the cliffside they climbed, in the early afternoon heat breaking quickly enough into a sweat. When well away from odd eyes she took his hand. As the sun and heat moistened her, she removed her small jacket. From the waist up she was bare.

"She's an Indian woman, all right," he thought.

Moreover she was a Chickasaw woman. Among the encroaching white men they were high in repute for their beauty. "Some of the Chickasaw women are described as being of surpassing beauty," one enamored Englishman was heard to exclaim. In 1761 Maj. Robert Rogers described them as "far exceeding in beauty any other nation to the Southward." Cushman averred, "Seldom have I looked upon specimens of female grace and loveliness as I have seen among the Chickasaws in their homes east of the Mississippi River. Their eyes were dark and full and their countenances like their native clime. They were truly beautiful and, best of all, unconsciously so. Oft I was at a loss which most to admire—the graceful and seemingly perfect forms, finely chiseled features, lustrous eyes and flowing hair, or that soft, winning artlessness which was preeminently theirs."

Taffy at this moment was an incarnation of these extravagant adjectives from the literate fascinated Englishmen. If Rutherford had been gifted as some of these other admirers, he would have wrapped her in the gauze of poetry.

She paused now and then, reminding him that he still was short of breath, and he'd feel the wash of fragrant wind across his face. She'd search for the occasional sprig of ginseng, or perhaps dig an Indian turnip. They'd climb higher then, and she would pull up the twisted bitter root, esteemed for diarrhea; and wahoo, for stomach ailments. She might skin a young dogwood for the bitter inner bark that was a cure for fevers; and mandrake root for women's menstrual pains. There would be other and more mysterious gatherings for remoter ailments, which she would explain but he did not understand. At length they reached the summit of the hills, where the tall timber was heavily chestnut. She looked against the sky, checking the fruits and finding them still unripe. Here the air was free, and there were birds about, though the time of their singing had passed with the emptying of the nest. A red flash of wing was a cardinal; a blue flash a jay. High against the gray-blue afternoon sky on the topmost limb of a stark dead chestnut sat a hawk, motionless and watching. In an open spot she did find a yellowing pawpaw with mottled sunshine in its freckled fruitiness, and she kneaded it and fed him the gooey pulp, none too ripe but savory enough. When she smiled, the sunshine and sky were in her dark eyes. There were springs here, and the earth under the oaks and gums was moist. At a pool of clear water she drank from her cupped palms and then washed the roots. One was a long writhing thing that she bruised and fed him in small bitter-sweetish chewings. Once when he would have spat the roughage out, she said "Uh-ah," and made him swallow. "No, no," she shook her head. "Good." These words she had learned. A faded memory of the taste grew on his taste buds, and it came to him the root was the fabulous sarsaparilla, presumed to thicken the blood and restore male potency. He laughed, remembering, and she smiled with him, though she may have had no idea what had amused him. The root was the oldtimey aphrodisiac.

She led him to a cool mossy spot, seated him next to the spring, and divested herself of the short skirt which was her other garment. She was not totally nude. She wore a very small triangular guard over her pubic spot, held in place by thin strong thongs of some animal skin. He made no effort to avoid staring. When she followed his eyes, she undid the garment and allowed him to inspect it closely. It was woven of hair—human hair, she gave him to know, drawing down a strand of her hair. It was a beautiful bit of intimate weaving, a fragment of female sexual vanity. She talked, and somehow he interpreted her words as, "Only the virgins may wear one." He was puzzled as to whether she was enticing him, prepared to sacrifice her virginity in this sylvan bed. He thought that her body was more muscular than a young white woman's. He remembered his wife, who at the same mature youngness had still been supple and slim. Taffy's curves were not as suave. She stood there demure waiting, and he returned the garment. She did not put it back on, but sat down in the mushy minty backwash of the spring overflow and played like a child. She coiled her hair high and stretched in the cool bed, flecks of sunshine pieing her body.

She talked and he talked, and without understanding they communicated. He did not say all that was in his mind and emotions. He must soon be going. He loved her. But he had no wish to possess her body for a moment's satiation. If she were virginal, she should wait for her man from the tribe. But, perhaps, she was not a virgin. He knew nothing of her—if her man had died, been killed in war, had quit her, or she had quit him. Perhaps his sentimentality was erecting around her an aura of romance after the manner of song writers and poets who followed and glamorized the Indian woman—when she was young, before childbearing and labor had toughened her to leathery flabbiness and her breasts were like purses of buffalo hide, when her soft features had dried to a criss-cross of leather like the back of a lizard.

On a final day she took him two miles down a trail to a cliff where the dead were buried or cremated. Here were holes filled with ash, charred bones, and charcoal. There were mats about where the dead had been wrapped and rolled till the flesh decayed, after which the bones and hair were removed and washed and tanned, and the bones polished and kept about the lodges. He had observed such relics in the privacy of the domiciles.

And so she had spoken to him of life and death, and offered him love; and had invited him to her arms and into the ways of her people.

If the change had any meaning to Rutherford beyond a shock he should have been prepared for, it was how the wilderness could gobble up memories, peoples, men's schemes, and leave few clues of the human passions and hopes and dreams that had once been vivid and alive in it. Before his party left the region he heard that New Madrid, a thriving post on the west side of the Mississippi, had sunk into the river, and the quakes had annihilated a couple of other settlements in that region. So he returned again to North Carolina with a good report of his enterprises. He would return again some five years later, by which time the land fever was at a high pitch, and settlers were shoving in by the ancient war and trading traces, pausing only by the threat of Indians.

By 1818 Washington was trying to do something about the situation. At first the Chickasaws said they had no lands for sale. But when it was made known to the chiefs that the Great White Father did not like that answer, they reconsidered and at last made the deal which came to be known as the Jackson Purchase. General Jackson of Tennessee and Isaac Shelby of Kentucky opened the negotiations, and the deal was closed at the Old Town of the Chickasaws, near Tuscumbia, Alabama, after 20 days of trading, much of it secret, with the chiefs, who made profit by agreeing to what later in the exodus westward of the Indians became known as the "Trail of Tears." The Indians were paid $300,000 in fifteen installments, and sundry gifts and the usual relatively worthless baubles. Part of the initial funds were put up by speculators from North Carolina, South Carolina, and Tennessee. The balance was presumed to be paid by the U.S. Senate when the treaty was ratified; and the Senate had little choice, now that things had gone this far. The speculators who had put up cash returned home with reports that dimmed by their glow anything Rutherford and other prospectors had made. They spoke "in raptures." Rutherford, though he probably would have abhorred the accusation of mishandling the Chickasaws, warmed up his old surveys and remembered these amounted to almost a million and a half acres—claiming a cut of 600 acres out of every 5000. It would make him one of the wealthiest men, in terms of raw lands, of his day.

No sooner was the pipe-of-peace spittle dry on the treaty paper than the rush, comparable to the gold rush in after years, set in. The ancestral lands of the Chickasaws, which now included the fabled realm of the Mound Builders, were rudely trampled by the boot-shod paleface aliens from the north lands. Rutherford was right in the middle of the land-office rush. He knew the land grants in all the Mound river countries—Wolfe, Forked

Deer, Obion, Big Hatchie, Reelfoot, Loosahatchie bottoms. In a year or so he was only one of a hundred land surveyors, though his name was never lost among the big operators—Richard Hightower, James Vaulx, Joel Pinson. The tale went that the farther south one journeyed the more fertile became the dirt. Though the hilly backlands had thin soil, they still would grow good corn and cotton, and the timber being smaller, clearing would be easier; in fact, the deep bottomlands would not be finally opened until the edge of memory of men still living today. Hilly rolling country was less sickly, and here sprang up the communities, villages, more formal towns. But it was said the Obion and Forked Deer rivers were unequaled for navigation. The largest size steamboats of the time could churn up the muddy waters of the Forked Deer, Hatchie, even the Wolfe. Keel boats and flatboats moved at will except in seasons of low waters. Their freights would consist of corn as farms grew; cotton, wheat, going out; dry goods, manufactured items, farm machinery, harness, flour, sugar, coffee, tea, whisky, coming back; and if you happened to be a traveler on foot you crossed the streams by swimming, rolling a log in and hugging it until you reached the other bank, or wading up to your neck. On horse or mule you plunged your beast in. Ferries grew up here and there, and only in recent years have such ferry names been dropped, as Lane's Ferry on the Obion.

The Chickasaws were gone. They'd beat out the "Trail of Tears." It began at the Mississippi crossing at the Indian Mounds at the mouth of Wolfe River, went over into Arkansas toward Little Rock, turned northward along the high ground known as Crowley's Ridge, and eventually wet the dusty western dirt till the "poor Indian" was well segregated from his great white brother. If any of the rising rich suffered qualms about "robbing the red man" of the land of his birth, they did not record it. In truth, save for a few men like Rutherford—and other leaders—the literacy level of the onrushing emigrants was sufficiently low that an impressive percentage could not write. The argument ran that the Indians had had thousands of years to make something of all this fertile dirt and contrived to erect a culture consisting of some mounds here and there along the muddy rivers. Well, move over and let somebody in who could do something with all this wealth.

7
The Unlettered and Unremembered

Mostly the first settlers around 1818 to 1820 came from North Carolina, Virginia, East Tennessee, and a few from South Carolina. They were poor white dirt-farmers. They came along Grinder's Trace in jolt wagons, by muletail, or even on foot, crossing the Tennessee at the old Indian crossing later known as Reynoldsburg where some enterprising fellow built a ferry of a log raft, powered with big paddles. And so they entered the promised land while still there were Chickasaw Indians who remained for the salt springs, by special dispensation. A reporter who followed the exodus with an idea of picking up a few thousand acres of prime land and later establishing a newspaper took a keen view of the day and time.

"Until a short time before this date (1817) there was not a single white settlement, nor a white man's cabin, in the newly acquired territory, save the 'trading post' that later became the city of Memphis. But hard upon the heels of the surveying parties the speculators and squatters began to explore in search of locations for homes. Soon the smoke from mud chimneys began to curl over log cabins, and from innumerable camp fires, and within a few months the whole of the Purchase or Western District was known to the enterprising pioneers. Its boundless resources, its grand possibilities and its glorious future were foreseen."

Now our verb-slinging pioneer breaks into rhapsodies.

"Imagine, if you can, the delight of the first settlers in this fair land. Its soil was untouched by the plow; its primeval forests had never known the woodsman's axe, and were alive with song birds; deer roamed in large numbers through the shady woods and grassy vales with nothing save the savage wolf, the panther and the catamount to dispute their rights of possession. There were bears in abundance; the beaver had never been disturbed in his rights to the waterways; the raccoon then, as now, sought its nocturnal meals in the streams and lakes. Wild fowls skimmed the bosom of its waters, with none to molest or make them afraid. Annual fires had kept the forests free from fallen timber and undergrowth. (He did not add that most often these fires were set by the Indians for the express purpose of keeping the forests in good pasture for the buffalo, deer and elk.) In season the luscious wild strawberry grew on every hillside, and the wild plum abounded. Autumn brought its harvest of nuts and persimmons, while the wild grapes hung in purple festoons from vines that embraced thousands of trees. Its lakes and rivers and creeks teemed with the finest fish. It was truly a fair land. Its landscape was undulating and rose and fell like waves of the ocean. Wild flowers shed their rich fragrance everywhere. The forests were clothed in regal splendor in summer, and when winter spread her snowy mantle over the earth no fairer scene upon which to look was ever presented to the human eye. Its climate was genial and mild, and its gentle winds carried the bloom of health upon their wings. Its winters were short and mild; its summers were long, but were tempered by the luxurious growth of vegetation that covered the landscape.

"There was no ruggedness in its landscape; it had no towering mountains, no deep valleys, but it possessed a sylvan beauty, a calm and quiet peace that gladdened the hearts of its beholders."

Now that no Indians lurked in the "fen and jungle" or behind a tree or stone to spring upon the unwary traveler, the emigrant could wagon along all day without fear of attack from a savage foe. The mule driver dozed at the

The Unlettered and Unremembered 93

wagon tongue while his old woman or the boys "hooed" the cattle along. There were, of course, certain enemies that still lurked, mostly by night—bears, panthers, catamounts; and woe betide any mule or horse or cow that strayed from the campsite. The oldest boy in this "march of civilization" had better stay awake and keep the camp fire roaring and his gun handy.

Nevertheless certain disquieting rumors kept seeping back from this Canaan Land. To go beyond the Tennessee River, they said, was to go to an early grave. Some spoke of it as "Death's Valley." Summer complaint and swamp fevers killed folks off like flies; there were billions of mosquitoes, gnats and horse flies—a small yellow fly that would bite the cattle and cause milk fever and to drink the milk would kill folks; there were snakes, skunks, bats— bats would bring bedbugs; and worst of all, and the hardest to do anything about, were the haunted spots where Indian bones had been buried for 10,000 years, and if the Redskins weren't around in person, their ghosts were, to lay you low with lockjaw, bone spavin, and cause your teeth to fall out.

But such tales merely caused a few bad dreams. The wagons creaked on, and West Tennessee loomed through the oak, beech, gum, hickory, poplar, ash, walnut, maple, mulberry, cherry, and cypress. The buffalo gnats maddened the beasts and the mosquitoes tortured the settlers, but always toward the sunset were the Indian lands.

Our scribe took note of the characteristics of these folk. Aside from their poverty, he observed their general lack of book learning. "But," he said, "their arms were strong and their hearts were brave as the eagle of the forest, and as true as the needle to the pole, and as generous as the bounteous nature that surrounded them. They were prompt to resent an insult or an injury and generous to forgive. Their hospitality was limited only by their capacity. Their doors were always open to travelers and their hearts to appeals for help. Their wives and daughters were worthy of their husbands and fathers; they were not endowed with conventional graces and accomplishments that would characterize their descendants. But they possessed strong minds, strong bodies, and pure habits. They could milk a dozen cows morning and evening, harness or saddle a mule, or they could ride it without a saddle; they could yoke a pair of steers or call the hogs; they knew how to load a rifle and how to use one. They could plow, chop wood, burn brush and logs in the clearing, card, spin and weave the cloth that made theirs and their fathers' and brothers' garments. They wore homespun frocks and big sunbonnets that protected their rosy faces from the rays of the sun as well as from the impudent stare of those who had no right to gaze upon their beauty. Their cheeks were painted with the rosy glow of health; they were strong of limb, strong in will and pure in mind. They were modest, timid, and reserved, and endowed with all the graces which constitute the charm of true womanhood."

We are told the sons scorned cigarettes and high collars, ironed pants, and suchlike tokens of an affluent society. They wore coonskin caps and shoes lasted at home of cowhide, deerskin, elk. They drank whisky, chewed tobacco, and swore in earth-shaking goddamits. "They were fearless and courageous, enterprising and industrious." Aside from hunting wild critters that quickly enough became scarce, their chief pursuit was seeking to seduce the wood-chopping, brush-burning modest damsels who could plow and roll logs—and these modest females all too often listened to their soft talk and yielded to the fearless and courageous yokels. In the beginning there had been no schools in the backwoods. I find no reference to a date when the first log school house was heaved up in Mound Builder country, but it was some years certainly after the land-clearing, log-rolling, brush-burning and new-ground busting had got well under way.

"The sons and daughters of the household received their

instructions at their parents' knee, and the Bible was their library. Amid such surroundings the people were happy and contented and their wants were easily gratified. Exercise in their various occupations gave them health and voracious appetites. The forest and stream supplied their table with meat; corn for bread was to be had for little effort. They lived near to nature's heart and worshipped nature's God."

Among the earliest of these noble settlers were the names Waddell, Hargrove, Roderick, McIver, Porter, Brown, Doak, Shannon, Murray, Dyer, Woolfolk, Brodin, Alexander, Duncan, Stewart—to name a few at random.

The smokes of a thousand log heaps early darkened the spring skies. Clearings and log cabins were everywhere. Joel Pinson and his chainmen had come and gone. James Rutherford, too, had made another visit and returned home. Settlers still pressed in, in increasing numbers. "The emigration is astonishing." "The Western District begins to assume the appearance of a civilized and thickly settled country." Considerable towns had sprung up. Jackson, Tennessee, had some 700 population. Land could be bought cheaply, largely because of lack of money. "Twelve to fifteen hundredweight of cotton can be grown to the acre," James Deaderick said in 1826. "The appearance of the western district is in the summer season very beautiful." He spoke of the grass—buffalo grass—upon which the cattle fattened and milked well until autumn drought and heavy grazing charred it down; and the fertility of the soil for cotton. But already bad farming methods and erosion of the sandy soil were taking their toll. Education was rearing its knot-head above the snags and stumps in the clearing; a certain John Holden had a school of 35 pupils in one of the towns. His salary was $225 a year and he paid $4 a month for board. Since the school was a subscription affair he probably collected about $150 of this.

Yet the truth was that away from the towns—500 population was a considerable town before 1830—the clearings were gaunt and ragged and filled with half-burnt snags and charred stumps, and the ground between was choked with tangled weed of cotton. The dwellings were logs, probably half, just a single log room with a plank kitchen at back; the slightly more pretentious had a "roof-room" in the loft; the affluent two-mule farmers had a double log house with dog-trot, and if the family were large, a log kitchen and eating room in a back L. There would be the log smokehouse, and maybe a pretentious log barn; or just a skinned pole barn for the one-mule gentry. There'd be a sizable garden, a hog pen, chickens. And of course the farm horses and mules and milk cows.

Doctors were scarce, and midwives took care of the population explosion. Summer complaint kept the babies within bounds, but malaria reduced all members of a community. Typhoid fever insisted on its cut, and around the crude churches, among the stumps, the dead were buried by the hellfire Methodist and Baptist preachers. The mortality rate among the wives was high; widowers casting around for fresh wives could be discerned among the newground stumps when an unattached female appeared in the settlement. These valiant folk marched to church once a month to listen to wearisome sermons on the wages of sin; and in the fall of the year they renewed their faith in hellfire by listening to the evangelists who promised them eternal roasting if they did not mend their ways. Yet the consumption of whisky and fornication seemed to continue undiminished. Withal it was a frontier society, in a hard crude land.

Yet in the millennia long gone this harsh land was a land flowing with milk and honey—buffalo milk and bumblebee honey. As the plowhand turned the new ground more often than not he bared to the hot sky the Indian weapons that made West Tennessee a country of peace. The arrowheads and spear points that became every country boy's prize collection of artifacts were used in hunting, not in warring. The tribes to the south and to the north had a tacit agreement if they met in the western hunting grounds they would, even though hostile, not attack each other. Their quest here was food, not fight. In times past great herds of buffalo had ranged here, especially in their autumn migrations. We have recorded tales of their uncounted numbers.

Adair speaks of this in his *History of the American Indians*.

"Not only the Indians but the whites, particularly the French hunters out of New Orleans, were responsible for the extirpation of the buffalo from the region east of the Mississippi." Williams in *Beginnings of West Tennessee* makes a point of the same tale. In early times the American bison ranged in great herds throughout the lands where the Pinson Mound Builders journeyed to slaughter their winter meat. The herds moved deeply into Georgia, the land of the Etowah Mounds, and especially into Tennessee and Kentucky. One traveler reported, "Colonel Wm. McIntosh, the brother of General Lachland McIntosh, my grandfather, has often told me that he had seen ten thousand buffalo in a herd. My father, whose Indian establishments extended to St. Marks, was constantly supplied with buffalo tongues, until as late as 1774, as my mother has often stated to me."

None of the De Soto narrators mentions the animal, however. The flesh and butter were food (the only milk products known to the Indian); the squaws used the wool to weave clothing; the skins were bedding. The hide was a symbol of protection, and given as a pledge. Lovers presented their brides with it as a love token. They believed eating bear's flesh by woman gave her fecundity and made child-bearing easy. Next to the buffalo tongue, the hump and rump were the choicest. This land where the white man broke furrows was the crude, raw, forsaken hunting grounds.

Possession undoubtedly lent a certain rude beauty to

the picture. But the newcomer, particularly if she chanced to be a fastidious woman, saw through the gloss of ownership to the ugliness underneath. A lady by the name of Henrietta Fitzhugh was such a person. She came down from North Carolina by way of Nashboro and took the trace to Indian lands in a vehicle described as a gig. She fetched along her fashionable crinolines in bags attached to the back of the rig, and they hit the long muddy trails across West Tennessee in the rainy season—that time of year the Redskins used to say the "sky leaked." When the team plunged into those muddy swirling fords Henrietta's pantalettes got drenched, and her pretties suffered much from the filthy deluge. So bad were the rains and floods when the party crossed neighboring counties they had to detour towns like Lexington and Henderson, in the flatlands, because the roads were knee-deep in mud; and so they kept to the dismal ridges where the scenery oppressed Henrietta as being remarkable for "nothing but sterility, high hills, and sickly mean-looking people." One of her chief gripes was against the taverns, their keepers and the beds. Her description of one keeper seems vivid enough to catalog the type.

"This man is living on extremely rich land with scarcely a comfort around him, his house an open half-finished log barn; he is a lazy, opinionated, red-faced fellow who twists his legs around the porch bench, barbecues the King's English and sets up to entertain his customers with a dish of politics and leaves all the work for his wife to do. . . . I could not help smiling at a remark made by the Hostess, a fat good-humored dame. She observed to me, 'You had better persuade your husband not to move to this country.' 'Why?' 'Because all the men become lazy, they sit down all day long and talk of accumulating wealth and leave all the work for the women to do. They'll promise to fix everything so wonderfully well, but never get beyond the half-built log house.'"

Henrietta added, "They seem to think of nothing but accumulating wealth, and it really seems to avail them little."

It was not till she reached Jackson that disillusionment really struck her between the eyes. There, from all the glowing accounts that had gone back to her home, she expected to see spacious homes, after the manner of some she had passed through in East Tennessee—Colonial semi-mansions that can still be seen in the gracious old towns like Elizabethtown, Kingsport, Greeneville; but to her horror all she saw were somewhat refined specimens of the shacks and log houses of the outlands. In fact, if there was a daub of paint in the entire "city" of 675 souls she did not mention it in the daily diary she kept of her journey. One of the black boys motioned to the houses on a main street.

"Gentle-folks' houses."

Henrietta saw more open farmlands and a certain air of settled life and prosperity, but the flourishing city she had anticipated wasn't there. So on through Jackson, where there were stumps still inside the town limits, and cow-barns and hogpens, and south across the Forked Deer on the road to Bolivar, where her brother lived. If she hadn't been so grumpy, she might have observed an Indian mound as she went out of town, and certainly along the road they followed, after a good dinner at a place near the river where the fish was prime, old rises of earth were visible. At a place afterward named Medon there were clusters of mounds on near lands already opened. But the lady's grumpy eyes were on the winding road, that went down hill and uphill, picking its way at last over the 30 miles from Jackson to Bolivar. It was land that today is mostly wasteland, deeply eroded, with gullies which one could throw a house into and have to search to find it again; but in the spring of the year it is lovely beyond words with the virgin bloom of dogwood.

Henrietta left no record of how her equipage crossed the Hatchie River a few miles east of Bolivar. The river must have been pretty much at flood, and this early it's unlikely a wooden bridge that later crossed the murky stream had been built. Probably there was a crude raft ferry. If she'd turned off to her right down the river two miles or so, she'd have come upon an ancient Indian town as old as the hills, and some of the best preserved mounds that exist on this once well-populated waterway. She was a lady and her heart was in her crinolines. Maybe at Bolivar there was "society."

8
City of Cisco

In the early 1880s a jaunty young man by the name of J. G. John Guy Cisco fetched his knitting and job printing press and box of hand-set type to Jackson and set up shop off Court Square to produce a county newspaper he called the *Forked Deer Blade*. He had a cargo of verbs and adjectives of which "Progress" was one of the most important. He was a personable fellow and his selection of *Forked Deer Blade* for his venture, perhaps without his being aware of it, was something of a key to his personality. For one thing, Forked Deer is a euphonious pair of words. Blade suggested some sharp talk coming up—as proved to be the case. No sooner had he installed his secondhand printing press, which was powered by a sweating buck Negro turning a fly wheel, than he set forth to mingle with the populace—to solicit advertising, write up personals, and acquaint himself with the city fathers and other bigwigs. Almost from the first issue the *Blade* began to stir the townsfolk. John Guy began to agitate for gravel streets, abolishing of all hog pens within the city limits, and circumscribing the keeping of cows by the citizens. This animal husbandry was practiced by the retired farmers who left the farms, both the opulent ones and the eroded lands, and moved to the city for hydrant water and gas lights. Cisco swelled with civic pride and would tear these rural gentry away from their country raising and make them into city slickers. It wasn't long before John Guy was the subject of dialogs around the grog shops, taverns, and court square. The *Blade* prospered, because citizens who smelled the hog pens at twilight in the hot summer evenings shared his crusade. The cows were less objectionable. As for the horse barns, everybody had them and what everybody has to smell becomes socially acceptable.

It was a long day from 1820 when Joel Pinson's crew came upon the Indian Mounds. In the intervening 60 years there were great numbers of people who were born and raised in Madison County who had never even heard of Pinson's Mounds.

But our hustling young newsman had an insatiable curiosity, as well as a verbal genius that adored the purple metaphor. In his riding forth over the county to solicit subscriptions and clasp hands with the simple yeoman farmers, he heard tell of some big piles of dirt off the old road from Jackson to Selmer—now Highway 45. He turned his horse off into a narrow dirt road toward the east, forded the Forked Deer, climbed a rise to a well-cleared second bottom, and there had his first view of the Mounds. A less imaginative man would have grunted in inarticulate wonder, maybe smoked a pipe of tobacco, and turned and gone back to glad-handing the prospective subscribers. Cisco was filled with wonder. But he was anything but inarticulate. He rode along the farm road to the first large mound, and dismounted, let his nag graze, and he climbed to the flat summit. It was not at this first visit that he began his measurements. But he found presently that the mound was about 40 feet high, and about 150x200 feet in size—larger than an ordinary city building site. Large trees and undergrowth choked the top, making it difficult to judge the size, but he estimated 150x75—something like that. One great poplar reared above everything else, and he found it four feet thick. Much of the top was dead but it was a proud old tree at that. He guessed its age as around 250 years. Narrow paths ran here and there where farm animals, mostly goats, had nipped the vegetation; but he explored the mound fairly well, and let his imagination prank with phantasies.

Some quarter of a mile away loomed the great mound. It took another visit and some more accurate measurements to get at the size of this dirt pile. He established its height as close to 80 feet—somewhat under; but the great trees growing on the summit gave the illusion of perhaps 200 feet. The base was 300x370 feet, and though he found it hard to judge the dimensions of the summit, he figured on 40x60 feet. From the top he could see a long distance in all directions—eastward to the line of hills between three and four miles; westward to the snake-crooks of the Forked Deer and leisurely "big" road, mostly dust now in the middle of the summer; north to the farmlands and woods and south to the timbered regions that remained uncleared. There were birds about, and the winds tousled his sweaty hair. There wasn't much he could do but sit on a dead log and ooze nostalgia, and wonder, "Well, what the hell!"

He spent a long hour just studying the smaller mounds that were readily visible from the top of the large one. He counted some 35, many little more than knolls in the corn fields, but a few rearing high out of the levels and well timbered. He left the locality musingly, deeply moved by a haunting sense of a previous civilization on the spot. Later in town he met with a friend, Colonel Pick Jones, and in talking with Jones he added more lore to his bag of nostalgia. "When I was a boy I rode a horse for a distance of six miles on a line of earthworks that connected and partially surrounded these mounds."

Cisco had already started his crusade to rid Tennessee of whisky, but he abandoned his prohibition urges to crusade for the Pinson Indian Mounds. He had begun a history of Madison County in installments in the *Blade*. Now he published the first report on the relics.

It is only fair to our hero to give some generous samples of his choicest prose. The reader is to remember, of course, that it was an age when writers strained after the mouth-filling word, the lofty rhetoric, the classic allusion. It permeated even fiction of that day, as one notes in Mary N. Murfree's stories of the Tennessee mountains and mountain folk. Let us bravely at it, then.

"Eighty-three years have come and gone, years fraught with changes of vast importance in the history and progress of the world, since the first white family settled in what is now Madison County, Tennessee. The territory was then an unbroken, untrodden wilderness, the only inhabitants of which were the wild beasts that held undisputed possession of the dark, shady woods from time beyond reckoning.

"The bold and hardy pioneers found a country as fair as any upon which the sun had ever shone, fresh from the hand of nature, untouched, untarnished and uncontaminated by the hand of man. For centuries unnumbered it had been the abode of the red men. Its forests had afforded them shelter from the suns of summer and the blasts of winter. Its hills and glens and its clear running streams had given them an abundance of nature's food, while the skins of animals taken in the chase had supplied them with clothing.

"That a prehistoric people had at one time populous villages and communities in what is now Madison County is evidenced by numerous remains that still exist. But the names of these settlements have long been forgotten, even if they were ever known to the whites. Who these people were, of their tribal relations, of their social institutions, of their manners and customs, of their language, whence they came, and when, we know absolutely nothing. All their history and traditions perished with them."

Cisco then goes on and tells of a rare artifact he found at the south end of Market Street in Jackson, west of the Illinois Central Railroad, at an Indian mound inside the city limits. "I found a stone pipe of curious workmanship, and a number of arrowheads." John W. Campbell owned a farm a mile and a half west of Jackson on the old Denmark Road, where there were several mounds that Cisco excavated in the year 1880. About five feet from the top, near the original surface, he found a pit filled with ashes, some charred human bones and partly burned wood, and flint chips but no arrowheads. It was a pretty meager wage paid for some heavy digging. Yet it did show a method of burial practiced by the Indians, that of interring the dead in a bed of charcoal or ashes, and a crude cremation.

He went on:

"These mounds are silent monuments of a forgotten people. They bear no inscription of deeds of valor in war or the chase; nor of love and devotion of family or of tribe. They are dead monuments of a dead people. They bear no inscriptions as to their builders, who they were, whence they came, whither they went; and speculation is useless.

"Southeast of Jackson ten miles, and north of Pinson three miles, is one of the most interesting groups of aboriginal monuments in the Southern States. There are probably 150 mounds in this group within an area of six square miles. The largest of them is mentioned by Judge Haywood in his *Natural and Aboriginal History of Tennessee*, published in 1826. He gives the height as 96 feet. But this is an error. I measured it in 1880 and found it to be 72 feet high and about 1000 feet in circumference at the base. About one-half mile northwest of this mound is another of peculiar form, being pentagon in shape. It is 20 feet high, with five faces sloping to the top at an angle of about 45 degrees. The five sides are each about 100 feet. This mound is flat on top and has an approach at one corner. There are several large beech and oak trees growing on this mound," and he goes on then to mention the great poplar.

"To the south of this mound 50 chains are what are called the 'twin mounds.' They are about 12 feet high and are what the name implies. There are many other mounds in this group, some quite large, and others so small as to be scarcely noticeable. They have all been more or less reduced by the white man's plow that has gone over them year after year for almost three-quarters of a century.

"These mounds are on the north side, in a sweeping bend of the south branch of the Forked Deer River, in a fertile region in which there are numerous springs of pure, sparkling, freestone water." Colonel Jones rode his horse here, and Cisco found traces of the old earthworks outside the plowed fields. "The builders of these stupendous works are gone; their bones have crumbled into dust, and save these mounds of earth, a few stone implements and fragments of pottery, there is nothing left to tell that they existed. They left no history, no records, not even a tradition."

He must have sighed deeply as he finished this apostrophe to tragedy. But he took time to extol the attractions of the Chickasaws, a warlike and valiant race, who came along in time to claim the region if not to absorb the population. "The warriors of this tribe are a large, well formed, fine-looking body of men, and their women are reputed to have been handsome, modest, chaste and not as dark in color as most of the Indians were." It's an interesting note, this; for a fair skin and pale face, attributes of the white man, were in some esteem even by the Redskins.

Cisco wrote much of the Mounds; he made talks; he kindled some small fire of enthusiasm in Jackson, so that folks picnicking Sundays would go to the Mounds for their fun. He published a long history of Madison County in the *Blade,* and later it was republished nationally in the *American Historical Magazine.* There the Mounds were brought to the attention of national persons such as Carl Miller, archaeologist of the Bureau of American Ethnology, and W. E. Meyer, Tennessee archaeologist and author of *Art and Archaeology* and other books, both of whom eventually visited the Pinson Mounds and made extensive investigations of the area. It was Meyer who gave the Pinson Mound complex the name of "City of Cisco," honoring the young journalist. But J. G. Cisco did not wear well in his land of forgotten Redskins. His stirrings in local politics, and crusading against the Demon Rum, got him into such hot water that Cisco had to tote a pistol in case of personal attack. He hardly lasted out the 1890s. His genius for slinging hand-set type brought him a call to greener pastures in form of an offer from the L. & N. Railroad to be their public relations man, and he took leave of the little dirt-farmer pig-wallow West Tennessee town with a farewell to the misty ghosts of long-gone Mound Builders.

Still and all, he must have departed Jackson with a sense of quitting the homeplace. Here he had published successfully a first rate newspaper for his day and time in a town the size of Jackson. Extant copies (dated in the 1890s) show eight pages well illustrated, some with woodcuts done by Cisco himself. Here he had drawn national attention to himself and his labors as an amateur archaeologist. He had collected probably the finest collection of artifacts from the Pinson Mounds, which eventually found itself in the archives of history in Mississippi. He had established some considerable trade in books and stationery at a shop on Main, across the street from the courthouse. He huckstered pictures, moldings and music. His home in an old directory is given as "ws Cumberland, ne College." An oldtimey ad follows:

J. G. CISCO
Wholesale and Retail
BOOKSELLER AND STATIONER
Dealer in
MUSIC, MUSICAL INSTRUMENTS, PICTURE
FRAMES, MOULDINGS, ETC., ETC.
Orders by Mail Solicited
33 Main Street, Jackson, Tennessee

Cisco must have enjoyed about a quarter of a century's work with the L & N in Nashville, for he was buried in Riverside cemetery in Jackson April 24, 1922. He was born April 25, 1844. His wife Georgia Pursley is buried with him, and so is his daughter Bertie F. Cisco. No date of the daughter's birth is given, but the retention of her maiden name indicates she never married. She died May 12, 1928.

Stanley Horn, Nashville historian and author of *Army of Tennessee,* University of Oklahoma Press, is authority for the tale that in a fit of rage Cisco slew Bertie's seducer with a knife in Nashville. So the publisher-bookseller-archaeologist retained his fiery habits after quitting Indian Mound country, though the shadow of tragedy fell long across his after years. Maybe this is one of the reasons that he studied mounds no more, writing nothing of them, though he was in the heart of the Middle Tennessee mound country. This was the Harpeth complex, itself a very populous and extensive civilization of the Mound Builders, some 20 miles west of Nashville. It is doubtful, of course, that this was an actual extension of the Pinson Mounds, though certainly the two populations were in communication with each other by overland trails and waterways down the Cumberland, into the Ohio, down the Mississippi, and eventually up the Forked Deer.

If you have ever driven along old Highway 70, as we have, you've paused to study the beetling crag that supports the curious earth work that is the famous Harpeth Mound. The highway itself is the old east-west trade route —and mayhap the war trace in hostile times—which has been designated as the Cisco-Harpeth Trail. Archaeologists think of this mound with its companion across the river as one of the most spectacular of all ancient sites in Tennessee.

"It has two divisions," as Lewis and Kneberg describe it in *Tribes that Slumber,* The University of Tennessee

Press, "one of which is on high ground, protected on the river side by precipitous bluffs and on the other side by defense works" similar probably to those at Pinson. "The entire hill top has been leveled off and terraced, creating a plaza about 1,000 feet long and 500 feet wide. One large mound and two smaller ones had been built near the edge overlooking the river bottom. On a terrace below the plaza, two more mounds had been constructed. The entire area enclosed by the fortification is over 300 acres."

Today it is a verdant pasture, lined by recent dwellings on the highway on one side, and a large "amusement hall" where the Nashville go-go crowd can roller skate, dance, drink beer, and enjoy the blandishments of the juke box (and perhaps a beverage stouter than Coca-Cola, for we discovered an empty Old Crow bottle in the refuse behind the place that sunny morning when we'd have preferred seeing ghosts of Redskins cavorting in the rows of Indian corn in the bottom).

The account goes on, "Less than a mile away, where the river makes a deep loop, lies the other division of the site. Almost completely surrounded by the river, except for a narrow neck, it occupies level bottom land. There, another broad plaza with one enormous mound and a number of smaller ones had formed a second ceremonial center. If, as seems likely, this was a single large town composed of two widely separated divisions, its population must have been very large."

We have stepped astray 150 miles not for the sake of the Harpeth Mounds, but in wonderment that Cisco apparently did not fare forth on his horse and visit the locality, view the splendors of a slumbering past, and gather a saddlebag of artifacts, which at that time must have been fairly plentiful. Better still, he might have published another monograph on Harpeth, thus further immortalizing himself in the scrolls of the archaeologists. Mayhap he was too busy in his spare time chasing the seducers from Bertie with long blacksnake or mulewhip, horse pistol, and knife. It's a pity. John Guy was good at that sort of thing.

Instead he promoted his railroad, one line of which follows almost exactly the highway and Indian trails, and indeed the Harpeth Mound hears daily the snort and roar of the iron horse, the uncouth racket of which would have made the noble Redskins wet their breech clouts and pretty maiden-head caps. But "progress" has its compensations. The Redskins, scared white, could have relaxed to the charm of hideous jazz and hillbilly down at the juke joint, and beguiled their upset with tranquilizing draughts of Budweiser and snorts of Old Fitzgerald.

9
The William E. Meyer Expedition

William Edward Meyer was Tennessee's most noted archaeologist. His fame was not confined to Tennessee. He was a collaborator of the Bureau of American Ethnology of the Smithsonian Institution at Washington, D.C., and author of the important book, *Remains of Primitive Man in Cumberland Valley, Tennessee*, as well as articles in many archaeological journals. He missed none of the important mound sites in Tennessee, and few of the long abandoned village sites. His diggings and delvings in the dirt fetched to light new discoveries of primitive Indian life. One of his most important discoveries was that of the hitherto unknown Indian citadel on the summit of the tall, long, narrow double-faced precipitous bluff on the point of land between the Harpeth and Cumberland Rivers at their junction in Cheatham County, Tennessee. He wrote in *Art and Archaeology*, "This natural fortress extended along the summit of this thin double-faced bluff or promontory for a distance of 3110 feet. This fortress-bluff is from 150 to 200 feet in height. It can be scaled in very few places, and at these places only with great difficulty." It must have taken our agile mound-chaser many grunts and much sweat to negotiate this difficult approach, which was further fortified by breastworks and palisades. In his prime Bill Meyer was, presumably, a tough husky hunter for lost tribes.

Not the least of his achievements was his running down of the clues to the mystery of Old Stone Fort. This is not a mound but an enclosed area of 40 acres guarded by 10 to 15 foot stone-and-earth wall, with but a single entrance that was capable of being closed against an enemy by a ponderous oaken gate. It's about four miles—as we recall—from the town of Manchester in Middle Tennessee. The earliest historians of Tennessee had noted the spot, but no one knew its history. There was no local tradition concerning it. There it was, a fortified site between the forks of Duck River. There were, we remember, elevations at each side of the gate above the rest of the wall; and at intervals these watch towers were posted. Though there was a vast amount of loose stone for building material, nevertheless, it had been a monumental task to erect this structure by hand. And in the quiet of that summer day, in the isolation of this hidden region—we had to park our car off the highway and take a stony road some distance and then a rugged footpath the rest of the two miles to reach it—we could only sit and soak up the romance and nostalgia and wonderment at the whole business. We were always like that in the presence of these forsaken habitations of Mound Builders. Who were they, and where had they gone? The questions challenged Bill Meyer, but he did something about them: he eventually worked out, by a lucky coincidence—only dedicated archaeologists know how to utilize these coincidences—the answers.

In 1919 he found a copy of the old "Franquelin's 1684 Map of La Salle's Discoveries, Paris, 1684," in the Library of Congress. This map furnished the first faint clue as to who built this ancient fort. Researching it, Meyer established the fact that the fort was at one time inhabited by the ancient Yuchis Indians. These Indians later lived on the Savannah River and elsewhere in South Carolina and Georgia. This presumably was after they permanently abandoned the fort. Meyer established no date for the exodus; he states elsewhere, "further researches showed the Old Stone Fort to be the famous Cisca which De Soto tried in vain to reach in 1540." We are left with the question whether De Soto lost his way in the wilderness or whether the Indians had already departed. In any case

Meyer found the Yuchis busy in warfare in the South between whites and Redskins, and a remnant surviving to be living with the displaced Creeks in Oklahoma.

We have, of course, departed from our main story, Meyer's visit and research on the Pinson Mounds, but the point seemed well to make: the study of the Great Mounds was in competent hands when finally, in January 1919, Meyer came to Jackson, contacted Cisco, and headed south of town to dig and delve in Pinson.

Meyer's field notes have come into our hands, thanks to Dr. John B. Nuckolls, a prominent urologist in Jackson, who today wears Cisco's scalp in Pinson archaeology. Much of this material for obvious reasons is quoted verbatim. Who Meyer's companion was on these long tramps through the wintry fields around the Mounds is not stated. But winter in Tennessee land can be a messy and somber season. If the men didn't wear boots in the mud, it's safe to assume some time within the two weeks they wished they had.

"Few objects were found on the surface during Mr. Meyer's two weeks spent at this place."

We wonder if this was not the writing of J. G. Cisco.

"For instance, while red jasper seems to have been the favorite material, yet there is very little found considering the extent of the group. This curious fact was noted by Mr. Meyer who spent much time searching the fields about the mounds. He and I walked over the place during our visit of January 17, 1919, and were unable to find more than three or four fragments of pottery, and one arrowhead, and some chips of camden chert. How this place could have been occupied as it was long enough to construct 35 mounds, one of which is probably the largest in the state of Tennessee, is another of our archaeological mysteries.

"The theory that suggests itself is that the place was immediately abandoned after the mounds were constructed. This fact cannot be determined until after further explorations. At any rate until the mounds and walls are actually shown in the survey of the group. Preparations were made by the Indians for one of the largest fortified places in either the Tennessee or Cumberland Valleys, yet smaller places [have] shown signs of vaster occupation."

On second thought, this could not have been written by Cisco. Cisco, for instance, would have explained readily enough the paucity of artifacts around the old Indian town. He himself had a couple bushels of choice stone axes, tomahawks, spear points, and arrowheads. He had a rare old Indian pipe. What is more, the land had been under cultivation for around 75 years. Boys had haunted the locality for arrowheads. Ownership of the lands had passed through many hands—the Murphys, Marshalls, Ozier, Thedford, Waddington. Then the Saul family bought in the farm upon which stood the Great Central Mound. In plowing each spring the ploughboys had turned up just about everything of value as deep as 12 inches. Naturally, then, when two strange palefaces came snooping around, they found few bones. To conclude that the Mound Builders had pawed and scraped and toted dirt enough to build 35 mounds, and then rolled up their knitting and left seems premature at the very least.

The following notes are in Meyer's handwriting:

> In January 1919 Mr. Cisco told me that Col. Pic Jones, living at Jackson, Tenn., told him that in 1840 he had ridden along the breastworks in and about the Cisco group for a distance of six miles. In 1877 Cisco saw the remains of the breastworks or roads in Ozier's fields, is not certain about seeing them in Wattington's fields. Cisco had in the eighties or nineties a collection of arrow and spear heads from the Cisco Group. Many of these he got from Ozier and Wattington. Thurston illustrated some in fig 120 fig 1 & 3. (Not shown in MS). Fig. 1 was about 8" (inside) 10" long.

No. 3 about 10″ long. Both 1 & 3 of flint of typical East Tenn. appearance. Appearance, very much in color and appearance of Humphries and Henry Co. Specimens.

Pinson neighborhood settled [says Cisco] about 1823.

The main mound on Murphy land was 72′ 2″ when measured by Cisco and one of the college professors of the College of Jackson in 1878. The hole in the large Murphy mound was dug by local school teacher about 1870—found nothing. The digging in one of the Twin Mounds on Ozier farm was done about 1888 probably by Sam Lancaster (who later became famous as a good road man). No record of what he found. Do not think he found anything other than the sandstone rocks now about the old unfilled hole.

Rock (? word looks like pork) in mound with five equal sides, each "angle" about 90′—flat top has several beech trees on it near 12 in. diam. Angle of slope 45′.

South of the above mound, in a cultivated field, is a twin mound 8′ to 10′ high, about 20′ long & 15′ wide.

Within one mile of the big 72′ mound referred to on other page there are many small mounds and many others have disappeared before the plow. If any have been excavated Cisco was not aware (of it). This field has furnished many thousands of fine relics & flint stones and pottery.

West from Jackson ten or 15 mi. in vicinity of Denmark are a few mounds. Cisco has some fine relics from them, copper beads, gorgets, etc. Oval Mound, 5′ high, 15′ long, 10′ w, on hill 300 yards n. of Campbell's Levee Road 1 mi. W Jackson. Excavated by J. G. Cisco, 1885, found few arrowheads, flint chips, and in hole below original surface of soil found charcoal, ashes and burned bones. This is on Campbell's Farm.

On same Campbell Farm—¼ mi—nearer Jackson—Cisco excavated a larger mound. Found nothing of importance, except the pit in center, containing ashes, burned wood and charred bones. "Took bones to be human."

A small mound, in edge of river bottom, near I. C. Shops. About 3′ h 15′ in diam. Contained fine sandstone pipe and a few arrowheads. Two modern brass crucifixes—not corroded—found 15″ below surface of mound.

2 large mounds—150′ long—100′ wide 8′ h. flat on top, been cultivated for years, in level field, 100 yards from river, in old field, near Love's Bridge, 9 mi S. of Jackson and near Forked Deer River, no further information. This is the old town at Johnston's farm.

North from above 2 mounds outside the field, at edge of bluff, begins a line of earthworks, plainly marked. After entering the field they disappear—(obliterated by the plow). Early pioneers say they extended several miles & embraced in their enclosure near 100 mounds of various sizes. Col. Pic. Jones, a pioneer, claimed to have ridden a distance of five mi. on this embankment. It still can be seen where plow has not leveled it down.

About 2 miles from the above 2 mounds, on old Henderson's farm, now Sam Ozier estate, a most interesting group of mounds. The largest in a field not far from spring branch —72′ high (Haywood says 96′). Trunketed pyramid, 1000 ft. around base. Not explored. 300 yds. w. of this mound, in flat. . . . Specimens

Here ends this handwritten set of field notes. We do not know how much more there may have been in original ms, now in the Smithsonian. But Meyer was just coming to the two principal mounds of all the 35 he mapped, and we are curious. In his last note he says, "not explored." We wonder more. There are possible errors we should note. The date, pencilled in, of January 1919, does not coincide with the date of 1916 Meyer gives in his article "Recent Archaeological Discoveries in Tennessee," published in 1922 in *Art and Archaeology,* and confirmed in a letter written by Matthew W. Stirling, Director of the Bureau of American Ethnology of the Smithsonian Institution, to J. H. Gilbert, Washington, D. C. "At the time of Mr. Meyer's visit about the year 1916, there were approximately 35 mounds in the group as well as traces of embankments which supported the palisade surrounding the area." Stirling noted, "According to Mr. Meyer's survey, the central mound is 73 feet in altitude which makes it, next to Cahokia in Illinois, the highest mound in the entire country." Further in his letter he adds, "The Pinson site is . . . one of the largest and best preserved groups of the so-called Temple Mound period."

In Meyer's article—one wonders if, for all his devotion to archaeology and integrity in factual report, he took time when he wrote his article to check more closely on his conclusions when he stated, "This mound (Great Central Mound) is about sixth in size among the great mounds of the United States." We shall consider this question of *size* further on, especially when it is measured merely by *height*. Pinson undoubtedly ranks second in the matter of altitude. There are other factors in support of its importance—the vast area of its cultivated acreages; the probable number of inhabitants; obviously the widespread lesser mound groups within the ready vicinity of Pinson— to cite just one such neighborhood, the Johnson farm group of ten mounds. Though many were modest in size, two were major mounds—one rectangle 200x200 feet at the base, 100x100 feet on top, and 20 feet high; the other 140x155 feet, 60x90 on top, polygon in shape and approximately 10 feet high. These mounds had cubic contents of 18,518 earth yards, and 4818, respectively. The farmers on the land had gradually reduced many of the low flat mounds, though even so most can still be discovered.

One great service Meyer did was have E. G. Buck of the Patton Engineering Co. survey and measure all the 35 mounds in the Pinson group, as well as the ten of the Johnson group. His official figures follow:

PINSON MOUNDS

Table showing size and volume of various mounds in the old Indian Village near Pinson, Madison County, Tennessee.

No. as shown on plat of town.	Shape	Height in feet	SIZE Base	SIZE Top	Contents Cu. Yards	Owner of Land
1.	Polygon	6	90x120	60x80	1,527	Waddington
2.	Rectangular	3.5	90x100	70x50	722	,,
3.	Rectangular	4.5	95x100	45x55	1,065	,,
4.	Circular	1.5	80	Point	654	,,
5.	Polygon	32.2	240x230	100x100	34,346	R. L. Ozier
6.	Twin-Circular				21,000	,,
7.	Circular	1.5	40	21	44	,,
8.	Oval	2.0	90x160		533	,,
9.	Oval	73.00	300x370	36x60	92,300	J. Murphy
10.	Polygon	6.5	130x200	70x140	2,700	J. J. Marshall
11.	Rectangular	3.5	170x180	110x130	2,915	J. Murphy
12.	Oval	7.0	150x190	88x30	3,266	,,
13.	Circular	3.5	150		1,500	,,
14.	Circular	2.5	100		242	,,
15.	Rectangular	60.10	160x165	105x117	6,666	,,
16.	Circular	3.5	125	Point	151	,,
17.	Oval	3.5	120x160	Point	698	,,
18.	Circular	6.0	150	Point	1,309	J. J. Marshall

Mounds in the Mist 118

19.	Circular	4.0	150	Point	873
20.	Circular	3.5	175	Point	1,039
21.	Circular	4.0	160	Point	993
22.	Circular	1.0	120	Point	140	J. J. Marshall
23.	Circular	2.0	100	Point	194	”
24.	Oval	3.0	150x175	Point	745	”
25.	Circular	2.5	150	Point	500
26.	(Point in ridge or embankment being point in known location of old line of breast works around the town.)					”
27.	Circular	4.0	30	Point	28
28.	Rectangular	14.0	205x215	130x140	15,763	J. Marshall & R. S. Price
29.	Rectangular	10.0	130x140	95x105	6,740	J. P. Thedford
30.	Irregular	7.5			1,444	”
31.	Circular	3.0	80	Point	654	R. L. Ozier
32.	Circular	3.5	80	Point	700	J. Murphy
33.	Circular	4.0	80	Point	800	R. L. Ozier
34.	Circular	1.5	25	Point	12	”
35.	Circular	15.0	100	50	?

PATTON ENGINEERING COMPANY
Jackson, Tennessee,
By: E. G. Buck—1917.

(A COPY WITH CERTAIN OMISSIONS)

Taken from Meyer's report. The names of the farmer owners of the land were written in by hand in original.

Meyer in his *Art and Archaeology* report, September 1922, wrote in part:

"Recent archaeological discoveries made by the author in Tennessee show that state to have within its borders some of the most important and interesting remains left by the stone age man in the United States. Very little has been known about some of the great ruins. Amongst these great and almost unknown remains may be cited the ruins of the city of Cisco. . . .

"It is hard to realize that in the State of Tennessee ruins of a great and ancient walled city with outer defenses measuring fully six miles in length, with elaborate outer and inner citadels, with 35 mounds of various sizes, should have remained almost unknown beyond the bare fact that near the little railroad station of Pinson, in Madison County, there were some mounds and inclosures.

"The author visited this site in 1916. He found in the thickets and swamps and woodlands along the south fork of the Forked Deer River the remains of an ancient and fortified city together with its outlying towns and settlements. They were so close together that doubtless their cultivated fields and small isolated truck patches formed a more or less continuous cultivated site for a distance of about 12 miles."

This city itself, Meyer says, extended along the high bluffs of the river for some two and a half miles. "It was probably defended on the river side by a continuous line of wooden palisades along the edge of the high bank." The pole-log palisade was the typical fortification of not only the Mound Builders but Indian tribes all over the timbered regions of North America. Further protection was afforded by the river and great swamp to the westward. The length of the outer defenses was a little over six miles. "The walls of the inner citadel and the other inner defenses add five-sixths of a mile to this total." Though cultivation had destroyed parts of the long embankment, Meyer found sections of it in fair preservation in the thickets and woodlands, and old farmers about the place remembered fainter traces and tales of early settlers. "Of course all traces of the wooden palisades have long since disappeared."

There were the 35 mounds, ranging from some no more than a foot high to the mighty Great Central Mound. "This great mound is 73 feet high; its base is 300x370 feet; and its summit 38x60 feet. It contains 92,300 cubic yards of earth. . . . It commands a view of the surrounding country for many miles in every direction. At one time it probably had the great house of the king on its summit."

He makes the point that it is about sixth in size among the great mounds, one in particular that resembles a bird with outstretched wings—birds were sacred in the religious rites of stone age men.

"There is abundant evidence showing this city was the central city and capital of a large region; that it had a population of several thousand, and was built by some conqueror-king. The great fortified city was occupied only a short time after its completion. Then the conqueror-king was overthrown. His stronghold was seized and destroyed. It was left desolate and never afterward occupied."

Meditations on the life of prehistoric men in Tennessee charm our distinguished digger in the bones of time to some of his greatest flights of rhetoric.

"During the untold centuries since man came into what is now Tennessee many quite different savage peoples have lived at various times in this region. They toiled and worshiped, loved and fought, even as we the latest comers, do. Then in the course of long years came fate in the guise of enemy or pestilence or omens, and they were driven out. Their wigwams decayed and fine forests slowly grew on the sites of their villages, which became buried beneath the black loam wherewith nature so kindly and tenderly covers the scars upon her breast—scars which mark the struggles and heartaches of her children. Time comes when all knowledge of these former inhabitants has been long lost. Comes some archaeologist with pick and spade and uncovers these ruins of buried homes, and from the few relics found therein, with infinite patience and labor, slowly works out the broad outlines of the life of these vanished people. These relics, in the hands of those who have given them years of toil and study, become keys to the gateways of a great and unexplored region, lying silent and deserted, just beyond the present ken of men. The archaeologist enters the gateway his researches have unlocked. He wanders alone down the vast silences of the dead centuries, feeling the exquisite thrill which comes only to those who tread where man before has never trod. Some such thrill has come in a small way to the author, who has devoted a large portion of his life to an endeavor to solve the problem of prehistorc man in Tennessee."

William Edward Meyer was born near Fountain Run, Barren County, Kentucky, on October 5, 1862. When he was about six years old, his family moved to Carthage, Tennessee, and there he spent the rest of his life. He attended the Carthage public school, then entered Vanderbilt University, where he took his degree. Declining the principalship of a large school in Michigan because his parents thought him too young, he settled in Carthage, organized the first bank in Smith County, and promoted bridges over Cumberland and Caney Fork Rivers. As a highway commissioner he fostered good roads in Tennessee. He took an active part in the development of navigation on Cumberland River and for many years was president of the Cumberland River Improvement Society. During the First World War he served as fuel administrator for Tennessee.

His interest in archaeology began while he was at school. He spent his vacations in research work in that field, and though active in business found time daily to study archaeology. One year he camped with his family for two weeks on an Indian mound at Castalian Springs, collecting many rare aboriginal relics. In time, through field trips and correspondence, he covered the state. In 1919, he moved to Washington, D.C., to pursue research at the Smithsonian Institution, working with Dr. J. W. Fewkes, Chief of the Bureau of American Ethnology, and other investigators. A paper by him, entitled "Two Prehistoric Villages in Middle Tennessee," appeared in the 41st Annual Report of the Bureau. His interest widened with publication, and he developed a study, "Stone Age Man in Tennessee," which he broadened into "Stone Age Man in the Middle South." His next contribution was "Indian Trails and Remains in Tennessee." This finally became a report on trails in all states south of the Ohio and Potomac Rivers and east of the Mississippi.

In the midst of these investigations, he was suddenly stricken with a heart attack and died on December 2, 1923, at the age of 61 years. He was among the very earliest scholars in Indian life and lore in the Mound Builder area of the United States.

10
Mounds in the Mist

I remember the first time I saw the Pinson Indian Mounds.

In a vague way I knew of their existence. In the university library I had run into an article in what may have been bound volumes of an historical magazine which detailed the strange and forsaken relics of a vanished civilization. There was mention of some 60 mounds—I'm speaking from memory now—and a vast area where in prehistoric times a numerous population had flourished. Two of the large mounds were named, accompanied by photographs. There was a map, I recall. The place of all this fabulous, lost people was only 60 miles from my college. It fascinated me. The romance, the apparent tragedy and mystery of the Mound Builders' disappearance—it hit me in the heart of my romantic and emotional nature. I resolved some day to run down there and see all this for myself.

But I was in the first year or two of teaching at the post that I held the rest of my career, and somehow I just didn't find time under my heavy load and outside duties to visit the Mounds. But the spell lasted, and when a time came that I might satisfy myself, I couldn't find the article to refresh my mind before the visit. I think the ghost of some Redskin must have sneaked up behind me that day in the library and put a spell on me while I napped from overwork.

One of my outside jobs for the college was visiting high schools and talking to senior classes about our offerings, and two counties assigned to me lay on Highway 45 which led through the village of Pinson 10 miles below Jackson, Tennessee, a couple miles east of which the

Mr. and Mrs. Laymon Shoemake, with their children Helen, Henry Lee, and Margaret, live at Chucalissa Indian Village where they add the richness of their ancestral heritage to their present-day opportunities to live abundantly. (Photo-Courtesy Chucalissa Museum Memphis State University)

mound region is located. It was an early April day that I drove down to Bolivar. You remember this is where Henrietta's brother lived when she came into the Western Territory to find uncouth folk, soiled settlements, and disillusionment. I took the same road her stagecoach had followed that day. It was blacktop now. The land was worn out, eroded, overgrown with snow-top dogwood,

Among those who prize highly the rich heritage left them by their ancestors and keep alive many cherished traditions are Mr. and Mrs. Esbie Gibson. At Chucalissa they are able to wear their native dress, make fine cane baskets and other intricate craft. (Photo-Courtesy Chucalissa Museum)

Mounds in the Mist 127

Memphis State University students eagerly watch and note findings as they excavate village area at Chucalissa. (Photo-Courtesy Chucalissa Museum, Memphis State University)

the tree the Indians used to debark for basketry, boil the bark as a cure for swamp fevers—malaria—in thicker brew as an abortion medicine, and mixed with sarsaparilla bark, for restoring lost manhood in fading braves. The redbud was declining but still vivid splotches where the old Indian trail to the Bolivar Town and Mounds led; and the oak leaves were the size of squirrel's ears—corn planting time for the Indians. You may remember the Redskins planted a fish with each three grains to the hill. They believed the fish imparted its spirit of nutrition to the ears of maize—not a bad substitute for the principle of fertilizing. The white men who settled on their lands would have done

Mounds in the Mist 128

well to emulate them before the clearings washed away into the yellow dirty Hatchee, Forked Deer, Obion, leaving these gullies and scraggly timber as a monument to their unbridled greed.

Choctaws placed the body of the dead onto a bier made of cypress bark and mounted on four forked sticks fifteen feet high. After worms had eaten the flesh from the body, the family assembled and wept quietly while the bonepicker dismembered the skeleton, tearing of muscles, nerves, and tendons that might be left. These they buried and then deposited the skeleton in its resting place. There was no singing—no dancing; all left weeping. (Photo Courtesy Chucalissa Museum)

A Chucalissa house reconstruction of the type once used by the Choctaw Indians of Mississippi. (Photo courtesy of Memphis State University)

A group of Choctaw girls in their native dress. Choctaws throughout the southeast did not cut their hair or shape it to a definite pattern but allowed it to grow full length. (Photo Courtesy George Day Studio)

But I was thinking none of this that sunny day I drove down along the blacktops and through the white caps on a day's break from the uninspired monotony of Freshman English. What helped in this happy oblivion was Sue Marie.

Let me present Sue Marie. She was a saucy, fruity child, soft as lazy feathers, blond as wild moonbeams, babydoll with a sexy knowing insolence, my student "secretary" who posted my rolls, checked on grades, and changed the shrubbery in the vase on my desk, and decorated my office with her sculptured youth. I admit at times her springtime display upset my natural lechery, but a man needs the Indian herbs and potions of Youth at times to dissolve the rheumy deposits in his joints. Sue Marie did this by substituting for the daughter I never had, and being as possessive and affectionate. She had a taste for good music, tormented a certain acceptable Chopin from a piano, adored me for the books I wrote, swore one day she would write the Great American Novel, and readily dropped into all my enthusiasms as if she had invented them. She knew about the Pinson Mounds though she'd never been there; and she said she was going native one fine day and live in trees naked, and eat acorns and snakes and have a baby by the Spirit of some dashing Brave. (She had the baby all right, but not by a spirit.)

Her folks lived six miles west of Bolivar, and she accompanied me because she could spend the day at home while I harangued the prospective graduates at Bolivar High School.

We were a trifle late about starting home. From Bolivar to Jackson, the old Chickasaw Trail, is Highway 18. You pass through the villages of Medon and Malasus, two slumbrous gatherings of pretty homes—more interesting to me were the mounds scattered on the nearby farms; and then some couple miles south of Jackson you intersect Highway 45, in ancient times the Cisco and Savannah

Trail. We turned into this at dusk, picked up a couple sandwiches and cokes at a joint on the way south, and resumed our journey to Pinson, seven miles on. On the left of the road is the historical marker, "Lost City of Cisco. Two miles east, the famous Pinson Mounds . . ." We left the rusty little rural railroad town to the right and went into what then was a sandy-dirt country road, which crossed the shallow Forked Deer on a wood bridge that rattled under us. A day had been, just outside the memory of old residenters, that this was one of the water routes for freight and passengers to the new land; and 4,000 years ago the route of travel, save the overland trails, for the Indian migrations and traders. Now it was a muddy creek with no more romance about it than a string of dirty wash. Reeds grew at the shoreline, now drifting into darkness, and we could hear the croupy

Plaza and reconstructed houses at Indian Town, Chucalissa village. (Photo Courtesy Memphis State University)

Choctaw Indians in front of Temple Mound; others in group represent worshipers come for ceremonial to honor Chief. (Photo Courtesy Chucalissa Museum)

croak of amorous frogs. Sue Marie said once, "I wonder what's in that noise to make a lady frog lay eggs and have little frogs?" We wriggled through some more sand and then climbed through a shallow cut out on a wide level of farmland, dim and ghostly in the first faint rise of a moon above the line of dark hills perhaps five miles to the east. All the land had either been broken for cotton or already bedded and planted. There was the smell of fresh earth in the sweet, wet shifting air. All this was Indian old fields. The little I knew of the region told me that corn—maize—had been cultivated here untold centuries. Present farmers were still cotton men.

The first mound rose out of this level in somber squat like an old woman enjoying a pe-pe in the shrouded gloom. Its name was Ozier Mound. It was tree covered, the tops

Temple and temple mound at Chucalissa. Choctaws were a group uncontaminated with the idea that they existed for the sake of religious organization. Their ceremonials were relatively simple and uncomplicated. (Photo Courtesy Memphis State University)

still thin; the old poplar that once had been its landmark was longtime gone. Far distant was a house, its lights shining dimly; but there was no other habitation. A great blank aloneness, choked a little by sudden spring night mist, clutched down upon mound and land. Sue Marie plucked at my sleeve.

"Let's get out and go see."

We crossed some rows of earth and peered up through an opening in the undergrowth toward the top of this hunk of Forked Deer mud. Awe is a hard thing to manage in words. Sue Marie shivered a little and moved close to me. "Boogars! Ghosties! Spooks!" Just what did the thing

Mounds in the Mist 134

look like? Let's drag in some statistics, though they won't help much. My book afterward said it was 32 feet high. It was in shape of a polygon. That means a figure of many angles and many sides. Close up, this polygon was a rise of ground covered with hazel, sassafras and persimmon brush, with a half-nude oak or beech sticking out of the underwear. The footway, which we did not immediately follow, entered by the northwest. It seemed the original stairway. The base, so my book said, was 240x230 feet.

Aerial view of Chucalissa. This restoration of a Mound Builder village recreates prehistoric Indian life with remarkable fidelity. Dr. Charles Nash, professor of anthropology at Memphis State University, has created with authenticity the temple and dwellings of a population estimated at its peak as perhaps 2000. The site overlooks the Mississippi River. (Photo courtesy Memphis State Univ.)

Neighboring villages invited each other to their "stick games," somewhat similar to LaCrosse. Men and women gathered the evening before the contest, each dressed in his finest apparel. They spent most of the night dancing to the sound of the drum and rattle; those who did not dance, sang. Each village had its own fire lighted in the middle of the prairie.

On the day of the match, the players—with their bodies bare and painted in all colors and with a tiger tail fastened behind and feathers attached to their elbows and heads—met. Each team had forty players who vied with such vigor that sometimes their shoulders were dislocated, but players never became angry. Unusual among southeastern tribes, women whose husbands had lost, came forth to avenge them. They ran and shoved just as the men and like the men, too, played naked. (Photo courtesy Chucalissa Museum)

Mounds in the Mist 136

The lot where my old house just off the campus stands is 90x200 feet. So a couple of my humble mansions could be piled on the base and there would be enough dirt left over for the juke joint that prospers at my corner with the enticing name of Joy House.

"Come on, Sir Harry," Sue Marie said, coming out of her shudders. "Let's go to the top and stir up the skeletons." She took my hand in her plump warm one. We pressed through the overknit limber switches, and once she stopped midway of the climb to yowl, "I'm caught in a mess of briers!" I helped her free her skirt from the thorns. She removed the wrap-around garment, and underneath she wore white shorts. In the still thinly

Group of young Choctaw girls dressed for the day during which they may meet many visitors to Chucalissa village. (Photo courtesy Memphis State University)

sifted light it was a little difficult to dissociate her fair plump leg skin from white duck weave. "Here," she gave me the skirt bundle to tote while she pioneered up the rise to the flat top. We halted for breath and now some more statistics. It's a Mississippian Mound. The top was square, 100x100 feet. Goats must have been kept here to chew off the thickening undergrowth, for the vegetation was reasonably open. The trees were clear cut, and I'd have said they ranged from 50 to 75 years in age. Oaks, a gum or two, some clean-cut beeches, a tree I love. One large tree, but not the aged giant poplar, had been felled, the lumber cuts sawed off, and a knotty torso left, which was blackened by having been imperfectly cremated against the stump. We found cow chips in the thick grass. There was the smell of farm beasts, of gray pale night air, of dew, hidden flowers, and the wide fresh plowed acreages on every hand. Sue Marie was close enough to me, still clinging to my hand, for me to smell her hair and body. Her fragrance was youth and female. They were ghosts as wraithlike as any hovering spirit of the Mound Builders in the winds and trees, as stuffed with romance as the thought that engineers, bless their unimaginative souls, said that this mound contained 34,346 cubic yards of prehistoric West Tennessee dirt, and every last pound of it—a cubic yard weighs a ton, I ween—was toted by patient females, in baskets woven from willow and pawpaw bark and in leather burden pokes made of buffalo hides. Old squaws with naked dehydrated tits, sucked dry by the young females with firm tall breasts toting burden baskets on their heads. Miles and miles away. Somewhere I'd read there were no signs of earth having been taken nearby. This incredible tonnage of silt and mud and clay had to come from somewhere, but God only knew. I suppose in a way I thought of this, as mist seeps into the bones; but anyway that was the way of it. Sue Marie was there to fill my senses with the smell of youth and woman. You can't think clearly like that, but you can have a world of wondrous feelings and eerie yearnings, while ghosts tousle your hair.

Picnickers had been here; we found their camp fires, the garbage of their lunches.

"I'm hungry, Harry!" Sue Marie suddenly wailed.

"My God, wench, you got a hollow tube for a gut?"

She felt in my pocket. "Don't you have a candy bar or something?"

"I'll call up the spirit of an Indian brave to give you a raw fish."

She gagged. "Reckon I'll just have to starve."

By this time the moon had broken free of the hills and timberline toward the east, and its radiance, reddened by low distance and the mists, had a strange and haunting veillike quality. I liked to think that 10,000 dead Indian women and girls, falling and creeping into the land they could no longer tote, leaving no bones behind them, were rising to burnish the night. Their patient substance wove back and forth across the bloody moon, somehow mocking me and this girl and our car and this day and its greed and abundance, and reaching for our grief to share its compassion. I drew the girl close, wondering at how toil could turn her fair skin and milk sweet flesh into leather and coarse gristle, as might have been in a primitive or prehistoric day. Small wonder the worst epithet a man could use for his woman was "squaw." I said, "Let's go around the base of this lump of dirt and have a look at The Great Central Mound."

We picked our way back and around to a point where we could look across the half mile of intervening prairie flat. We stopped; I gasped, Sue Marie's breath caught in wonder. Saul's Mound—named after the man who had owned the land for more than 50 years—stood there in the eerie moonlight in fantastic massiveness and brooding isolation. There was a wide halo around the moon, its light sifting through the nearer mists with a prismatic glitter—an effect really of stereoscopic distortion. This mystic illumination clutched and clawed at the earth heap, cloaked with wintry gray-green timber, until Mound and trees scratched the back of the dew-damp stars. I made no estimate of its size. Yards and tons and altitudes have no measure for the mystery, the illusion and phantasma, of the toils of ancient ghosts, the tears of dead souls so long buried that even their bones have rotted. The mound itself made me think of a great dead woman whose monster breast remained for trees to grow upon like hairs on a pubes. Upon all this the glittering moonlight fell, wet and chill; and a man and young girl gazed at it with the salt of wordless awe in their damp eyes, and a dry voiceless tension in their tearless throats. We made small sounds and clung to each other; and I knew then such another moment would never come again. It did not need the wafting gossamer of webs of rutting spiders, weaving in poetry across our line of vision, to emphasize or even make articulate the shiver of knowledge that this was once in a lifetime, and even it would not have been quite so if we had not been together to share it.

"Sir Harry!"

"What?"

"I have been here before." I looked into her limpid eyes. "But I haven't."

I nodded, shaking off the spell. "I know. I had the feeling too—for a moment. It's called Deja Vu—'seen before.' I haven't either."

A rustle of night air broke the spell, and we laughed shakily. "Let's go see that awful thing," she said, and we started across the plowed field by a turn row. The distance was deceptive, farther than we'd thought. When we came within the vicinity of the mound base, we could see still the buttresses of the pyramidal Mound. The wind rustled in the trees. The moonlight now was gay, nearly brilliant.

I had a thought that Mound Builder Indians might once have been people from Egypt. But, then, there was nothing secret about the shape of a pyramid. The Egyptians could have thought of it and the Mound Builders in a cruder shape thought of it, and the two never heard of each other or dreamed. Men's minds have a way like that. Men's bodies grow like that—the Negro in a black soil, the Indian in a red soil, the white man in a white soil; and if we admit a God why could He not readily have knocked together the different bricks of structure without letting His right hand know what His left was fashioning? The scientific men wearied me with their struggles forever chasing down to one original source the beginnings of men and their ways. So I let my dead and gone Mound Builders think of their own pyramids. But I could wish they hadn't worked the hell out of their women.

"Let's climb to the top," Sue Marie said.

"Mygawd no!" I said. "No! Let's walk around the thing and look up at it."

"Aw, Sir Harry, I want to climb it!"

"You can't. It's full of snakes and bats."

"Aw you old sissy college professors are scared of snakes and bats! Well, I'm not. I'm fixing to climb up!"

I caught her arm. "Nothing doing, young lady! I've got to deliver you to that dorm mother by ten o'clock and we're going to be late now!"

She yanked loose. "You stop me, big shot!" But when I pleaded with her to let's walk around the base first, she yielded. "Okay, Sir Harry, but if women could carry all this dirt and build the Mound, while the men sat on their fannies, then I'm man enough to climb it—see?" So we walked around the mound. The land had been mowed like a lawn, and I looked for any depression in the near ground to indicate that the dirt had been excavated near by. Actually there was a slight upward slope toward the base. I couldn't think the Indians had carried their good farm dirt here—it was too hard to clear, and too precious to rob from their maize. I did not step distances. My book had said it was 300x370, and adding the figures we have just about a quarter of a mile. There was some difference of opinion about its height. One of the earliest historians said it was 100 feet tall. Later and probably more accurate men of science gave its height as 78 feet, and finally 73 feet. That's the dirt. The trees are bonus. That night I went along with 100 feet for the Mound and 150 feet for the tallest tree, and that's why in my eyes the brown-wet breast in springtime oak-and-beech lace suckled the stars, with the honey of history. Let's heave in the tonnage of dirt while we're at it, and I report meaninglessly that it contained 92,300 tons, counting a ton to the cubic yard.

"Aw well!" I sighed. "Let's get on to the top of this thing, and maybe I can tell Mother Blacky that we had car trouble and were delayed. It's an old gag with the young bloods but maybe my professorial robes and smear of gray will save you from being campused a week."

"It'll only make it worse. Come on." She started ahead.

I tagged along, my joints creaking at every upward step; and I would have you know that the slope of this primitive pyramid was at a degree to make me puff and grab bushes to escalate my ascent after this indefatigable female. "Mygawd!" I kept thinking. "Why'd I ever get into this mess?" Now and then my foot would slip on the wet leaves of last year's fall. But the route was reasonably open; and I imagine it must have been the stairway of the famous old chiefs who shinned up the Temple Mound to communicate with the Great Spirit. It had been kept open by goats, scientific diggers, and boys hunting arrowheads and other artifacts. Picnickers shunned it, naturally, for it took work to climb the golden stairs to the flat area on top given as 36x60 feet. One hardly noticed this flat top, however, from the ground. It was, again, a "Mississippi" Mound. We'll come to that after a while. This would place its age as not less than 1000 years, and perhaps the base had been laid while Jesus was blessing the loaves and fishes and changing water into wine. I'd have settled for a loaf and glass of red wine when we at last got to the summit.

I grabbed a sapling and Sue Marie muffled a shriek when a nocturnal bird swooped down at us with menacing click of bill, and veered away into the shadows. "My Lord!" Sue Marie gasped. "I thought you said they were only snakes and bats—"

I said with a show of nervous bravery, "It's nothing but a hoot owl!"

Moonlight sifted through the half nude branches, muted by the young leaves, but we could see the partly open area that in ancient times had been the site of the ceremonial temple—according to one authority; or the palace of the "king" according to another. The "king" idea had never set well with me, inasmuch as the Indians, none of them that I'd ever read about, ancient or recent, had a king in the sense of the traditional paleface kings whose crowns in latter years had set so uneasily on their heads. Tribal government really seems, in examining it at a distance, to have been a fairly good parliamentary democracy, with authority derived from the people through some deed of valor in battle, or respect due him for the gift of statesmanship; and to suppose the Mound Builders were different sounded absurd to me. So I dismissed the king explanation for the building of the Great Central Mound, as if there had been a shadow of Egyptian Pharaohship here whose slaves swarmed under his command to shovel dirt and heft it aloft to his honor. Standing high in the spring sky, with earth-laden winds wafting cobwebs across my face and making it itch, I surmised something greater —far greater—than man had energized human ants to lifting high the Pinson Mounds. Though God is presumed to be dead, we'll find an explanation in God. I think to the

Mound Builders God was alive and very close.

Sue Marie had resumed her lightsome tone and chatter. "Sir Harry, why don't we spend the night here—"

"Yah," I muttered. "Why don't we?"

"I could dream of my copper-bellied brave, the father of my child, and you could dream of your brass-tailed squaw—" She broke into a shrill female snicker at the erotic implications of her nonsense. She kicked up a mattress of dead leaves from last year's fall.

But I was peering into a shallow excavation, maybe six feet across by ten feet long, unevenly filled with leaves, branches, loose earth leaving a hollow maybe two feet deep. I did not risk a foot in the treacherous hole. I surmised artifact diggers had sweated here, and perhaps men like Cisco and Meyer had manned a curious shovel. It could also have been a sunken area from old ceremonial fires, a collapsed grave, even the site of a "temple" where human sacrifice was practiced in misty times gone by, an influence of the Aztec and Mayas, with whom in long gone ages some authorities believed the flat-topped temple mound was borrowed, to become known by archaeologists as Mississippi Mounds. For a brief while in a situation like this you can believe almost anything, though after a while I began to question a lot of authoritative speculation, based on nothing sounder than my own sensitive intuition.

What was real were the farmlands lying under the spring-sweet full moon. I went here and there to gaze out across the eerie distances, painted by dim gold, where maize once again blossomed, and cotton still had not greened the earth on the steady rows. This was still the day of the one-mule, one-Negro, one-plow husbandry, and instead of Indian women toiling, I could imagine the dark small ghosts of nigger-mule cotton culture. All this silent night painting smeared away into a starlit impressionism. The one dark line of break in the night was the distant eastern hills, probably five miles away, where most of this mound-earth must have been brought by my squaw-virgin slaves. Any direction I looked was this tender desolation, with its haunting promise of fecundity.

This land, I knew, had been cleared of the tall trees and thick underbrush that had grown up since the exodus of the Mound Builders into oblivion. The white man with his axe and saw had opened the fields again where the Indians had harvested their chief crop, maize—corn. But a time had been when these thousands of acres had sustained a population of anywhere from ten to fifteen thousand, not to count the scores of adjacent mound-settlements within a radius of 20 miles. I could think that the great chiefs who used to lightly govern the folk had stood as I did tonight, watching the plantings, savoring the fat harvests in the autumn. Maybe even this hilltop had been the scene of the corn festival, the place of their banquets, and the hole on top was really the barbecue pit over which tons of venison and bear meat, and hundredweights of fish from the Forked Deer were smoked, half-cooked, and sizzled to various stages of indigestibility, for the heap big chiefs to have the bellyache from in the midnight hours. I had one final look from this vantage point, for enemies lurking in the distant forests. Did the Mound Builders put the dirt pile up as a look-out? Even an Indian would not be that big an idiot. The spies need only have climbed any 200-foot poplar tree left standing for the purpose, and see farther than I was seeing tonight. Yet some of my "authorities" suggested this as a possible motive for the Mounds. I shook myself to clear my head of the fogs, and turned to search for Sue Marie, leaving the ghosts to their bones under the earth.

She was waiting. "Let's go, Sir Harry. You'd better be rehearsing your story of the flat tire for Mother Blackie."

11
The Mounds and I

Like Chaucer's pilgrims enroute to Canterbury, I had eagerly awaited this April day. For I, too, was to visit a spot enshrined; theirs was the tomb of Thomas à Beckett, and their reasons for going varied. But mine, so many generations later, was a group of Indian mounds little more than half a hundred miles from my home, and my reason for going crystal clear. I must view these Pinson Mounds, scale one or more of them, and if possible project myself back to these days, so many hundreds of centuries ago, when they were fulfilling the mission for which they were so painstakingly created. Then I would write of my emotions and reactions for this book, *Mounds in the Mist*.

Unlike the Canterbury pilgrims, I had no plans to stop at an inn or to meet a group of people. I wished to lose sight of modern scenes and sounds, to avoid influence or interpretation of any other person, to yield myself completely to the "feel," the sense of belonging, the spirit of Pinson Mounds.

The day dawned fair; a new, young season permeated the air. Even my little Buick seemed attuned to adventure as it sped over the modern highway to this place primitive. I had chosen to make my trek on Sunday because my classes at the university prevented my going on a weekday. Then, too, Sunday for me had always been a day of worship, and I knew I would sense God's holy presence in the quiet stillness of this simple rustic setting. And that Sabbath morning was vivid with virgin April, the soft warm winds pregnant with springtime. The young leaves were feather fans in the shifting breeze. Highway 45, from

Martin to Pinson, was practically empty at this pre-church hour; hence, I could look aside occasionally at the gorgeous array of red azaleas and white dogwood as they vied for attention and with the poet proclaimed, "Beauty is its own excuse for being."

The village of Pinson, nestling along the highway, seemed a relic of that better day when it celebrated Joel Pinson's discovery in 1820. A line of non-descript buildings on the west side of the slab, a car or two, a native, seemed worthy of a picture. I stopped long enough to make a shot and then took the modest blacktop east across the region which, in Indian days, had been a vast swamp. The road was on an embankment to a concrete bridge over the river. At one time, I was told, this inconsequential drift of yellow water was an avenue of traffic— for the Mound Builders once, for the white man in historical times. Just across the bridge the rise set in, rather abruptly, and I saw the eroded bluff which, according to legend, is part of the ancient embankment that for six miles surrounded the town. I decided to park the car, set up my camera, set the self-timer, and photograph myself against the legends. This accomplished, I drove over the ridge and emerged on the wide level of fields that once were Indian corn land. Across the flats, a couple of miles, Pinson Mounds appeared as tufts of summery trees. In a few minutes I was at the base of Ozier Mound. I stood gazing at this mass of earth almost in disbelief; true, I had felt a sense of awe when I read from archaelogical files and viewed old drawings of Ozier Mound, but I was hardly prepared for its vastness. I could but feel how small a thing man is and yet how great the work of his hands. Verses of scripture tumbled about in my mind as I paused, recalling measurements of this mound; now, but only now, were the mathematical figures truly meaningful. I climbed to the top by a grassy, friendly little path and stood in the center of the clean bosky plateau. Under-

Aerial view of Cahokia. Photo made in 1930. (Photo Herbert George Studio)

growth had been cleared but big trees fringed the locality —a pair of oaks, a huge hackberry, an elm, a gum. The winds were soft—fragrant with new leafage; the sifted sunshine was drowsy. Birds fluttered here and there, but in this late forenoon they were not singing. I felt a great aloneness, ghost-haunted by the spectres of men, long dead, who had celebrated life atop this man-made mountain. I was 40 feet above the surrounding flatland. So flat were the farmlands that I had the feeling of a great loftiness. Looking toward the west, I traced the plowed ground and distantly, perhaps two miles, the slight elevation that guarded the old Indian lands—perchance the flattened out earthwork that had, in ages past, guarded the citadel. Little dancing dust clouds advanced with the gusts of wind. To the north ran those distant hills that

No clues have been found to indicate why the Mound Builders pulled down the temple atop Monk's Mound and abandoned the site. There is no evidence of burning or other depredation. Archaeologists have theorized that prolonged drought in the Mississippi Valley around A.D. 1500 might have made it difficult to victual such a large population. The trading empire built by the Indians collapsed. Something of the same sort of calamity may have dispersed the Pinson Mound Builders. Or Etowah, or Moundville, or Emerald. (Illinois Div. of Parks photo)

legend declared had furnished the earth for these immense temples, and folklore insisted had been carried in baskets by the Indian women. This may well be more than legend, for here there were no barrow pits such as those which furnished dirt for the great mound at Cahokia and the beautiful mounds at Moundville. Some said the

The Mounds and I 149

dirt had been scraped from the surrounding land, but I could see no evidence of this. Beneath my feet the ground was hard, long-packed through so many centuries. Again I set my camera and photographed myself against the sunny far-off Indian fields.

And in a twinkling I passed, as it were, through the eons of time and space. It was as if I were a reporter for a great city newspaper or a candidate for a Ph.D. in Anthropology interviewing the chieftains who sat in council smoking their peace pipes and listening respectfully to my myriad and all-but-reverential questions. Did the women indeed carry the dirt? Archaelogists have little patience with this

Yes, give me the land that hath legends and lays—
That whispers of memories of long vanished days.
    (Photo courtesy of Division of Parks, Springfield, Ill.)

idea. Were the aged, the newly wed, the great-with-child exempt from dirt-carrying? How were the dirt carriers chosen—by lot, favor of the gods, for their skilful hands, for their strong arms and sturdy backs, or for their status

The American Indians who lived in the Mississippi Valley between 700 and 1500 lived in large towns and under well advanced social, political, and ceremonial systems. They built with mud, thatch, and perishable wood. Their huge earth mounds, their only remains, show traces of structures in hard-packed interiors. They made pottery and stone implements as well as some copper and stone art objects and ornaments. The latter, however, were rare, and most of the existing specimens were looted from Indian cemeteries by 19th-century collectors and have since vanished into private collections. (Washington Univ. Magazine. Photo from Memphis State University)

Silhouette against the ages.
Sunset on Monk's Mound (Washington Univ. Photo Service)

in the tribes? Who directed them in their tasks and how were they organized—into cohorts, companies, or groups? How many, in what order, and how many hours per day did they work? What rest intervals were given them and how were these determined? Among the women themselves, who were the leaders and how were they chosen? Did petty jealousies arise, thus delaying the work? What penalty was meted out to the lazy, the careless, to those who had no desire to work? To the grumblers? Who determined the place, position, size, and number of mounds to be built within a specific area? Where did they get the dirt for this mound? How far did they carry it? How big were the containers and were these the woven baskets?

In what order did they bring it—single file, two abreast? Who cleared the trail for them? Did they come through the trail at a dogtrot or what was their normal pace? Did they trudge slowly to the muffled beat of drums? Were they happy, believing they were serving their god or pleas-

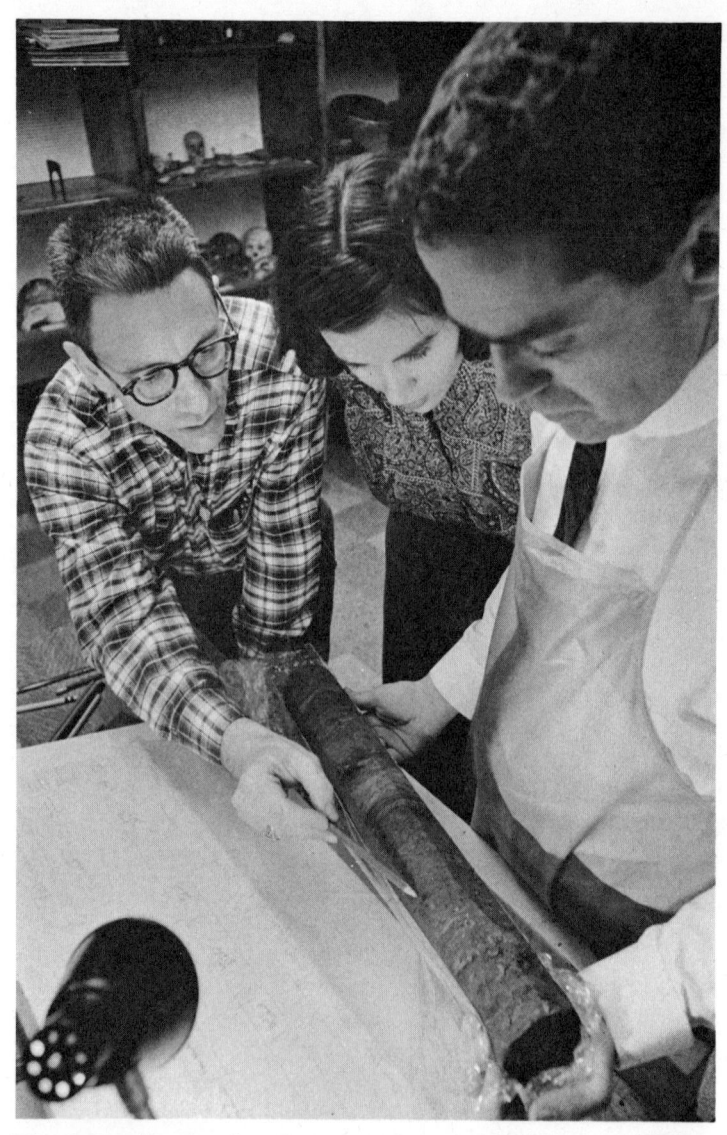

The eternal quest for the past. A core sample from Cahokia Mound is removed from its casing for study in the laboratory. Dr. John W. Bennett, professor of anthropology at Washington University, St. Louis (left); Gail Schroeder, graduate anthropology student (center); and Nelson Reed, research associate, check the marks of the centuries (Washington Univ. photo)

The Washington University archeological team at work atop Monk's Mound, gigantic prehistoric earthwork across the river from St. Louis. The team is taking core samples at various levels of the enormous mound. (Photo Washington University Service)

James Porter, archeologist in charge at the site, does some first-hand exploration near the summit of the Mound. Porter is an authority on the use of miscroscopic thin-section analyses of pottery fragments. (Photo Washington University Service)

Simplicity of design and pleasant location in this reconstructed Temple Mound at Chucalissa is representative of original purpose and structure of Choctaw temple mounds (Photo Courtesy Chucalissa Museum)

ing their men? Did they sing, chant, gossip on the way or was theirs a work of patience, of silence? What of their work-a-day dress? Was it the apron that afforded scant coverage from the waist to midthigh, leaving breasts and backs bare? Was space between them, if they worked in rows, adequately comfortable for arms and motions? How were their feet shod? By what technique did they pack the dirt that finally made up the mound? Weary, grimy, and sweaty at the day's end did they then have to prepare meals and settle members of the family for the night? If not, whose chores were these? On the whole, were these Indian women slender or husky? Did mound-building make them muscular of limb, coarse of skin, and thick of body? Who determined the purpose of this Ozier

Mound? Did this purpose affect the height? Why was it so named? What role did the women play after they finally completed their work and saw the great plateau crowning their labor?*

Mid-morning sun filtering through the trees suddenly snapped me back to the reality of the present. I tapped the firm, solid ground and once more noted its texture, roughness, and hardness. So much of the imperceptible almost overwhelmed me; I gave Ozier one long wistful look and took the camera to the car.

Only a short distance away stood what we call the Twin Mounds. I could have walked, but I am not one to shun modern comforts though I love ancient cultures. Besides, the way was dusty and the day had become quite warm. The air-conditioned car offered protection from heat and dust; in its comfort I mused over the legend that tells of a chieftain and his wife being buried here. Sometimes these twin mounds are called the King and Queen Mounds; that seemed most appropriate as I moved slowly toward them. A romantic at heart, I sensed the rounded dome-like tops as the upper part of a great heart; between the two lay a slight, recessed sort of valley up through which a path eased ever so gently. And then I stood at the base of these twin mounds looking upward, but the idea of their summits forming part of a great valentine persisted. As I stood there alone, attempting to visualize the two people supposedly buried within these mounds, great goose pimples popped out on my skin; my flesh turned cold; my heart all but stood still. Tears began to trickle down my cheeks; an unuttered moan came from my heart. I wondered which of these two died first, which was left lonely. I wondered if they had offspring . . . perhaps they had several stalwart sons and a bevy of beauteous daughters; I hoped they did and that their life together had

---

* Further research revealed the answers to many of my questions and they are included in the context of the book.

been radiantly happy—that they had found each in the other total fulfillment. Unable to trace their ancestry or their descendants, I could but surmise something of their background, their courtship, their wedding ceremony, their sharing day-by-day incidents and events with each other. Perhaps they watched their children grow, sensing characteristic family traits and observing each phase of the young lives as uniquely fascinating as the one preceding it. Of course, these two dreamed dreams, saw visions, and held ambitions for themselves and their people. I wondered how many of them came true—how many were realized.

My thoughts thronged in upon me in an unusually disorganized train, for now they had wandered to that ancient day when these two potentates assumed power and from their mighty throne ruled a vast domain. Though they may have ruled with undue coldness, cruelty, and harshness, I hoped they did not; somehow, I saw them living, loving, and ruling with compassion and consideration, seeking always what was wise for the group, what would bring greatest happiness to the individuals within that group.

Feeling the hard earth beneath my feet, I thought again of the weary women and any others who dug, packed, carried, and then pounded the dirt into such mounds as these. Perhaps this was a work of love—perhaps not. Far out from the days of my past learning came floating to me images of august potentates holding sway and wielding powerful scepters. To some, memorials had been erected; shrines had been built; some of those from antiquity are yet seen by tourists traveling in strange lands. Momentarily, just as I had felt upon viewing some of these so I felt now. And I could but cry out with Shelley in the words of Ozymandias:

> Look on my works, ye Mighty and despair!
> Nothing beside remains.

For what remains of this pair and their reign lies hidden not in their own mighty works but in the great twin mounds that serve as their resting place but built with other hands—some, perchance, grudgingly and unwillingly. I moved away from this spot not sadly but somewhat meditatively.

Passing Ozier, I drove by the gravel road to the narrow blacktop and turned east. A few, but very few folk rambled along the way; the inhabitants seemed to have fled with the Mound Builders. On my right, a quarter of a mile away, a neat white frame dwelling appeared; it looked clean and well-kept, but deserted in this Sabbath emptiness. Just beyond the yard a small, rutty road turned off to the right toward another white house hidden in a woods. This grumbly little lane was enough to baffle the pathfinding skill of a city-bred woman: in fact, the washouts across it made the whole lane look like a series of irregular and inconvenient washouts. Then horror upon horrors! I must cross a sagging wood bridge. Could it have been used by the women wagging dirt for the Great Central Mound? Certainly not, but it sagged ever so mournfully and was indeed a relic of the past. Beneath was a rather wide ditch with a trickle of spring water lazily lying six feet below at the bottom. Just now I was not the "competent, able-to-take-care-of-yourself Mildred"; I felt more like some of my pet names such as "Kid," "Baby," or "Dinks." How I wished there were a man at the wheel of that Buick! Almost any man! I'm sure I would have said, "Here, you take the wheel, I'm afraid."

I closed my eyes, gulped my heartbeats, listened to the low-hanging limbs of a tree shriek as they brushed the top of my car. Then, I eased into the hollow of the planks, just knowing every second I'd break through and hit the muddy bottom. Well, in that extremity, I was sunk for there was not a soul at the farmhouse. My only thought besides terror was that this, in ancient times, must have been the spring stream that watered the land above the Mound fields. When I rolled safely off the bridge, I opened my eyes and thanked God for taking care of a reckless woman. Then I climbed the ruts up to the yard of the farmhouse, where they dissolved into the yard turf. But it was a used route; I drove through a wide, open farm gate, swaying to the pot holes; I now crossed a pretty lawn-like locality belonging to a deserted tenant house, passed a weathered barn off to my right—brown with time and smelling still of hay, farm tractors, and forgotten mules. Then I was on a fairly easy dusty road going back into the open fields. The whole area seemed dazingly dead, any sound oddly loud and out of place as the winter weeds crunched under my tires. I kept on the roadway some distance till I came to plowed land; though the road went on, the furrows broke heavily into the ruts so I left the car, took my Nikon and tripod and trudged by the dead road in the direction of Great Central Mound that lay crouching in the silence of an unforgettable emptiness. Pushing through a fence-row growth, I stopped at an electrified cattle fence and took stock of the business of getting over a strand of wire too high for my long legs, yet hardly high enough to ease under. After easing camera and tripod through the fence, I lay on my stomach and edged discreetly beneath the wires. Gathering my picture-taking equipment, I moved on by foot toward the great mound. It is truly an awesome sight!

Briefly I stood at the base of this incredible mound and wondered if I dare climb to its top. I yielded to the impulse and ere long was on the broad, open plain that forms the top of Great Central Mound at Pinson. Imagination took wings: there were the Pinson Indians hosting some of the neighboring tribes who, dressed in strange fashion and showing their native village by markings on their backs, had gathered in a giant enclosure surrounded by high posts carved grotesquely at the top to represent the veiled faces of women. I imagined the old men in council or gossip over tribal affairs; young men carrying the ceremonial wand before them as a gesture of friendship and cordial hospitality to their guests; comely Indian maidens moving about with mincing steps in that grave traditional "way of a maid" in the presence of tribal patriarchs. I heard the deep, full-throated directions of the mature women as they placed their small children in care of half-clad giggling girls who would attend them during the evening ceremonial. I could not seem to sense just how this ceremonial began or ended but felt sure that bonfires lighted the dusk before twilight came and that as the sun set in a great fiery ball, excitement spread over young and old. Silhouetted against that great open space, bodies of guests and hosts swayed rhythmically in tribal dances that culminated in a sort of grand finale as three lovely Indian virgins, chosen for their beauty, approached the point of setting sun. Here, in simple but exquisite ceremony, they pirouetted and twirled about—their shining, perfumed bodies in perfect harmony of dance and song. They swayed to the now tenser beating of the ceremonial drums which were, on this occasion, bits of hide stretched across wide-mouthed jars more decoratively appropriate than the typical drums used for other purposes, for this was a gay evening of ceremonial merriment.

Suddenly the muscles in my throat tightened, and I stifled a cry of woe. For on the same spot—atop this very same mound—I saw these very same Pinson chieftains and these same neighboring chieftains in war paint and feathers! A fire had been lighted at the left; two vessels of water were at the right. The Pinson chief was yelling in incoherent shrieks, his young braves echoing the battle cry; he gesticulated wildly—rolling his eyes in rage, striking his thighs and rattling his weapons. His neighboring chiefs imitated his every action; but the tribesmen stood rigid, watching intently until he poured water from one of the vessels. Then, of one accord, all turned toward the sun to pray that as this water has been poured upon the ground so may the blood of their enemy be spilled over the earth. With solemn deliberation, he moved to the other vessel and with water from it extinguished the fire, thus exhorting his followers to extinguish the enemy. At the end of this blood-freezing ceremony, the Pinson chief, painted red, walked alone in solitary pomp; close at his heels followed his braves, also wearing the red war paint. Here and there, darting in and out, war-bedecked heralds directed them in their weird march against the enemy.

I can not relate the fearful atrocities of the war, but at its end I saw the remnant return in glory. Proudly they bore the legs, arms, and scalps of their adversaries; these they attached most solemnly to tall poles erected for that purpose. In the meantime, women made widows by this recent affray had gathered that they, as a group, might approach the chief and with long, loud lamentations beseech him to avenge the death of their husbands, to provide for them and their children, and finally to grant them permission to marry at the close of the appointed mourning period. Having heard their passionate plea, the chief admonished them to return home, cut off their long hair, scatter it over the graves, place cups and favorite weapons as memorials, and trust in the communal tribe for sustenance. When their hair had grown long enough to cover their shoulders, they had his permission to marry. With bowed heads and tear-filled eyes, the women accepted the ultimatum and grievously moved away to do as bidden. I wondered about the number of eligible men remaining if the women waited that long; for there would be famine, pestilence, disease, accidents, and other wars!

Now, my thoughts patterned a Swiftian digression: after war, peace would settle for a time over Pinson village. There would be hunting, fishing, target-practice, foot-racing, tough and tumble game-playing, dancing, singing, love-making, and feasting. Upon the thought of feasting, I felt a slight twinge of hunger, looked at my watch and knew I should leave further reverie to another day. Carefully I chose my way down, down, down the steep slope of Great Central Mound. Back to the car and then a retracing of the route to Ozier where I sat in pleasant shade eating the lunch and sipping the iced coffee I had brought from home. How long ago that seemed! As I ate, I gazed out over the good, calm earth and into the shadowy mists beyond. This had been an invigorating day; my remembrance of it would be forever cobwebbed with emotions ranging from joy to dejection, from hurt to exaltation. And I had, like the Canterbury pilgrims, a story to tell.

Eagerly I started the drive home. I could hardly wait to pound out of my typewriter that unforgettable experience on Pinson Mounds. Perchance, sooner than I now dreamed, those vivid emotions would become hazy and dim; but now while they were indelibly etched in my mind, I lacked only the writing of them to bind together the mounds and me.

12
The Rise of the Great Central Mound

"Who were these mound-builders?" asks Paul Radin, one of the admitted authorities on Indian cultures in America (*The Story of the American Indian,* Garden City, 1937). "Unquestionably they were Indians, possibly even the ancestors of the Sioux and Creeks. Yet they clearly possessed a civilization immeasurably superior to that of the latter tribes. We have no means of ascertaining today what type of government or what type of ritual the mound-builders had, but recent excavations have shown that some of the mounds were used for ceremonial purposes and for ceremonies possessing an elaborateness for which we find no counterpart among" Indian tribes today. . . .

"The mound-builder civilization had a very wide distribution. Its monuments are today scattered from the Atlantic to the Mississippi and beyond, and from Florida to central Wisconsin and Michigan. . . . In fact all aboriginal culture east of the Mississippi merely represent what has been salvaged from the great mound-builders."

Radin makes a strong point of two Mound Builder complexes which he regards as among the most important, if not the most important, colonies of this lost and mysterious population. These are the Cahokia Mounds in Illinois not far from St. Louis, and the Etowah Mounds in Georgia. Georgia, he thought, was in the center of the true Mound Builder culture. "The famous Cahokia Mound stands as a remarkable structure. Situated in the midst of a group of about sixty artificial mounds, it rises to a height of a hundred feet . . . the most extensive of all mounds north of the Rio Grande. Four terraces lead to the top, and it embraces an area of twelve acres. Though

The Great Kolomoki Mound at Blakely, Georgia. It is 325x200 feet at the base, and 56½ feet high, and dates around the 12th and 13th centuries. It is estimated that a population of 2000 dwelt here at one time, leaving behind the huge temple mound and many lesser burial mounds. (Photo courtesy Georgia Dept. of State Parks)

everything else about it may be doubtful, one thing is clear, that it must have taken many years to construct, and that it presupposes a very extensive sedentary population."

Of the Etowah mounds, "Situated in the midst of a fertile Valley, the Etowah mounds occupy a central position in an area of some fifty acres. . . . The central mound rises some 65 feet above the level of the valley, and is quadrangular in outline with a diameter of 225 feet. As seen today, shorn of vegetation, its outlines stand out sharply." In the same mound group are seven more mounds, three of them very large in size.

Mounds in the Mist 164

AERIAL VIEW of Etowah Mounds. RIVER AND MOUND C EXCAVATION IN FOREGROUND.
"The Etowah Valley was occupied for about 500 years between A.D. 1000 and A.D. 1500, and was the center of political and religious life. At its peak several thousand people lived in this fortified town, which was surrounded on all sides but the river side by a stockade of wooden posts and a deep moat." Within the palisade the people lived in windowless clay-plastered houses, with earthen floors. A basin-shaped fireplace occupied the center, with a hole in the roof for the escape of smoke. (Photo Georgia Historical Commission)

One begins to wonder if Radin ever visited Pinson, or even heard of these magnificent Mounds. Let's make some comparisons—admitting, of course, that size is not necessarily a full measure of importance of anything. The Great Central Mound today is 73 feet high, though an earlier

MALE AND FEMALE MORTUARY FIGURES CARVED FROM WHITE MARBLE WITH TRACES OF THEIR ORIGINAL PAINT—FROM MOUND C.

Mounds in the Mist 166

The Master Farmer Village A.D. 900–1100 (Macon Plateau Period). An artist's conception of their village of 1,000 years ago. Also an effigy-headed portion of a water bottle, a conch shell dipper and a plain water bottle. (Photo by Staff; Courtesy National Park Service, Ocmulgee National Monument, Macon, Georgia)

measure placed it at 78, and first estimates, visual and faulty, said 100. We have noted the base measurements before—300x370 feet, a circumference of 1340 feet. Adjoining the Saul Mound is the Ozier Mound, 32 feet high, 240x230 feet at the base. Nearby, almost in the very shadows of these mounds, is the famous Twin Mound, the only known one of its type. Then melting away into the distances lie the other 30-odd mounds, which thanks to the ploughboy's mule and plow range from little knolls to

The Rise of the Great Central Mound

almost imperceptible rises in the levels of the cotton lands. Myer found 35 excellent mounds. Williams, perhaps the earliest historian of West Tennessee, noted more than 100. The actual neighborhood in ancient times would include the large mounds on the Hatchee near Bolivar; the mounds on the Obion, Forked Deer, the several mound groups at Reelfoot. Within easy day's running distance by an Indian runner, who could cover 100 miles in 24 hours, lie the splendid mounds at what is now Shiloh battlefield on the Tennessee River, and the vast mound, so far unnoted here, at the headwaters of the middle fork

The Great Temple Mound of the Master Farmer period at Ocmulgee. Over 40 feet high and containing about 1,000,000 basket loads of earth. (Photo by B. Berg; Courtesy National Park Service, Ocmulgee National Monument, Macon, Georgia)

The restored ceremonial earthlodge. Master Farmer period. (Photo by Bernard Berg; Courtesy National Park Service, Ocmulgee Monument, Macon, Georgia)

Diorama showing political and religious leaders holding council in the earthlodge. Master Farmer period. (Photo by Staff Courtesy National Park Service, Ocmulgee National Monument, Macon, Georgia)

THE SOUTHERN CULT

Throughout the South, ornaments of stone, shell, and copper, which once belonged to priest-chiefs, are all that remain of an ancient religion. Chief god was the Eagle Man shown on the wall above. Others were the winged or plumed rattlesnake, the turkey, the ivory-billed woodpecker, and the mountain lion.

The religion of the historic Creeks recognized many deities from the Southern Cult. Religious concepts may have come originally from Mexico, but their growth and decline in the South were an independent development.

Some symbols of the Southern Cult of religion with some reproductions of shell gorgets depicting their use. (Photo by Staff; Courtesy National Park Service, Ocmulgee National Monument, Macon, Georgia)

of the Obion at what is now Paris, Tennessee. The immediate plantation of the Mound Builders at Pinson included approximately 7000 acres, of which some 500 surround the Great Central Mound and Ozier and Twin Mounds.

It requires no trick of the imagination to assume that Pinson in height was second only to Cahokia, and in extent of area and neighboring mounds and maize lands surpassed Cahokia and Etowah.

Why was it overlooked so long by men who devoted their lives to a study of primitive American cultures, specifically the Mound Builders? Partly, perhaps, because of Pinson's isolation. More, we venture to say, because of the indifference of early settlers and later citizens; and even such vandalism as the highway engineers who so ruthlessly bulldozed down the beautiful central mound at Reelfoot, mindful only that tourists and motorists save a split second from Union City to Samburg. Anyone with

Mounds in the Mist

EXCAVATION OF MOUND C DOWN TO ORIGINAL GROUND LEVEL.

Hundreds of burials have been excavated from this mound. Millions of baskets full of earth from nearby barrow pits went into the building of the three principal mounds. Mound A, the largest, is 53 feet high, and covers several acres. A thousand years ago it dominated the valley of green waving corn, the principal bread food of the Indians. They had beans, pumpkins, fish, mussels, wild nuts, wild fruits, and edible roots. Bones from refuse pits are largely of wild turkey and deer. In their 500-year sojourn here the Etowah Indians became highly skilled in many crafts—copper, shell, bone, flint, wood, cane and clay. They crafted baskets, cloth of fiber, hair and feathers; and pottery of art and beauty. They manufactured axes, arrowpoints, and knives. Burial practices indicate their belief in a hereafter. (Photo Georgia Historical Commission)

The Rise of the Great Central Mound 171

BURIAL UNEARTHED IN EXCAVATION OF MOUND C. Notice the tools of this exacting excavation, so bones may not be disturbed: small brush, syringe, spoon, trowel, scoop, whisk broom. A skeleton as perfect as this must be allowed to dry slowly, until a degree of original hardness is restored. Meanwhile it must be protected from rain by tarpaulins. (Photo Georgia Historical Commission)

an eye for antiquity could have made a gentle curve in Highway 22 a half mile away and saved the mound for generations more intrigued by America's lost past. Probably the bulldozers came by their disrespect naturally. The migrants into the Western Territory were the least folk to concern themselves with these prehistoric hills of earth. If they had had bulldozers themselves, they'd have saved the roadbuilders the bother. We noted earlier they were,

Mounds in the Mist 172

in general, poor folk; mostly they were uneducated if not totally illiterate; and people like that, worthy as they may be in other respects, are not noted for intellectual curiosity about anything, least of all aboriginal inhabitants. Their passion was for land and the more level the better. Eventually the farmers in the Pinson area managed to plow down all but the loftiest Mounds. Archaeologists like

AERIAL VIEW, Etowah Mound group, near Cartersville, Ga. MOUNDS A AND B IN FOREGROUND.
MOUND C IN LEFT-CENTER BACKGROUND POSITION.
Etowah was one of the most populous towns of Mound Builder prehistory. Some authorities place Georgia as possibly the heartland of Mound Builder culture. More than most states below the Ohio River Georgia has preserved these ancient relics of a lost civilization. (Photo courtesy Georgia Historical Commission)

The Rise of the Great Central Mound

Meyer came for a brief study, and Cisco labored long in behalf of the Pinson group. Only in recent years, through the indefatigable agitations of men like Dr. John B. Nuckolls, Seale Johnson, the book publisher of Jackson, and other dedicated souls have the Mounds at last been placed under the supervision of the Tennessee State Park System's Department of Conservation.

Four thousand years ago, more or less—give or take a thousand years here and there in a misty pre-history of ten-fifteen-twenty thousand years—the Mound Builders appeared in what became southeastern North America. Archaeologists, who stutter heavily when they speak, and hem-and-haw with many maybes, generally believe the original of these aboriginals came from Asia by way of the Bering Strait, survived ice floes and grizzly bears and fanned out southward, populating the new world in the image of ancient China, Japan, the Middle East. One admits that the Indian of today resembles Chinese and Japanese more than Caucasians. There are some authorities who believe the immediate forefathers of the Mound Builders hailed from Palestine and Turkey. They had a heritage of coarse straight black hair, high cheek bones, squat muscular bodies, and a yellow ochre skin. Their earliest appearance in what we know as Mound Builder country was in Georgia, and the radiocarbon date assigned to them is 2000 B.C. Since this technique of establishing dates seems variable—the socalled Paleo-Indian period may range from 12,000 to 6,000 years ago—we have only a convenient jumping off place in this timeless endless while of existence. In any case they were a fruitful folk. They multiplied exceedingly fast and replenished the lands from the Gulf of Mexico up the Mississippi River to the Obion River, and eventually as far north as Wisconsin and Minnesota. Though the Indian is credited with being a lazy rascal, he didn't mind sweating through the pores of his females to heft a lot of loose dirt from the

Gulf to the Great Lakes to build himself more lordly monuments.

When the tide of migration washed up the river later named the Forked Deer by James Rutherford, the Indians found just about the nearest to the Garden of Eden as any spot they'd left in the old world. A climate that would make anybody's mouth water—long warm to hot summers with plenty of spring rains; short cool winters with only occasional cold snaps, going as low as zero. On the average, these blasts of winter ran to three or four and their duration was three or four days. The land just off the river was densely timbered and level and fertile. In the woods were all manner of small game—rabbits, ground hogs, opossums, 'coons, squirrels—and the large beasts—deer, bear, elk, buffalo. The air was alive with wild fowl—turkey, pigeon, goose, duck, blackbirds—and the river teemed with fish—cat, buffalo, carp, perch, crappie, bass, mud turtle. If a Redskin could get his women into the woods to clearing the land, he could himself char out dugouts for navigating the waters; and after the beans and corn and squash and rest of the garden sass came on, he could feed his fat belly and wax amorous on vitamins and relax in the shade with his pipe of tobacco—for this land grew a weed that was beyond his vocabulary to describe. If that wouldn't make any man settle down and start raising a big family, it would be because he was a hermaphrodite (of whom there were many). After a man had a gutful of boiled vegetables seasoned with bearfat, and a roll in the slat-hay with his squaw, and a good smoke or "chaw" of tobacco, he could contemplate such ideas as God, the nature of Spirits, the formula for standing in with these unpredictable critters, and planning a big mound.

It is not to be thought the Mound Builder was a philosophical man. If he really did descend from the ancient Hebrew people, who eventually evolved the most chaste and moral, not to say beautiful, philosophy of Deity, the

The Rise of the Great Central Mound 175

Mound Builder lost his impulse to beauty and piety in his centuries-long wanderings over the inhospitable earth. But he did—eventually—arrive at a fairly universal conclusion of a Great Spirit—a monotheistic God—and a sense of immortality, an extension of his own sense of personal dignity that he felt was worthy of survival. It was about this time that he felt the urge to erect mounds and temples. Just what this time was we have no radio-carbon measure. Archaeologists seem to be of the opinion that some of the Indians drifted southward along the Pacific Coast and eventually wound up in Central America—Peru, the Mayas, Mexico—where they developed a marvelous culture and civilization that astonishes us to this day by the magnificence of its mounds and temples. These folk used the building materials at hand, which were denied the Pinson people—stone. One thing is obvious. They had more art in their gizzards, more highly developed sense of beauty, than the Tennessee brethren. But considering the Pinson fellows had nothing except mud and female labor they acquitted themselves pretty well.

In any case those slowly drifting centuries were the halcyon centuries of the Mound Builders, and down in Tennessee, where it was so pleasant to drift, where fried pigeons practically flew into their mouths, they knew the good life—the best years of all their time. The Indians in other sections of North America were busy killing themselves, or packing up their families and taking off to safer places to avoid getting killed, while down at Pinson they happily vegetated, raised more Redskin babies, took in more new ground for corn and beans and pumpkins and tobacco, until finally they had a population estimated up to 15,000 souls, and covering up to 13 or 14 square miles—and 100 mounds: The Great Society.

If we arbitrarily establish this date as about the time of Christ until about 1000 years ago, we at least can have something to work on. Pinson was a prosperous and stable community, founded on man's oldest resources—good land, equitable climate, abundant natural sources of food and clothing, and reasonable peace.

The Mound Builder enjoyed a settled home and three meals a day as well as any pale face who a few thousand years later would stare at his mounds and wonder what manner of man this was. He knew a long era of dreamy tranquil centuries. Archaeologists adore their classifications, and the delver into prehistory dirt has called this the Archaic Age. From its earliest beginnings it lasted 8,000 years. Probably no Indian lived long enough to note any change in his way of life. A Mound Builder would wake at dawn, listen to the birds, read the signs and omens, make a dash for the Forked Deer and churn the water to muddy suds, and emerge to squat at corn which his squaw boiled in an earthen vessel over an outside fire. Our Builder would increase the calorie potential by some venison, bear, rabbit, bird, whatever. He'd have fish for noon, cornbread, a kind of hominy, some more meat of one sort or another, and spend the afternoon hollowing out a log for a new boat. He'd make much merry with his buddies. For supper he'd have a hunk of bear, a chunk of cornbread, in season some fruit, and during the summer vegetables. He'd have gone to bed with the chickens if he'd had chickens. He had no cow, no shoat, no horse, nothing but a hound dog. At least a dog. Sometimes for variety he ate the dog. In the night he would enjoy his woman. It was a brief business and destitute of lovemaking. After so many years—usually 35—he'd have ground his teeth down to the gums, developed pyorrhea, gastric disorders, arthritis, or maybe he just got killed in war.

Some sideline activities he may have enjoyed were making arrow points of flint, pecking out stone axes, shaping scrapers of bone and stone for de-hairing hides for winter clothes, blankets, in the autumn when the corn harvest came off filling the common granary to tide the village through the winter. He might before he died take a long journey on foot from Pinson to Bolivar, Shiloh, Eva, Cairo, the Harpeth town, perhaps even as far away as Cahokia, where some more ambitious Builders were supervising their squaws and daughters toting dirt to build a monument. He'd trade and traffic and pick up any new ideas floating around, check on the pastoral qualities of the females—no doubt during his sojourn in any strange town he'd enjoy a lady of the occasion provided by the chief; and go home from this globe trotting refreshed in spirit, and no qualms of conscience for stepping out on his squaw. In fact, before he departed he likely told his neighbor to shack up with her in his absence. Our Pinson man believed that what was tobacco for the gander was wampum for the goose.

Among the trophies of his trek might well have been a new dance step. He adored to dance. He danced at every opportunity—when he'd scalped his enemy or dodged his enemy and saved his own scalp; he danced when the green corn was in milk and again when it was dry in the shuck and ready for jerking and housing in the common crib. He danced when he married and when he died his kinfolks and neighbors danced at his funeral. He danced when rains came, and when there was a protracted drought he danced to make rain. His dance was a weird and incoherent hoochy-coochy of many gyrations and hideous grimaces, the more repelling the more meaningful he thought it. His woman danced with him, but he did not touch her person; men and women did not embrace, clasp hands, or otherwise fraternize. But the women danced with more decorum and grace, swaying their nearly naked bodies with becoming rhythm and a certain beauty. Their eyes would become dreamy, and the hypnotism of the tempo softened their features. The singsong that passed for music, along with the drumbeat, and gourd rattles might have a quality of melody with the women; but the racket that issued from the men in the name of song would have made a Forked Deer bullfrog hide his head in shame. There is nothing in the surviving musical literature of the Indian to convince us the Pinson man could even carry a tune. But he danced and cavorted.

It became necessary eventually to have some spot dedicated to this form of pleasure, and from the small center ring in the congested area of the village where early dances were performed, our Pinson man had his women tote dirt and build a low flat mound. Though archaeologists like to speak of this as a ceremonial mound, it really was a spot where our man could kick up his heels. The earth became packed, and time and population explosion widened the spot. The Pinson mound devoted to ceremonials, when we visited the Mound area years ago, was maybe a three-foot rise above the surrounding fields and was growing cotton almost man-high in irreverent disregard of its original holy purpose. The ploughboy had marred its outlines, but this was the mound probably which Meyer listed as being 3.5 feet high, and 160x170 feet in dimensions. At what time it came into the Woodland Culture is of no importance. But mound building was a mark of Woodlanders.

Another mark in the slow turning of centuries was the change in the Pinson man's weaponry. He'd traded in his old model spear for the latest model bow and arrow. In some ways this was as earth shaking for him as the exchange of the horse-and-buggy for the Model T was for a more recent paleface culture. Our man's bloody horizon was increased immensely—in the battle, in the hunt, in the agility of his curiously skilful body. He had to modernize his arsenal—small arrowheads for small game and birds; the heavy head for the forest beasts. His skills in chipping had to be refined, and he made use of different flints. Thus his commerce widened as he trafficked with other tribes for these other flints; and he must needs also

The Rise of the Great Central Mound 179

teach his hands more accurate skills in chipping, making shafts, and in shooting. He searched out new woods for his bows—elm, young ash, hazel. If it took a few centuries to develop his industries, he had plenty of time. In the end, he became exceedingly expert with his new weapon.

Inevitably he had a look at his domicile. How much his squaw helped in pointing out to him his old shack was about to fall down or the termites were eating his posts we can only surmise; but knowing women we suspect it was considerable. A woman's way is like a termite's: she just keeps gnawing away without making much noise till along comes a big blast of wind and hail and blows the old wigwam away and peppers the man of the house with ice cubes the size of goose eggs—old timers tell of seeing such hail stones in West Tennessee; and our Mound Builder turns to house building and puts up a new dwelling. If the new house was much more substantial, larger, it was still uncomplicated: Four corner posts sunk 8 to 12 inches in the ground, a runner from post to post attached by bark or leather thongs, walls of bark or animal skins, and a roof of thatch. Some of the earlier houses were made by thrusting green slender saplings in the ground, and arching the limbs over till they met on all sides, and then weaving them in basketry patterns for roof, and adding bark or thatch.

At last our Pinson man had become "sedentary population." He liked this feel of permanence, after a few thousand years of shifting from pillar to post. Plenty of meat and cornpone; enough war with enemies to keep his hand in at killing. Now and then, of course, he was embarrassed by stopping an enemy arrow and landing in the happy hunting ground; but by and large life was good. His women were growing more comely over the centuries. His squaw and daughters took on that soft layer of coppery meat that makes a female nice to pinch. He was not unmindful of this pleasure. His lands had widened; his neighbors had grown numerous; likewise his enemies had increased, casting covetous eyes at his prosperous corn patches and plumping females. To protect himself and his possessions our Pinson man decided to fence in his properties. It would take a little time and some rail splitting, but one day he got his neighbors and women folks on the job of heaving up a dirt fence next to the Forked Deer, about six feet high, and on this he stuck posts into the soft ground to form the first lap of his palisades. This was going to cost him sweat, but somebody had to do it. He didn't want a lot of lowdown bastards swooping down on him and eating all his corn and raping his wife and daughters, or hauling them away as slaves. A good fence should help prevent that. "A good fence," the man said, "makes good neighbors."

How long this chore took we can only surmise. If the threat were urgent, the work could have been accomplished within the span of a lifetime. It may have engaged our man a couple of centuries. He had only his stone axe for getting out his post timber, and he would select hardwood from this new sense of permanence. He could cut young trees, oak and chestnut and walnut, by using fire—building a fire at the base and when the tree was mostly burnt in two, push it over, scrape off the char to something of a sharp point, and top it the same way. The six or more miles of this palisade required thousands of timbers. If trees on the average were a foot, say, more than 5,000 were needed to each mile. Thirty-odd thousands of timbers, with stone axes and fire; and the job begins to loom as man-size. The timbers had to be set firmly, tamped in close, or an enemy could push them down.

To find trees of appropriate size the Pinson men had to range farther and farther into the forest, going perhaps more than ten miles in all directions. Their best cuttings would be up and down the Forked Deer, or up the creeks from the river. The logs they could float down to the town. But forests near the streams were apt to be made up of large trees, and so again they were compelled to work back into the rolling lands or low hills. Any way they went about it, the job was staggering. They had no wheels, no beasts of burden, no saws or axes or mauls and wedges to split some of their logs in two. We find no evidence—no stone wedge—to indicate wood splitting. Yet day by day and year by year, one century into another, they logged out timbers, set them in the 6-20-foot banks, and erected fortifications that held a potential enemy at bay. Even when the outer palisades were completed they still had an inner palisade to build around the growing Great Central Mound. This was an estimated extra mile. Evidence of these earthworks, though the posts had long since rotted, were clearly visible in 1860, as reported by old settlers; and today, dimly but unmistakably, the inner breastworks in spots are discernible. By the time the posts were all set in those prehistoric days the first section of the wall was decaying, and had to be replaced. Once the job was started there was no end of it.

Meanwhile in those years, those centuries, the Great Central Mound was steadily rising. We say steadily advisedly; it rose layer at a time. The age of Woodland Culture had merged into the era of Mississippian Culture, so named because so many of the Mound Builders lived on the Mississippi or rivers which emptied into it, as the Ohio, Missouri, nearer by, the Obion, Forked Deer, Hatchee, Reelfoot. As the Pinson man got down to mound building in earnest, he fell into what archaeologists call the Hopewellian Culture type of mound—a rounded mound on top used for burials. Of the scores of low mounds in the Pinson area, so far as any one knows today they were not burial mounds. Mounds levelled by farmers have disclosed no bones. Was the Great Central Mound started as a burial spot to some great chief, held in reverence because of his bravery and wisdom, or fear because of his dreaded tyranny? Perhaps the answer will be found when this mound is excavated.

When the question was presented to Dr. Nuckolls, his reply was, "The nature of the silt lands in this region is such that human bones disintegrate in two or three hundred years."

We may never know whether a great "king" was buried here.

We do know, however, that in East Tennessee and Middle Tennessee, where the soil content is heavily limestone, well-preserved skeletons of related Mound Builders have been unearthed.

To return to the building of Pinson. However the first low mound was started, back in the dim early Woodland mists, it likely was no more than three feet above the level of the surrounding ground, and perhaps some 25x35 feet. We hazard this simply as a guess. On top of this earth heap a "temple" was erected. It was a flimsy pole-and-thatch affair that the first big wind blew away, if indeed the contraption didn't catch fire when the priests kindled some sacred fire inside it, or just outside. The squaws and young girls were yelled up, then, told to get their baskets, and fetch more dirt. For months they hustled in soil, raised the mound level, and increased its dimensions. The men knocked up another temple. The chief moved into his sumptuous new quarters, the priests and sorcerers and medicine men resumed activities, and a century or two or three came and went till the termites ate the temple down, or a cyclone hurled its bones five miles out in the forests, or another fire destroyed, or even some new and more ambitious chief thought he'd look more important a few feet higher off the ground with some more yard space. Once again the squaws were requisitioned. Thus another eon came and went and another layer to the Great Central Mound was built. Each layer was harder to build than the last, for more earth was required, and it would not do to dig it from the cornlands, for it took time and toil to clear land for corn and beans, and the increasing population demanded more ponebread and beans. Our noble women and girls had to range more and more distantly, digging in the woods a mile away, and sorting out the roots and humus that would not pack well in the mound. Thus the Tower of Babel lifted steadily, and the higher and larger it grew the more ambitious became the chiefs and medicine men and priests, and to the naked sweating females it did not matter whether this was the Woodland, Hopewell, or Mississippi Culture—it was one hell of a hard job. They moved like ants, going and coming, climbing a hundred feet to deposit the last baskets of dirt, beating a trail to the five-mile hills, meeting and passing and breaking their backs; but theirs not to reason why, theirs but to do and die. And many died.

Had our Pinson man been asked why, he'd have been surprised why anyone asked. He could have pointed to the great cathedrals in Europe, or the Egyptian pyramids, erected on the bones of slaves. Since he did not know this answer, he probably rolled his eyes and shrugged. Men just do these things.

In the end, the Great Central Mound and its host of lesser mounds were erected. Five hundred years? A thousand years? Why do you ask?

Years ago we often traveled from Memphis to Clarksdale, Mississippi. Along the highway we'd pass the Great Coahoma Mound. It was the trinity mound group the Mississippi Culture Mound Builders adored having their women folk build. It was there we first heard the legendary tale that women and girls carried the earth that went into them. We'd park our Model T off the pavement and sit and stare in wonder at the curious pattern—the main large mound situated near what a long time ago was the bank of the Mississippi River; the smaller, flat mound

Mounds in the Mist 184

a stone's throw south of it; the wider ceremonial mound across the road to the east, now growing cotton. The south mound was symmetrical, perhaps ten feet high, oval, top neatly rounded. We'd cross the cotton rows and climb to the summit of the central mound, press through the weeds and briars along the top, and pause at some gravestones where the first plantation owners had buried their dead after starting to reclaim the delta from the swamps. There was a very old tree here, and some smaller ones nearby. We could see spots where campers and picnickers had built fires to roast weiners, or fishermen in the sloughs and swamps close by had spent the night when running their set-hooks. Save for the highway it was a lonely haunted spot, and once we heard owls in the rutting season give their weird mating cries, like strangled ghosts chortling through a hollow log. The winds came gently, cooling us, and it's easy to remember how immense the big mound was. Fifty feet high? More or less pyramidal, 125x150 feet? Romance and mystery and this spell of the past measure no exact feet and inches.

That summer we would drive the back plantation roads through this strange and beautiful yet ugly plantation country. We could be going along an empty little gravel road swinging around a gentle curve, when we would look over and realize there was a sheer nearly perpendicular drop of ten or twenty feet to a lower land level exactly like that where we were, save that it stretched away a mile, two miles toward the sunset. It took some moments for it to dawn on us that this was the bank and bed of the old river; that maybe 5,000 years ago that very lowland was the murky snarling waters of the Mississippi; and now the river ran five or ten miles away to the west. There was always this level land, broken only by these ancient beds. But we would pause, startled; coming around a fringe of timber, pinoaks and cypress, we'd find the remains of an Indian Mound. We then would know the

Mound Builders had been here; centuries and centuries and centuries ago they'd had their women and girls scrape up earth and fashion a mound, groping after something that startles us by its irresistible impulse toward what—Deity?

We have driven soberly through many a sunset, watching the declining heat waves change the distances to purple, painting now and then a small rise of dirt a faded vermilion, and wondered.

13
Squaw Work Never Done

For a thousand years the Pinson squaw went about her daily tasks with the stoic patience of a primitive woman who combined the functions of slave, drudge, concubine and breeding female. She had no memory of the past for happy recollection and no dreams of the future to upset her hopelessness. She must have rolled out of bed mornings with an increasing grunt as the centuries crept upon her, and moved about her work with creakier joints. All through the Archaic Age she fixed breakfast at dawn and sunrise for herself, her young, and her lord and master—thank the Great Spirit there was always plenty of fish from the Forked Deer and her man enjoyed taking them from the streams; she knocked up cornpone or boiled mush from meal she had milled with stone mortar and pestle; or over a crude grating above a backyard fire she smoked up a rabbit or hunk of venison or bear, disguising the rawness of the flesh with plenty of oak smoke. There was parched corn, too. The food might be served from a common wooden bowl, with the family squatting around and reaching. When every one tried to be sophisticated, the portions were served on leaves like the sycamore, that cupped well. In the next few hundred years she thought of wooden vessels that served as plates, bowls, even drinking vessels. These were made of soft white woods like box elder or white ash. They could be scraped out with small stone scrapers, somewhat like the warriors used in scraping the char from the dugouts they fashioned from logs by burning; or even bone scrapers from the sharpened shoulder blades of the deer and elk. Perhaps she washed them after meals or just put them out for the dogs to lick

Three grotesquely beautiful effigies from Ancient Buried City. The squatting female figure is one of the rare pottery patterns in Mound Builder artifacts. Though distorted by artistic convention, the woman's features are remarkably accurate and comely, in comparison with the harsh faces of the males; and the nude breasts are proportionately excellent. The bone needles in the foreground are of superior workmanship. (Photo Ky. Dept. Public Information)

clean. Besides the crude grating for broiling, she built an oven by digging a hole in the back yard, smearing the bottom with clay, and burning it until hard. This was the fire pot. She kneaded crude mud bricks and built a wall, over which she spread thin limbs and covered with a roof of bark, and perhaps clay. Roasting of meats and corn could be done by putting the food on mats made of split

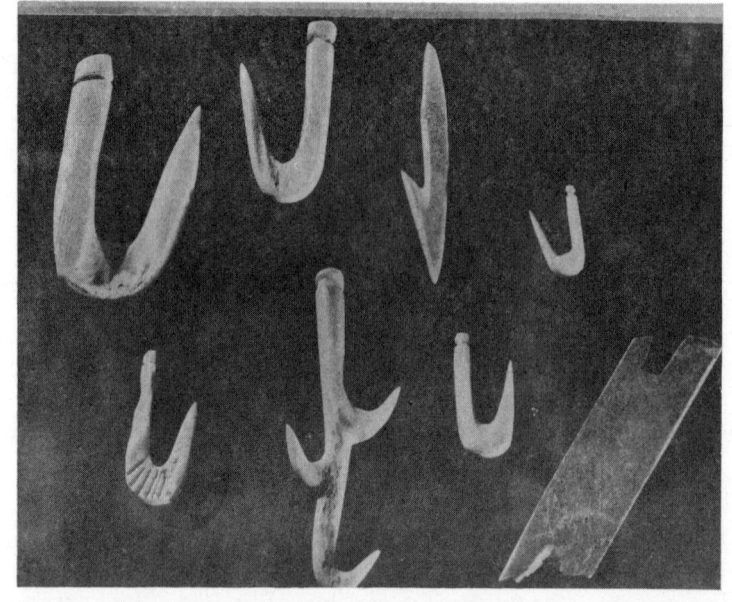

Types of bone and copper fish hooks used by the Mound Builders at Wycliffe. The population was sedentary and agricultural; the village was politically independent. In the backland maize, beans and vegetables flourished, but fish caught in the big rivers was an exceedingly important source of food. There were still great herds of buffalo feeding in the forests, to supplement meat ration. Note the ingenuity of the craftsmanship. (Photo Dept. Public Information, Ky.)

cane and laying hot coals in the pot, closing the oven off, perhaps replenishing the coals ever so often. Small fish and birds could be barbecued in like manner. Much of this food must be eaten without seasoning, for salt was one of the scarcities the Pinson people were chronically plagued with. There were no salt springs near Pinson; the nearest was three sleeps away on a river that became the Tennessee, near a paleface village three thousand years later named Eva. Dinner and supper consisted of more of the same. All this cooking and eating was done out of doors, back of the house. If it rained cats and dogs and put out the fires, the family ate raw corn and meats in the shack. In summer it was not too bad. When winter came, it now and then got too bad. But our downtrodden patient squaw

Near Wycliffe, Kentucky, is Ancient Buried City where excavations have revealed the remnants of an entire community. Over two hundred skeletons of adults and children are on display here. This area of Kentucky was inhabited in prehistoric times by a race known as the "Mound Builders."

Exhibits of thousands of artifacts—pottery, dolls, household utensils—give the visitor rare insight into the living conditions of a long-extinct people.
These burials are mostly of young children. (Photo courtesy Dept. of Public Information Frankfort, Ky.)

just made do as she could. Now and then she'd take time out to have a baby. Some other old squaws came in to help with the population explosion. Her lifetime litter, according to her fecundity—and Indian women were fecund as a rule—might add up to ten. Half these died in infancy. Though it was legendary that Indian women were delivered of young easily, it did not always hold true. Where preserved skeletons have been found, there have been mother and infant who died in childbirth. Then of course she had to serve her husband's bed at regular intervals. There is considerable evidence that she may have enjoyed this activity.

Fortunately there was no washing that had to be done. Our Pinson squaw wore her spring outfit till it fell off her in rags, and then she made a new dress. It was scanty. Mostly it covered her unmentionable in front, and left naked as a jaybird the rest of her body. If her buttocks hung out behind she did not see them. When she was young she had some awareness of her breasts, and probably a woman's pride in them. In this respect she was blessed with shapeliness. Her garment, then, was mostly just a leather thong to which she had woven a fringe of mulberry or pawpaw bark, beaten until it was the texture of flax, or even silk, and allowed to cover, as one outraged Catholic priest said some thousand years later, "her shame." In winter she wore a garment sewed of deer skin, but hung over her shoulder so as to leave one breast bare. This was more convenience than vanity. Usually there was a suckling baby, or one well along the way in her belly. The children went naked. Mostly the care they got, besides feeding—and the plentiful supply of food kept the urchins fat as mud—was periodic tanning. The squaw brewed a stout solution of red oak bark, red clay, and other dye stuffs, and painted her young ones with this smear to toughen their skin, render them less susceptible to cold in winter and blistering heat in summer, and preserve

The burial of a sun-worshipping priest, with the rare pottery of his office about his bones. The elaborateness of the ritual pattern suggests his high position.

The burial mound where these photographs were taken is in five distinct layers and contains 153 skeletons. Bodies were laid out on, rather than within, the ground. The largest mound of the group is 125 feet by 60 feet. Burial positions had no reference to direction. Artifacts found with skeletons indicate a highly developed culture and belief of the Mound Builders in immortality. (Photo Ky. Travel Div.)

Mounds in the Mist 192

them against the germs in small wounds of which she never heard. Girl children ran naked up to eight years, and then they started dressing like their older sisters and mother. There were no end of children after Pinson town had been populating a number of centuries. The wonderful climate made the folk thrive; the endless food supply fed them fat; and life for the Mound Builder, if ever, was good around A.D. 1000.

A thousand years ago Wycliffe, Ky., was an important commercial and religious center situated at the junction of the Ohio and Mississippi Rivers. It had a permanent population of 3000 to 5000, who carried on a flourishing trade with the transient traders moving up and down the two rivers from one Mound Builder center to another—Cahokia on the north, Pinson on the south. The burial in the foreground was of leather worker, the tools of whose craft were buried with him. (Photo Dept. of Public Information Ky.)

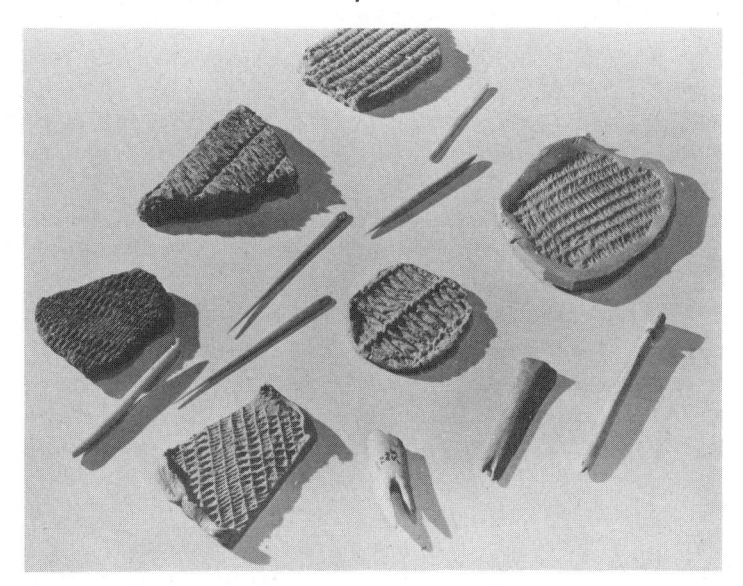

Excavations at Wycliffe were begun in 1932. The work was in the hands of trained archaeologists, who left remains as they were found. The photograph shows beautifully fashioned needles, punches for leather, and potsherds—fragments of pottery—with incisively etched cord and fabric impressions. The patterns were beat in by paddles in the hands of the potters before the pots were fired. Pottery is man's oldest skill, and the archaeologist's most enduring evidence. Ancient Buried City is owned by Western Baptist Hospital, at Paducah. (Photo Ky. Dept. Public Information)

One of the chief tasks of the Indian woman was producing young. In her most fertile years she often had a baby a year and there were instances where she might have one child in January and deliver another in December. We have fragmentary pictures of her busy in this work.

"As soon as the native woman has been confined she

goes to the edge of the water. She washes herself there as well as her infant. From there she comes back to lie down again, and fixes her child on the cradle which has already been prepared. This cradle is about two-and-a-half feet long and 8 or 9 inches broad. It is artistically made of straight canes running the length of the cradle, and at the end they are cut in half and bent back under to make the foot. The whole is only half a foot high. This cradle is very light, since it weighs not more than 2 pounds. It is on the bed of the mother, who is thus readily able to suckle her infant, which being in a warm cabin can not be cold however little it is covered. The child being rocked endways can not have the head disturbed like those rocked sideways, and in that way run the risk of being overturned, a danger the natives do not fear at all."

"The children of the natives are fair at birth, but they darken because they are rubbed with bear's oil in order to stand exposure to the sun. They let them crawl on all fours without having them walk on their legs, still too feeble to bear the weight of the body. They rub them with bear oil for two reasons: First, to render the sinews more flexible; in the second place, to prevent the flies from biting them when they are all bare and left to themselves in this manner. They do not put these infants on their feet until they are more than a year old, and when they begin to raise themselves up they always have a young girl of from 10 to 12 years to hold them under their armpits. They let these children suckle as long as they please; at least unless the mother finds herself pregnant, when she no longer nurses."

Next to having babies and seeing to their raising, our Pinson squaw looks to the garden and maize patches. We have long known that the Indian women had the care of the crops. As the centuries passed, the Pinson acres increased and crop after crop came to the harvest. The land gradually lost all stumpage and dead snags and be-

City of the Dead.
There are those who believe the burial cult of the Mound Builders helps to establish the quality of their culture: Hope of eternal life, one of the tenets of civilized faith, for one; the use of pottery vessels for food and drink into the future existence; the selflessness of these tokens, since they were precious; the preservation of earthly remains through the use of charcoal in the burials (the skeletons of Ancient Buried City folk are encased in this eternal element). Many of these burials are thought to trace back a thousand years, to A.D. 800–1000. (Ky. Dept. Public Information photo).

Mounds in the Mist 196

Wickliffe Mounds vary in size and original intent; they were built up of hard-packed earth to serve as foundations for temples and houses. Many are at least 80 feet long and 40 feet wide; the largest is about 125 feet by 60 feet.

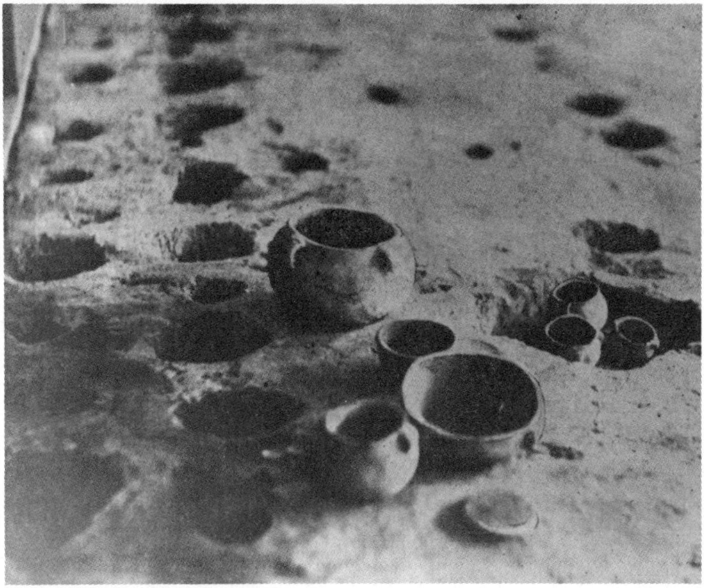

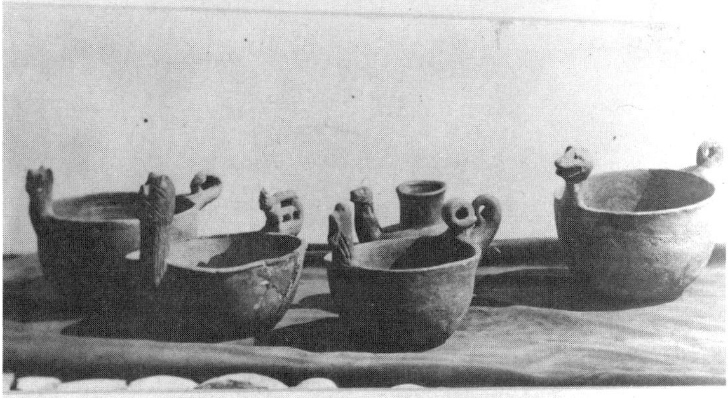

Wycliffe Mound Builders were a part of the Mississippian culture of prehistoric Indians that appeared in 900–1000 A.D. These builders left their traces from Wisconsin to the Gulf of Mexico and from the Mississippi River to the Appalachians.

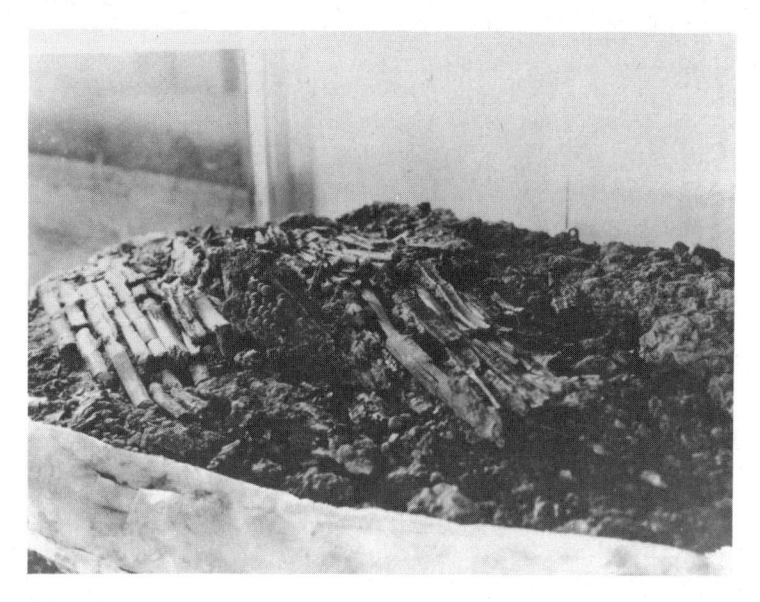

Though excavations began in 1932, much of the city is still undisturbed. Each finding is cataloged and each is displayed just as it was found. (Photographs courtesy of Kentucky Dept. of Public Information).

came fertile prairie. From the river back almost to the hills the fields greened richly under the summer suns, and the squaws and young girls scratched the alluvial soil with crooked-wood plows and bone and stone hoes. Weeds and grass were pulled by hand—"stoop labor." Not only the Mound Builders but the whole Indian race were a corn culture, as the white man was a product of a wheat-rye-oats culture. No one has ever been able to trace historically the origin of maize. It was corn from the dawn of history. It remained corn through the centuries, improving however gradually through some selection of strains. There was nothing studied about seed selection. The Pinson woman picked the largest ears, the fattest grains, to seed next year's crops. By the time the early explorers reached America the types were established and this new land was covered with thousands and thousands of acres of the grain.

Thomas Hariot, adventuring under the direction of Sir Walter Raleigh, voices the general amazement of those who saw Indian fields and Indian women tilling them in the year 1584. In astonishment he wrote: "*Pagatowr* is a kind of grain. It is called *maize* in the West Indies; Englishmen name it *Guinea wheat,* after the countries from which similar grain has been brought. The grain is about the size of our ordinary English peas, and, while similar to them in form and shape, differ in color, some grains being white, some red, some yellow, and some blue. All of them yield a very white and sweet flour which makes excellent bread. We made malt from the grain while we were in Virginia and brewed as good an ale from it as could be desired. It could be used, with the addition of hops, to produce a good beer. The grain increases on a marvelous scale—a thousand times, fifteen hundred, and in some cases two thousand fold. There are three sorts, of which two are ripe in ten, eleven, and at the most, twelve weeks, when their stalks are about six or seven feet in height. The third one ripens in fourteen weeks and is ten feet high. Its stalks bear one, two, three, or four heads, and every head contains five, six, or seven hundred grains, as near as I can say. The inhabitants not only use it for bread but also make food of the grains. They either parch them, boiling them whole until they break, or boil the flour with water to make a pap."

Kneberg in *Tribes that Slumber* examines the squaw work less intimately. "Maize or Indian corn had been domesticated in Middle America very early and had spread to the southwestern United States by 1500 B.C. Corn, second only to wheat as a matrix out of which civilizations are born, is a domesticated grass like wheat. Unlike wheat, whose various wild forms still grow in many places, corn has no known wild ancestor. Its origin is shrouded in mystery, notwithstanding the Indians grew hundreds of varieties. The most ancient examples that have been found belonged to the popcorn variety with small, flinty kernels. . . . During centuries of Indian cultivation, the primitive type of maize changed until an amazing variety existed at the time Columbus discovered America. Special kinds were used for meal, for flour, for popping and for corn-on-the-cob. The kernels came in assorted colors: black, yellow, red, white and blue."

Whether the squaw was in arid America, the tall mountains, the steamy jungles of the southern rivers, she could find a corn that would grow there best. Soon after Columbus found corn in 1492—and this may have been near the year our Pinson squaw laid down her hole-pecker and hoe for good—the grain had spread to Europe and finally to China.

"What wonder, then, that most Indians regarded corn with reverence and offered the first fruits of each harvest to their supreme gods."

All these fine words, if our Pinson woman had ever heard them, would have left her cold. To her, in April or

May of each year, it spelled going down into the land with crude plow and chopper, and along with her sister squaws and the big girls, breaking the surface of the ground and planting hills three feet each way—and a foot meant her foot, which was long, strong, calloused, and had the great toe crooked upward at an angle. These women worked naked save for a brief drape over their "shame." Sweat dripped off their noses and between heats in the land they'd go to the spring branch and lie on their bellies and drink. If the season were rainy, and crabgrass and weeds grew amain, the work force had to stay close and weed the crops. There would be plantings of the various ripenings, the 10, 12, 14-week types, so food would be coming in with a degree of regularity. Then between the corn rows would be planted beans—the type we know today as butterbeans, and the vine speckled bean, which would hug the corn as it grew tall and become known to us as polebeans. The squaws would plant pumpkins, melons, squash, gourds, and finally sunflowers. The sunflower seed, rich in oils, would be milled into flour to add to the cornbread. Sometimes the dried beans were pounded into meal to add to the bread. If all this was nose-dripping toil, it resulted in rib-sticking grub, when cooked with honest Simon-pure bear grease.

And so through the habitual well-rainy springs and summers, until the midsummer and fall droughts set in to dry the fodder and cure the harvest. It was then that our noble Redskin displayed his creative genius by going into the lands and jerking the ears with many mutterings and prayers of thanks for his squaw, while she and the big daughter hefted the baskets of corn on their heads and toted the gift of the gods to the crib.

The typical crib was elevated a couple feet off the ground, and was built of long supple saplings with the limbs woven to form a roof. Perhaps to increase the protection from weather, and particularly from the rat population that was always present, an inner wall and ceiling were made of woven oak splits and canes.

Kneberg, whose studies of the Mound Builders in the upper Tennessee region, can be related readily to Pinson, gives a picture in detail of house building. "The arts, crafts and customs of (these people) were a more constant part of their daily life than the periodic construction of mounds. The manner in which they built their temples and dwelling houses (and granaries) is one activity that reveals their craftsmanship. The first step was to outline the floor area with narrow trenches about two feet deep. Next, long saplings, four or five inches in diameter, set upright and spaced about six inches apart, were set in trenches which were then filled in and firmy tamped. Then, long slender poles were bound horizontally to the uprights to stabilize them. The roof framework, a remarkable piece of construction, was woven like a huge basket. Most Indians were excellent basket makers, but these people went even further by actually weaving the roofs over their heads. The weaving process began at the corners, using the end poles of the walls. First, the two end poles from opposite walls were bent inward and lashed together. Then, the same was done with the end poles of the two opposing walls and, as the weaving process continued alternating from side to side, all of the wall uprights became interwoven in an over-and-under pattern. As the work progressed, the roof assumed a dome shape. The result was an exceptionally sturdy type of roof construction, one that was able to withstand strong rains because it was actually a continuation of the walls."

The job was completed by lathing the outer surfaces with cane and plastering with clay. Grass thatching covered lath and chinking. The result was a weather proof building, whatever the use made of it. Temples and the finer houses of the chiefs were increased in elegance by woven cane mats on walls and floors, and lavish adornment was applied to the temple. But in case of the corn-cribs and house for the beans and pumpkins and squash, which were preserved as long as possible, the motive was protection against weather and rodents and itinerating animals. Coons and squirrels were almost as big pests as rats.

House-raising was man's work. But the squaws did their bit. And when the men had jerked the corn and filled the baskets, the flat-headed women who could tote heavy loads went trudging up through the dry fodder blades and dead bean vines to the beautifully woven granaries.

Through the summer, long before the harvest, there had been the seasonal tasks. Fruit gathering was one of the most important. The land that became known as West Tennessee was a fruitful land beyond man's remembering. As the fields opened and became old, wild blackberries sprang up in every cranny of open land. They waxed fat and richly sweet when the season was right, and bore even when drought was on the land. Our squaws and big girls took their pretty baskets and moved into the briars to contest with the birds for the berry crop. On occasions when the crop was heavy they set guards to scare the birds away till picking could be accomplished. Berries were the one natural source of sugar for the sweet-starved Mound Builder. He knew nothing of sugar. No sorghum or cane grew in the crops to sweeten his taste buds. Honey was nothing he had ever heard of—that is, bee honey, wild bee honey. The honey bee did not appear in America until the white man came. Then the bee spread swiftly, but too late to flavor the red man's jaw. All the natural sweet he ever knew, aside from fruits and maybe a sugar maple he skinned with his stone hatchet in the spring when the sap was rising, he had from the bumble bee. This fierce and beautiful insect nested in dead logs lying on the ground, in hollows of decaying fallen timber, and now and then in rotting knot holes in trees, living and dead. In his natural state he prospered, for bears, avid for bee honey, were respectful in robbing him of his winter hoard. The bumble bee by intuition knew the one vulnerable spot on a bear is his under-tail area, which is hairless. Our savage bumble bee would pop the bear right in his heel and send him lumbering down through the woods, squatting now and then and dragging his hind quarters to relieve the sting. The bumble bee had no annoying enemies, and his big capsules of strong clover honey made a nice gulp for our noble Redskin. The job of getting this delicacy was left to the squaws. Mostly it was accomplished by night, after a nest had been spotted, by moving in with a smoke torch and gassing the bee long enough to rob him. The bulk of Indian sweet was in wild fruits.

Wine was as rare a treat for the Mound Builder as was honey. The taste he might have would be in berry time. The squaw would place any overplus in an earthen crock—her craft in pottery making—and allow the wine to ferment from wild yeasts. Her lord and master would gulp the brew, and if the gallonage was sufficient get drunk and sleep it off. Nothing was wasted. The wined garbage would be swallowed along with the wine. Sometimes other fruits yielded a grog—wild fox grapes, if abundant; wild cherries when the squaws and girls would climb the cherry trees and pick them.

Mostly, though, fruits were consumed immediately— wild plums, the hard little wild crabapple, huckleberries, which grew abundantly in the far back hills; mulberries, hackberries, haws; persimmons, bulluses (muscadines)— a large single dark grape which grew on lofty vines in the deep forests. Finding these other fruits and gathering them fell to the women. About the last chore of the summer was hunting the pawpaws—a golden, pulpy, cloying banana-like fruit which the Indian children gobbled avidly, while the squaws salvaged enough for their men of the choicest not gnawed by the opossums. Deep in the Forked Deer bottoms and back against the hills the pawpaw groves grew at the edge of deeper woods. It would be in September.

Autumn nutting was one of the biggest gathering times. Women and children again went into the woods, ranging far and wide, carrying baskets for hickorynuts, walnuts, butternuts, acorns. The acorn was abundant, and was a staple food for Mound Builders and Indians everywhere up through the ages. The large white oak acorns were the best flavored, the fattest, the most plentiful. The squaws harvested these "beans," as the white man later called them, by the tens of bushels and stored them in the cribs along with the corns. They milled the meat into flour, mixed it with corn grist, sometimes added pulverized dried venison, and made a stout bread by adding bear's grease to shorten and add taste. At times if other foods were scarce they would boil the acorns like corn grains.

The quest for medicinal herbs, roots and plants was unseasonal and never-ending. When our squaw had a little spare time she went into the woods to dig bitter briar, sarsaparilla, ginseng, snakeroot, sassafras, Indian turnip; to chop barks of cinchona-bearing trees like dogwood; to scrape from wounds on the bark of the sweetgum the ooze which contained the balsam whose healing powers were fabulous; to gather leaves of the ivy creeper—"poison ivy"—which was held by the medicine men in high esteem for poulticing against wounds, and brewed and taken internally would relieve cramps of menstruation and avoid, when used as a wash, childbed fever when her own babies were delivered; and as populations grew, and forests receded, this task led her farther and farther into the woods.

But she found her highest creative satisfactions in making pottery and weaving basketry. These things would last. They were her art.

It is in pottery, and the remains of pottery—sherds—that the archaeologist today reconstructs the life and times and culture of these prehistoric folk. But to the Mound Builder squaw it was just another job, in which as the centuries passed she became more proficient and self-expressive. In the beginning her need had been for cooking and eating utensils. She had found mud—blue clay—in pockets along the bank of the Forked Deer which could be kneaded readily without crumbling, and when heat was applied—baking—would harden permanently and in fact might assume a glaze that pleasured her eye. She made a set of bowls and finally eating plates; eventually she used the material to fashion her cooking pots—her greatest forward step that really marked her passing from one age into the next. In the end she completed her whole table setting, and turned her hand to what has come down to us as some of the most beautiful pottery of primitive people—large basins, salt pans, long-necked bottles, jars with handles, pipes, ladles, and ornaments. The articles with handles presented a special problem: the handle might be a thick loop of clay with the lower end riveted through the wall of the vessel, the upper end folded inside the rim; but the bone rivet often charred in curing, and she developed a technique of softening the strips of clay so top and bottom amalgamated with the body of the vessel; and after drying she was now ready for a last gesture of artistry. Before firing, she painted a design with ochre, or vermillion, and burnt the pattern in. The English and French early visitors—intruders—saw and wrote down their marvel. John White wrote, "They made the most wonderful pots with which they cook their food over fires." But the French DuPratz gave the most detailed report, writing as if he were looking back through the ages at his Indian craftswoman.

"They go in search of heavy earth, examine it in dry form, throwing out whatever grit they find, make a sufficiently firm mortar, and then establish their workshop on a flat board, on which they shape the pottery with their fingers, smoothing it by means of a stone which is preserved with great care for the work. As fast as the earth dries they put on more, assisting with the hand on either side. After all these operations, it is cooked by means of a great fire. These women also make pots of an extraordinary size, jugs with medium-sized openings, bowls, two-pint bottles with long necks, pots or jugs for bear's oil, which hold as many as 40 pints, also plates and dishes. I have had some made, out of curiosity, on the model of my earthenware. They were of a quite beautiful red."

The red was obtained from ochre, smeared on the pots before the clay hardened, and then fired.

Dumont paid his respects to our deft-fingered squaws.

"What is more remarkable is that without a potter's wheel, with their fingers alone and patience, they make all kinds of earthen vessels, dishes, plates, pots to put on the fire, with others large enough to contain approximately four gallons."

Kneberg answers our question as to how these pots were made, from her lore of the upper Tennessee Mound Builders, in the Woodland Age. "Pottery vessels, used for most of the cooking, were enormous kettles that held up to five gallons. These vessels were made from local clays to which sand or ground-up rock had been added to prevent shrinkage and cracking during the process of manufacture. This process started with a mass of wet clay mixed with the rock. First, a long roll was made and coiled spirally to form a conical bottom for the vessel. Then, additional rolls were added as rings, one at a time, until the vessel was of the desired height and size. During this step, each coil of clay was firmly welded to the previous one before another was added. Next, the inside surface was scraped smooth and the walls thinned down until they were 1-4 to 1-2 inch in thickness. During the following steps, the vessel, still moist and flexible, was beaten on the outer surface with a paddle wound with cords or woven fabric." This surface finish was not particularly ornamental, but its roughness was practical because the vessel in use would become greasy and slippery. Then the pot was dried in the sun, a step that might occupy some days. Then came the critical firing operation. It was placed before a hot fire of oak coals until the material assumed a burnt hardness. After that it would be carefully put into the fire for several hours, until it became almost white hot. The change burning—later baking—made in the clay transformed it into the enduring substance of pottery. So durable was it that today the archaeologists trace eras and cultures by even potsherds—fragments—of it. The simple patient toil of the long forgotten squaw reveals not only the traditions of the Mound Builders but the woman's artistic expression—the soul of her as it came through her work-worn hands.

Her baskets were less enduring. But for their day and time they were her practical containers and burden carriers. Corn, nuts, vegetables, earth for the mounds—she built the baskets to sit on her head and toted them from here to there. Along the water courses up from the Forked Deer—the smaller creeks and spring branches—the tallest and most slender canes waxed supple in the drifting winds. The squaw and her tall girls moved into these and cut the choicest, trimmed the sharp leafage, and carried the bundles to the village. She picked those of size, and using butt cuts for heavy tote baskets and the more slender for the lighter jobs, she fell to building baskets. She laid a wheel of butts against each other for the bottom. Then in a circular pattern she bound them with thongs of leather, or in case of the heavy earth baskets, she used a ropelike material made by twisting the inner fibers of beaten barks. When the bottom was of size to suit her plan, she bent the canes upward by holding them with her foot. Then she wove in the warp material. When the basket was tall enough, she bound the canes together to form a rim. If the canes were too stiff, she limbered them by soaking them for a day or two in a solution of scalding water and wood ashes before trying to work them into baskets. For the heavy duty articles she used oak and elm wythes instead of canes, and kept them pliable by long soaking in the river. But it was in the beautiful smaller baskets that she achieved her highest skill and most vain accomplishment. With thin splits of cane often dyed brilliant reds and yellows and blues and browns she created basketry to contain her jewels, her intimate personal possessions, and perhaps her secrets, if she had such. That art has come down to us even today in the baskets which can be bought in marketplaces like Cherokee, North Carolina, where memories of our Mound Builder squaw survive.

Then, once in her lifetime, the mound had to be raised a layer for some great chief, to whom obedience was obligatory. Then would be days and nights of bent-back burdens of earth in the baskets she had woven in lighter hours. Legend has it that adultery was practically unknown among the Pinson wives. Where would they have found opportunity and energy for unfaithfulness?

14
Mound Builder Erotica

There seems to be sufficient evidence to warrant the assumption that the Mound Builders belonged to the family of Indians that historically were known as Natchez. We have noted earlier that these Indians of a common language were widely dispersed in the southern river valleys, notably the Mississippi. They were tall, strong, robust, and of a proud air. As a rule the men were handsome, and the women pretty and well shaped. The earliest report we have on the females was their well-proportioned figures—shapely hips and well turned breasts; and "they were generally quite agreeable in appearance." The men were sinewy, firm fleshed, with long thighs and legs "as if made in a mold." Their features were regular, their eyes black, their hair black, and coarse and straight. Their color ran to a light bronze. Men and women were generally clean. Though early ladies in America complained of their odor, the smell came not from the Indian but from the paint with which men and women adorned themselves. Often in summer and winter alike they bathed themselves.

We are to suppose, too, that a thousand years ago the Pinson people were not too different from the Indians the very early white men found in the vast Mississippi land, along the coast region that later became Mobile, Biloxi, and New Orleans and up the river to Natchez, which derived its name from the tribes along its shores. Among these first observers were men like Charlevoix, Dumont, St. Cosme, De la Vente, Iberville; and a thousand miles away to the northeast Captain John Smith, John White and Thomas Hariot—to name three. John White especially was an artist of unquestioned stature, and Le Moyne, the

Frenchman, equally so. From their reports, and paintings, we can piece together, along with the studies of the archaeologists, a fairly acceptable portrait of our Mound Builders, and this chapter will consider their habits in love, marriage, erotica, morals—in the sense of Judeo-Christianity the Indian had no morals; and the minor details of male and female adornment to enticement.

We have noted, too, how children—boys and girls alike—grew up in a state of abandoned nakedness. Part of this was due to the need of conditioning the young to the rigors of summer and winter with little or no clothing. Sometimes it was due to scanty materials for wearing apparel. Mostly it was because of custom. Nudity was so familiar, in young and adult, that it was as commonplace as the ways of animals. But that this display of body had an effect on early sexual experiment if not actual activity is not easy to doubt. It is probable that young children satisfied their curiosity. If the girls around seven or eight became sex conscious and started wearing a scanty girdle of soft skins, padded with a bland material in the crotch, it did not offer any great concealment. But around ten years when early puberty established itself, they assumed more the habiliments of adult females. Their mothers wore in summer a frail apron of fringed bark fabric, woven usually of some material like beaten mulberry bark which could be made into a linenlike cloth, and in winter a more ample garment made of the skin of deer, but they went bare of breast winter and summer. By the 12th year the menstrual cycle had started as a rule and in another year a girl was capable of child bearing. That the females, mature and immature, were noted for their comeliness could not fail of contributing liberally to enticement.

The boys, on the other hand, went naked until puberty. Then they assumed the breech-clout of the man. But all through these impressionable years they had displayed their bodies to the females, and by the time they became capable sexually they probably had developed a complete technique in the exercise of the function. We might say that boys and girls "had no secrets from each other."

So far as we can conjecture there was no special importance attached to such experience, beyond the normal physical and emotional sensations of erotic activity. Certainly there was no social stigma. Virginity and chastity, rather than being highly regarded as in civilized culture, were looked upon either as unimportant or as a handicap. "Some are found whose chastity can not be shaken; there are some who desire neither lovers nor husbands, although chastity among the savages is one of the least virtues. The greater number take good advantage of the liberty which custom gives them."

In the early stages this experimentation was more or less open, but time led the young to a more becoming modesty. They would adjourn to the nearby woods, which also afforded privacy for natural functions. It might be noted in passing that evacuation of human manures, at least for the women and girls, was a social affair, where females in groups repaired to the woods for relief, group protection against wild animals being a necessary precaution. Females used one locality, males another. As the villages increased in population and the woods receded, a problem tended to develop, but the Mound Builder was careful of disposal of human dung, lest is contaminate the springs and the cold spring branch that flowed through the land just north of the Great Central Mound, and afforded cold, pure water supply for the entire town. In this matter of sanitation the abundant insect life contributed its part. The green fly—the blow fly—was first on the job. A mound of dung would be covered in a moment. In a day or two the larvae would have completed the task. But there were also the great beetles that propagated on human and animal waste, and they burrowed in the spots to complete the disposal. There were no chamber pots, no privies. For this reason, as much as the desire of the Indian to have a detached abode for his family, Indian villages were dispersed along streams, such as rivers and creeks, and coastlines next to the seas.

But probably the greatest erotic activity was stimulated by the dances that followed the feasts and other celebrations. The Mound Builder adored his dances. We have noted this earlier. Dancing was an outlet for his aesthetic and rhythmic nature, and it was his chief social pleasure. In a monotonous life that was concerned mostly with hunting, fishing, fighting, and the unimaginative small business of an almost unchanging existence, the dance fired his blood and lifted his heart. We have the record of such a festivity, if not of our Mound Builders at least as accurate a portrait as we shall ever have of what went on erotically in Pinson Town.

"The dances are as follows: The women dance with the men and the boys with the girls. These dances are always by 20 or 30 together—as many boys as girls. A married man is not permitted to dance with girls, nor boys to dance with women. After they have lighted a great torch, which is ordinarily the dry trunk of an old pine, burnt in order to light the grand square of the village, and another opposite the cabin of the great chief, the dance master at the head of a hundred men and women, to the sound of a drum and the voices of the spectators, begins the dance at sunset, and each one dances in turn till midnight. After this the men retire to their homes with their wives and leave the place to the boys and girls, who dance from midnight to broad daylight. They give themselves to this pleasure many times, each in turn." The dance was like this, "When a youth has danced in that manner with the girl at his side or in front of him, he is permitted to lead her to the end of the village, into one of the groves on the prairies, where he dances again with her" in the manner of the Mississippi, when they return to the group and

Mound Builder Erotica 215

resume the dance as before. "They continue their dances thus till broad daylight, so that in the morning the boys especially are like disinterred ghosts, as much through loss of sleep as being fatigued with dancing with the girls."

What the girls looked like after an orgy like this our reporter did not say, but the inference is they stood up under the sex stimulating activity more stoutly than the boys. And though he is not explicit about what went on when the dancers were alone in the woods or down in the rows of maize, we are led to deduce that dancing was not all they were up to. The truth seems to be these celebrations, aside from being feasts of one kind or another—the Green Corn Festival, the Mid-Summer Feast, when maize was laid by, the Harvest Festival—ended in a type of sex orgy. The adults repaired to their domiciles for their pleasures, setting the example; the young took off to the bushes.

Inevitably what we know today as bastardy would result from such carryings on. The wonder is that the villages were not overrun by young ones of unknown fatherhood. But the importance the civilized Western Man placed on legitimacy did not trouble the Pinson folk. Inheritance, such as it was, was through the line of the mother. In truth, there was little to inherit of individual property in a society where everything was held in common. Civilized man has cherished legitimacy to preserve inheritance, though of course his nature is such that he esteems total possession of the wife as essential to his being. The Indian baby belonged to its mother. In case of an unmarried mother, the problem was of no consequence.

When our Pinson maid steps into history, her image becomes more clear. The earliest French, Spanish and English explorers have left sharp vignettes of her—and few are complimentary. Some of their bad temper may have been due to the wanton lass's transmitting syphilis, a disease native to the American Indian, to them. It was a dirty compliment in return for the white man's giving to the Redskin measles, mumps and smallpox.

Dumont wrote, "The girls let themselves out willingly to the Frenchmen in the capacity of slaves and mistresses at the same time," and for a few yards of some precious fabric "they remain with them in these two relations during the space of a month.... There are neither religion nor laws which forbid this libertinism [and] they abandon themselves to it without shame and without scruple, giving themselves sometimes to one and sometimes to another (man), their virtue never being proof to a present made to them, be it only a trifle. It is not that among these savage girls there is none who is wise, but it must be admitted they are very rare."

Another (Luxembourg) wrote, "These women who are not married have great liberty in their pleasures; no one can disturb them." And again, "I am not at all astonished that these girls are lewd and have no modesty, since their fathers and mothers and their religion teach them that on leaving this world there is a plank, very narrow and difficult to pass, to enter into the grand villages, where they pretend they are going after death, and only those who have disported themselves well with the boys will pass this plank easily."

Penicaut went on to add with a trace of bitterness, "One sees the consequences of these detestable lessons, which are instilled in them from the earliest years, supported by the liberty and idleness in which they are kept, since a girl up to the age of 20 or 25 years does nothing else, the father and mother being obliged to have her food provided, and yet in accordance with her taste and what she asks for, until she is married."

There is, of course, some discrepancy in this observation. Few Indian mothers, as we shall point out presently, lived long enough to see their pampered daughters reach the ripe age of 20 or 25. In a primitive society such as the Mound Builders, there was no place for laziness. The Indian girl toiled in the maize and vegetables along with the old women, and in the centuries when the Mounds were being erected she toted her basket of earth along with her sisters and mother. But these men were missionaries, and they saw through the glass darkly. Charlevoix observed, "We know no nation on this continent where the female sex is more irregular than this. They are even forced by the chief to prostitute themselves to all comers, and the woman for being common is not the less esteemed."

Du Pratz added his depressing testimony: "When the boys and girls have arrived at the age of puberty they associate with each other familiarly, and have the liberty of doing so. The girls, forewarned that they will no longer be mistresses of their own hearts after they are married, know how to dispose of [their favors] to their advantage in forming their wardrobe as the price of their pleasures, for in that country, as elsewhere, the rule is nothing for nothing. Her intended, far from finding fault with this, on the contrary values his future wife in proportion to the fruits which she has produced."

The men who came fortune hunting and soul saving contributed their measure to the maids' delinquency. They blithely took the fair creatures for mistresses, paid in bolts of cloth and baubles and cheap jewelry, and often left behind for future explorers and adventurers strangely assorted children among the coppery naked brats that ranged wild in the villages. One such traveller spoke of two girl children with beautiful chestnut hair and skin so fair as almost to be white—a mauve shade that was very lovely. He learned that this came about because of a shipwrecked crew that had remained in the estuary some months while they repaired their battered ship. One cannot help but wonder a bit at the emotions of the abandoned women when the ship again put out to sea.

But to return to our Mound Builder maid: If in all this free-wheeling carrying on she found herself pregnant, two courses were open to her. We are told elsewhere that "the girls, although given to their pleasures, have means of guarding against pregnancy." But now and then one might forget her pills, or the contraceptive failed. She could produce an abortion by going to the maize patches and searching out the mummied ears, misshapen by ergot, and eating these untasty vegetables. To increase potency, there was a species of wild cotton whose bitter root was a powerful amenagog. If taken in time this would usually restore her menstrual cycle. But abortion had its hazards. She might just go ahead and carry the child to its time. When the baby was born, her mother would ask, "Do you want your baby?" If the girl said "Yes," she took and suckled it and increased the Mound Builder population by one. The odds were even it would die in infancy anyway. But if she refused the baby, her parents either took and raised it, or if they did not want it, they would take the squirming creature out to the waste pit and either brain it or strangle it. Whatever disposition was made of it, the maid was not "ruined," though probably she was no longer a shy little Indian maid.

But once a girl married—usually between 23 and 25 years of age, as one observer states—her days of wine and roses were over. She had an average of ten or twelve years of childbearing, and Indian women—Pinson women in particular in that tranquil period around the year A.D. 1000 —were exceedingly fertile. They littered from five to ten children before dying of old age and toil around 35. It seems true that a few old squaws hung on into their 40s. But the life span of Stone Age man, judging from the skeletons excavated by archaeologists, was comparatively short; and 50 was an almost unknown age in primitive times. Thus we have to discount the reports of some historic writers that girls married only in their 20s. Most mothers would not have survived to see their daughters wedded. It seems much more probable that, like all primitives, marriage came much earlier, at the latest in their high teens. (The Indian had no sense of years; his calendar was by moons.) In any case the mortality rate in infancy was appalling. It has been estimated that half the babies died within the first year. There were the childhood diseases—a "summer complaint" that white settlers contended with in their babies; there were the winter ailments that carried off those the summer complaint didn't get. And there was head-flattening to finish the carnage.

One of the first things noticed about the John White water colors and the Le Moyne drawings is the flat heads of the Indians, especially those of the women. The custom rooted in the dimmest antiquity, and apparently was almost universal among the Mississippi and related folk, including the Mound Builders. One of the French writers has left a vivid picture of the process.

"They (the Indians) were not born so (with flat heads); it is a charm which is given to them in early years. What a mother does to the head of her infant in order to force its tender bones to assume this shape is almost beyond belief. She lays the infant on a cradle which is nothing more than the end of a board on which is spread a piece of the skin of an animal; one extremity of this board has a hole where the head is placed and it is lower than the rest. The infant being laid down entirely naked she pushes back its head into this hole and applies to it on the forehead and under the head a mass of clay which she binds with all her strength between two little boards. The infant cries, turns completely black, and the strain which it is made to suffer is such that a white, slimy fluid is seen to come out of its nose and ears at the time when the mother presses on its forehead. It sleeps thus every night until its skull has taken on the shape which custom wishes it to receive."

The reporter was gratified to add that the missionaries

on their arrival began to persuade the mothers to leave off this artificial blandishment, and later generations of Indians had round natural heads.

How much this custom increased the death rate we can only conjecture at this late date; but it must have been considerable.

A more direct method of butchering the babies was another custom known as the sacrifice of the firstborn. The first fruits from the fields were offerings to the chief—the corn, vegetables, squash, beans; and the first male babies were likewise given him. Soon after the first son is born a day is set for the ceremony, and the chief goes to the appointed place. There he takes his seat on a bench, near a tree stump two feet high and as thick, in front of which the mother squats on her heels with babe in arms, her face covered with her hands in sorrow. A friend or relative presents the child to the chief in an attitude of worship. The women of the village then form a circle around the chief and dance and sing in a great demonstration of joy. The woman to whom the chief passes the child all the while chants the praises of the great chief. Though it is largely a female ceremonial, there are men present, and one who is decked out in paint, feathers, and regalia befitting his office, waits to receive the sacrifice. The dance and song finished, this official accepts the babe and kills it, laying the sacrifice at the feet of the chief.

There can be small doubt that this practice of human sacrifice, together with other factors, resulted in a population heavily female; and this in turn had a marked effect on courtship and marriage. The scarcity of young men in proportion to available women gave our Pinson maid a narrower choice in a husband than if the sexes had been more evenly balanced. She took, pretty much, the first man who asked her. Another effect was widespread polygamy. Custom permitted a man to have as many wives as he chose. "Nevertheless, the common people generally have but one or two." But marriage was for good. "A savage is never seen to change the woman whom he once married. He keeps her until death." "What is remarkable is that in spite of the corruption and libertinism which reign among the barbarians, the bond of marriage is much more respected by them than among more civilized people." This would naturally be the observation of a religionist after we step a moment back into history. Was enduring love the bond that held man and wife or wives? Not likely—not in the sentimental sense that we like to think of marriage today. For one thing, family life was not private. Though each Mound Builder had a house to himself, he dwelt mostly, winter and summer, out of doors. His females went about the tasks of cooking, weaving, making pottery, tilling the fields, without intruding on his strictly masculine activities, such as hunting, fishing, warring. The friction of civilized living of husband and wife was lost in the hard business of living and dying. An unloved wife could hoe just as many hills of corn as a loved one; and though if our Mound Builder had more than one, and consorted with one in preference to another, the loveless one fed at the common bowl along with the favorite. There seems nothing in racial memories to indicate that she suffered the torture of the damned. Life never did promise her much, and wifehood was like the basket of wormy wild crabapples she gathered in the Forked Deer woods.

She might, of course, look back at her days of courtship with a sense of longing. For when a boy and girl had determined to marry, they went into the woods together, where the girl made a shelter of leafy branches and a bed of twigs while her young brave took to the deeper forest to hunt. When he returned with game, she had a fire going. They roasted a hunk of dripping flesh over the bed of coals, making their supper; and with night at hand, went to bed to enjoy their "pleasures." It is unlikely that either was a virgin. Since each had tasted many varieties of fruit, this apple from the tree in the Garden of Eden, under the dark Tennessee sky, to the faroff howl of a wolf or a panther, should have had a tang all its own. They might remain in the woods a night and day, or a week. It was, in effect, trial marriage. It contained also the honeymoon. If mutually satisfactory, they returned to Pinson Town and took up their lives together. For the time being they might live with her folks, until a cabin of their own could be erected of woven supple saplings and bark and thatch. Previous to this, however, the youth had paid his respects to her father and mother, to whom he had given befitting presents. There had been a feast and dance, celebrating the nuptials. In time our young Pinson man matured, and if his wife had sisters, and husbands were scarce, he married them, and they came to live at his house, and his tribe increased according to their fruitfulness. If his house would not hold them all, he would farm the spare wives out to his friends. Nothing was thought of this; sexual jealousy seemed one of the least passions of the Mound Builder.

Male concubinage seemed to have existed disproportionately among Indians generally, and was not confined to Mound Builders. The male concubine, the hermaphrodite, had the place of "chief of women." the earliest white men were quick to note this fact. Dumont gives us a picture: "It is certain that although he has the same dress and occupations as the women, he really is a man. Like them he wears his hair long and braided. He has, like them, a petticoat instead of a breechcloth. Like them he labors in the cultivation of the fields and in all the other labors which are proper to them, and as among these people, who live almost without religion and without law, libertinism is carried to the greatest excess. I will not answer that these barbarians do not abuse this pretended chief of women and make him serve their brutal passions. What is certain is that when a party of warriors or honored men leave the village to go either to war or the chase, if they do not make their wives follow them, they always carry with them this man dressed as a woman, who serves to keep their camp, to cook their hominy, and to provide, in short, for all the needs of the household as well as a woman might do."

The heaviest work, in battle and at the cabins, was loaded on them. The burdens of harvest, or the hunt, were toted by them. They carried the dead and wounded away from the battles. If they had any compensation at all, as implied by Dumont, it was in serving the "brutal passions" of the frustrated wives when the maize was tall and green in the blinding summer sunlight. What would happen to a wife discovered in this type of Lesbianism can only be conjectured. Adultery was almost unknown. Too many things prevailed to discourage it—the nearness of houses and density of population around them; the practical certainty of discovery and report; and severity of punishment. At the worst an adulteress could be put to death. She might be beaten, or her ears or nose cut off. There is one legend of a befitting punishment for a lady gone astray who was stripped naked, tied hands and feet to the ground, and all the braves nearby invited to rape her. One wonders if she was cured by this treatment. A Mound Builder might willingly lend his wife to a friend while he was gone on a journey, but he wanted none of this stepping out on him.

We asked Dr. John Nuckolls about this seeming prevalence of Hermaphroditism among the Mound Builders and reputed Mississippi Indians generally. His reply was, "True Hermaphroditism is very rare." In Hugh Hampton Young's book on *Genital Abnormalities,* he could find only 20 cases in medical literature that could be proven male and female tissue. Dr. Nuckolls himself had seen one at the University of Wisconsin. "There are, however, a much larger number of individuals who have congenital abnormalities due to hypospadias in the male, which is not too rare. In this case the male urethra fails to close at almost any point out to the end of the penis. When it opens in the scrotal area the scrotum is frequently present as two halves and the testes may be undescended. This would cause the individual who is all male to appear to have a penis and a vagina. It is a fact that congenital abnormalities are more prevalent in the underprivileged."

In his love life what manner of man seems to emerge from our conjectures on the Mound Builder? What manner of woman was his wife and daughter?

Our Pinson man killed without compunction, both beast and fellow man if his enemy. He could club a babe to death without batting an eye. He would torture an enemy with satisfaction. Was it likely, then, that he also was a tender man in his emotional life with his woman? We find it hard to believe so. For a brief time he may have known what we think of as love. It merged into a settled fidelity to his marriage vows. But a man who knew nothing of the aesthetics of art, literature, only the most rudimentary music, and had exercised his sexual function since puberty, was not likely to experience any of the romantic illusions that to the white man has been his great creative genius. The early observers called him savage. He was.

What then of his woman? Our Pinson woman seems to have been made of more tender substance. If she yielded happily to the urge of her flesh, and succumbed willingly to the blandishments of personal adornment, she still rarely if ever shared in the bloody activities of her man. There is a case on record where a man was brought to the village, captured after murdering her husband. The men stripped the killer naked, tied his hands and feet to posts, and made ready to butcher him by slow degrees. Our widow saw, not a murderer, but a well-proportioned young man. She moved into the torturers in traditional female style and cried, "Nay, nay! I'll claim him." The prisoner was unbound and delivered to the bereaved lady, who carried him home and presumably lived happily ever afterward with him—or as happily as an Indian squaw could. In any case she could not stand by and see a fine specimen of man done in. In the scarcity of the species one man seemed about as good as another.

Captain John Smith would have understood this woman.

15
"People of the Flints"

Joel Pinson's story shattered our delusion of a trackless wilderness in pre-fable Tennessee lands—the tale of tens of thousands of hoofprints of a thousand generations of buffalo, elk, deer, bear, panther, and lesser creatures on the way to pastures, prey, salt licks, springs and streams—and don't doubt that a butt-headed buffalo couldn't taste the difference between cold spring water and the murky swill of the Forked Deer; and breeding grounds. They had a taste, too, for familiar rutting retreats. Nor were roving wild critters all. The land was criss-crossed by scores of trails, traces, navigable streams, and other avenues of travel and trade by the countless generations of Mound Builders, Natchez, Chickasaws, Choctaws, and other historic tribes who beat their ways through forests, over mountains, across rivers in their restless pilgrimages from here to there, until some number of them settled down, built houses and temples and erected mounds. To suppose, however, that the Indian squatted down to vegetate and replenish this wilderness with his fecund females is to judge him wrongly. If there ever was a creature born with an itching heel, it was our Archaic, Woodland, and Mississippi Redskin. He admired to go places and swap cultures, trade pottery designs, learn new crafts in bone and metal, trade for flints, make wars, collect scalps; and if nothing else exciting suggested itself he was not above swooping down and stealing a fresh bunch of slaves, concubines and wives.

There seems small doubt that Pinson was one of the central cities of this vast network of trade, social and cultural exchange, and female pillage. We can assume that

View of lake, museum, and mounds (to the right). Four such lakes at Moundville were made by the Indians who used the soil for mound fill. When these "barrow pits" were filled with rain water, lakes were formed which served as a water supply for the Mound Builders.

it was the most important port of trade from the Ohio River down the Mississippi to the Gulf of Mexico.

We have noted earlier that all the worthwhile culture of the Indians that survived into the historic period was a heritage of the Mound Builders. Of all the Indians, they were the most polished and civilized. Many authorities would like to trace their arts, form of government—for primitive people it was a simple and direct democracy—and system of religion to the Aztecs, Mayas, and other Mexican and Central American roots; and their pottery designs and even the flat-topped Mounds which admittedly resemble Middle American temple pyramids such

Professor David L. DeJarnette, Curator of Mound State Monument Archaeological Museum, Moundville, Alabama, views the diorama of life at Moundville centuries ago. Such a scene might easily have been duplicated at Pinson. Diorama by Tom DeJarnette, Jr. (Photo courtesy Moundville Park Museum).

as the Castillo at Chichen Itza, Yucatan, and the Pyramid of the Sun at Teotihuacan, Mexico, can be traced to these influences. Yet, one can permit himself a shadow of doubt. When one views the Great Central Mound at Pinson, and the neighboring secondary mounds, he sees nothing there that an average Mound Builder might not have thought of for himself. It is the simplest and most primitive of all architecture: two piles of earth. The human species seems ingrained with a taste for toting dirt from one place to

Archaeological Museum built over *in situ* burials. Numerous displays and artifacts in the museum depict the culture of the Moundville Indians.

Twenty-five of these "Temple" mounds are located on Mound State Monument's 315 acre tract. A classic example of Middle Mississippian culture, Moundville dates from 1200 to 1400 A.D.

Mounds in the Mist 230

another; and if his females cooperate in the drudgery he will grow ambitious and design a larger pile. The archaeologist is intent on tracing influences back to their sources. The layman is less obsessed with this urge.

Be that as it may, the Mound Builders had an intricate and established religion and a regular priesthood. Though kings in the historic sense did not exist, there was a system of strong chiefs—who derived their authority from the people by virtue of their craft in war, power in oratory and persuasion, or years and wisdom; and below a network of lesser chiefs of lesser talents. There were distinctions of rank. They were skilled in the knowledge of medicinal plants and their properties, and their curative powers were augmented by religion and a good substitute for psychological medicine. The early French coming to America had good reason to respect these skills—or magic —as they have attested by cures little short of incredible. "It is extremely probable that this nation (the Natchez, most likely survival of the Pinson people into the historical period) in the days of its prosperity extended from the Wabash to the Mississippi southwardly and eastwardly to" what today is the Gulf of Mexico. "And it may be that their settlements were at all places upon these rivers and their branches where we now see the high places (mounds) which at the present day are attractive of so much notice." In their heyday the Mound Builders, though centralized in such gatherings as Pinson, Etowah and Cahokia, "extended from the river Manchers or Iberville, which is about fifty leagues from the sea, to the Wabash, which is 450 leagues from the sea; and it is probable that they extended laterally up all the rivers that fall into the Mississippi between these two extremes." Another archaeologist, Professor Jesse D. Jennings, University of Utah, commenting in a chapter of *Prehistory of the Lower Mississippi Valley* (University of Chicago Press, 1952) said, "Marksville period pottery is found in collections in a con-

Excavated burials in the south wing of the museum showing typical Middle Mississippian burial offerings: ceramic bowls, water jars, stone discs elaborately carved, copper ornaments and ceremonial weapons, and shell beads and gorgets.

tinuous zone along the bluffs and alluvial valley of the Mississippi River from Baton Rouge almost to Memphis."

Dr. John Nuckolls, our oft-quoted authority on the Pinson Mound Builders, stated, "All of which seems to add credence to my thesis that the Natchez were the direct descendants of the Marksville Hopewellian Woodland people (to which Pinson folk belonged). It is very likely that the customs and beliefs of the earlier people were continued down through the centuries more or less unchanged . . . as primitive people tend to hold to those things longer than we do. But, then, all of our religions

Professor David L. DeJarnette, Curator at Mound State Monument, examining *in situ* burials inside the museum.

have persisted for a couple of thousand years at least." It would follow that all their folkways tended to persist likewise down through the countless centuries.

Having thus fairly established the widespread distribution of the Mound Builders in both time and area, we can begin the study of their far-flung travels. To begin with, they came from a far-far country, across wide-wide waters. Within the historical era the Indian tribes had legends and traditions of migrations in the dim dawn of their history. According to the old men the Indians originated in Asia. They crossed to the North Continent by way of the Bering Straits. They then moved down the West Coast to Mexico, as we know that country today. Surplus population moved northward and eastward, to what at last

This Ceremonial Pipe was found at Beech Grove Trailer Court in 1955. This trailer site is on Route 66, several miles from Old Crib Mound on the Ohio River near Grandview, Indiana. Mr. Charles Raaf of Grandview, Indiana, owns the trailer court and formerly owned the mound. A Mr. William Suhrheinrich of Chicago, Illinois, now owns the land on which Old Corn Crib is situated. (Photo courtesy of William H. Kennedy)

Mounds in the Mist 234

Two boys from Fort Wayne, Indiana, look for relics at the Corn Crib Mound. The young man on the right is holding a bone found at the site. Professional archaeologists deplore these relic hunters. (Photo courtesy of William H. Kennedy)

became Mound-Builder land. "Archaeologists mostly agree that this was in fact just what happened—at least the Bering Straits crossing—but that this probably occurred ten thousand years ago." If we can accept a tradition ten thousand years old—questionable as it may be—we should readily go along with the Natchez tradition that at one time their nation extended over most of the southeastern United States, and the population was numbered as the sands of the sea. And over this time and distance the restless Indian tracks fell in the roving tracks of the brutes.

William E. Meyer corroborates these facts in *Indian Trails of the Southeast* (42d Annual Report of the Bureau of American Ethnology 1924–25): "More or less well established trails made by wild animals in search of food and drink existed upon the earth for long ages before the appearance of man, changing slowly as local conditions were altered by erosion, climatic shifts, or other causes. Man found the lands already covered with them and began using them because they led him to water and to salt licks and other places where the primal necessities—water, food, and the materials for clothing—could be obtained. Later they became media of friendly or hostile communication between the people themselves.

"There was far more travel among Indians than is usually supposed," he went on. "This was sometimes for barter-commerce, sometimes for visits of social, friendly, or religious character, and sometimes for war or adventure."

Meyer cites well-authenticated cases of Indians having gone on visits to a series of distant friendly tribes, covering from 1000 to 2000 miles, and being absent from home for two months or more. That Pinson Indians exchanged such visits with the distant Cahokia folk, or the Etowah towns near what is now Atlanta, Georgia, or to the far off south on the lower Mississippi, goes without saying. We can

Mounds in the Mist 236

give credence to the belief that in the beginning the first Indians did migrate from Asia, turned south to Mexico, and from there spread over most of North America. "A friendly visitor with a new sacred or social dance was always welcome in any Indian village, and great pains were taken to learn it." But sometimes the visitor brought something not the least welcome—a new scourge of fever, a fresh germ of flux, a revived outbreak of syphilis, and in due time as the white man came, the fatal measles and smallpox. Mound Builders followed the network of trails near and far for "barter commerce." Besides exchange of social and religious dances, they swapped skills in weaving, pottery making, fashioning characteristic weapons of

An Indian Peace Pipe found buried in a grave thought to be that of a Chief. Bones and beads were buried in the same grave. Authorities examining the bones say they are about 8,000 years old. (Photo courtesy of William H. Kennedy)

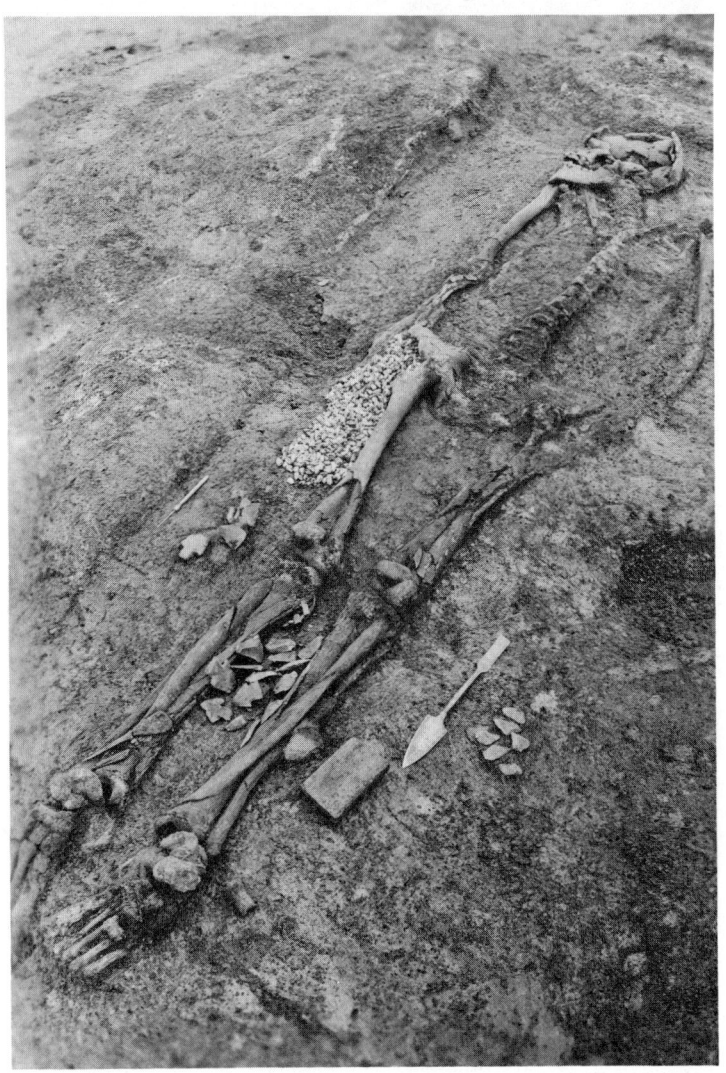

Burial from the Nowlin Mound, with typical Adena points, shell beads, and a stone tablet associated. Arrowheads of this calibre were used mostly for small game—in the Ohio Valley this would be large cane-eating rabbits ("cane-cutters"), squirrels, possums, skunks, groundhogs (a delicacy), and birds such as turkey, goose and duck, not readily slaughtered at close range. (Photo courtesy G. A. Black Laboratory of Archaeology, Indiana University)

Mounds in the Mist 238

the Stone Age—arrow points, ceremonial axes, spears, raw flints, choice woods for powerful bows; and the most adored by the Indian, beads of shell, copper, bone, and even gold. Much of the raw materials the Pinson Mound Builders did not have; somehow they must be bought from distant suppliers. Gold was mined in the far upper rivers in the mountains—gold is still found in Georgia and North Carolina in paying quantities, though artifacts of gold are rarely found in the excavations of mounds. Copper was brought down from the Georgia mountains; from

Overall view of the Nowlin Mound in Dearborn County, Indiana. This view shows something of the mound profile and log tombs *in situ*. It illustrates, as well, the use of hard-packed earth employed by the Mound Builders in their temple altars and ceremonial equipment, their burial arrangements; and the painstaking care of archaeologists in excavating to the core of primitive life. (Photo courtesy G. A. Black Laboratory of Archaeology, Indiana University, Dr. James H. Kellar, Director)

"People of the Flints" 239

a spot that in modern years has become a rich deposit at a place called Copperhill. To today's traveler it is a desolate region destitute of vegetation; not even a tree stands in the mining section. Here the Mound Builders in quest of metal, or traders gathering to barter with flatland buyers, dug plentifully. Shells were fetched from the sea—the Gulf, 600 miles to the south of Pinson. We are cautioned to bear in mind when considering this far-away and often rugged commercial travel that our Pinson trader followed the routes of easiest going: he avoided dense

Excavation of the Temple Mound at Angel Mounds State Memorial near Evansville, Indiana. This site is Middle Mississippian, which would seem to date it between A.D. 1000 and A.D. 1200. The dark dots on the surface and in the bottom of the altar trench are post holes left from the wood structures that topped the mound. Though the mound is not high—8-10 feet—it is otherwise large and commanded an impressive view of what must have been open cornlands in prehistoric times. (Photo courtesy G. A. Black Laboratory of Archaeology, Indiana University)

underbrush along the rivers, and stony ground in the highlands. In the wooded or mountainous regions the travelers were forced to go single file, and pathways were hardly more than two feet wide. But in open grassy prairie localities Indians would move in formations to suit their pleasure. Here trails might be wide and rambling. There was also the matter of burdens. This commerce was a job of the ablebodied men—the warriors; or in some cases slaves, also men, and the downtrodden hermaphrodites who served as beasts of burden. Women could tote earth for the great mounds and nothing was thought of it. But for the long haul it fell to the men.

One authority tells us, "The short-cut trails were indispensable to the Indians, for then news of an invasion or another matter of great importance could only be carried by messenger on foot, and [some Indians] were celebrated in this respect." Adair tells of a young Chickasaw who, on an emergency, and being pursued, ran from where Mobile, Alabama, is now located (a distance of 300 computed miles) in 42 hours," whereas a rider on a very superior horse rode the distance in just two hours less—40 hours. The messenger carried no provisions, depending upon such herbs as he could snatch up on the way for sustenance, and yet not allowing him a moment to eat or sleep, he travelled night and day at an average rate of over seven miles an hour for 42 consecutive hours." And while this Redskin demonstrated speed and endurance because an enemy was breathing down his neck, the qualities were characteristic of the bartering Indians beating out the traces and driving canoes along the water avenues of commerce. Distance and time did not deter the traders. Kneburg makes the point in Griffin's *Archaeology of the Eastern United States,* in discussing the Eva people (Archaic: radio-carbon dated 5200 B.C.), "They had wide contacts, trading with the Lake Superior Indians for copper and the Gulf Coast Indians for marine shells." Ar-

Barn on low, eroded mound in Spencer County, Indiana. Farmers in Southern Indiana river bottoms built homes and barns atop mounds to avoid problems of Ohio River spring floods. This mound rises five or six feet above high-water mark, and belongs to Archaic Mound Builder civilization. (Photo courtesy Glenmore Distilleries, Owensboro, Ky.)

chaeologists who have made close study of Pinson folk are of the opinion the town was a commercial and trading center for a wide territory, which today would embrace sections of Mississippi, Alabama, Arkansas, perhaps Missouri and southern Illinois, and practically the whole of Tennessee. Pinson had two natural resources in some ways exceeding the neighboring Mound Builder communities: a peculiarly fine clay for pottery which today makes spots in West Tennessee "the clay center of the world"; and a certain quality of tobacco which in modern times was of

Old Crib Mound on Ohio River five miles east of Grandview, Indiana. Corn cribs are now gone (1967) and much of the mound has washed into the river. Countless numbers of relics, bones, and artifacts made by mound builders were found on site in past many years. (Courtesy William H. Kennedy)

worldwide importance in the tobacco darkfired market (though this particular type has declined in competition with the lighter leafed cigarette tobaccos). Pinson hucksters trafficked in the leaf, and potters from near and far came for the clay. Salt deposits Pinson did not have, but Eva did, in form of heavily flowing salt springs; and in exchange for salt the Eva merchants—if such we may call them—paid the beautiful pearllike clam shells, of which the Tennessee River afforded countless thousands. Clams were one of the main foods of Eva folk. The refuse shells

"*People of the Flints*" 243

over the centuries they piled in layers as the town grew, one civilization on top of another, until the towns on the river bluff rose five hundred feet above the languid limestone girt river. The relics of this town remain today one of the monuments of our lost and forgotten Mound Builders. A thousand years ago it was a point of commerce for Pinson. They bartered not only mussel shells but pearls for the stringing of beautiful necklaces which charmed the avaricious eyes of the first white men who reached the backlands. The craftsmen at Pinson with incredible patience and a skill that baffles our appreciation when we

Corn Crib Mound on Ohio River, 5 miles east of Grandview, Ind. The cribs disappeared in the river at a time of high water, but the erection of farm buildings—houses and barns—on Indian mounds in overflow lands was common not only in the Ohio valley but over bottomlands to the gulf. Countless relics, bones and artifacts left by Mound Builders have been excavated over the years at this site. (Courtesy William H. Kennedy. Drawn from photo)

Mounds in the Mist 244

MOUND GROUP at REELFOOT LAKE

From a sketch made in 1936, before cultivation, erosion, and highway construction all but obliterated the mound group. For the sake of unity, the mounds have been compressed; in fact, they were about 300 yards apart. (Sketch by Kroll)

reflect the artisans used bone, burnt thorn ends, and the finest flint drills to puncture the holes in the pearls so fine that a woman's hairpin would fit. This work was done by men. Stringing the strands was left to the female craftsmen. They spun strands of buffalo mane, silken in texture, for the thread.

Kneberg tells us, "Fresh water pearls, skillfully perforated with very small drills, were a source of beads. One necklace contained a thousand pearls, and individual examples a half inch in diameter" have been found in Mound Builder graves. "The fabulous size and beauty of the pearls worn by the Indians impressed the early Spanish and English explorers who, seeing in them a possible source of wealth, secured as many as they could by barter." We can suppose these priceless artifacts found their way to the graceful necks of Spanish and English ladies of quality, while our alleged "beautiful Indian maidens, with midnight in their eyes, and blackgold and platinum in their long tresses" wound up sporting copper. The hallmark of Pinson craftsmen must have touched the precious flesh of our faraway pale beauties.

"Serpent Mound is situated in Bratton Township, Adams County, on the east bluff of Ohio Brush Creek near the village of Loudon. It is one of the few effigy mounds in the state of Ohio and is the largest and finest serpent effigy in the United States. Serpent Mound is an embankment of earth nearly a quarter of a mile long, which represents a gigantic serpent in the act of uncoiling. The greater portion of the body is extended in seven deep curves nearly to the end of the elevated surface on which it lies. Partly within the open jaws of the serpent is an oval mound of earth resembling an egg."
Excavations of the mound revealed no implements, burials, or ornaments of the builders. But nearby, low mounds indicated both prehistoric Adena and Hopewell peoples. (Photo courtesy National Geographic Society)

It may be said in passing that our attractive, expensively dressed young woman of today, if she is lucky, may wear a blouse buttoned with lovely Tennessee River mother-of-pearl buttons; but she'd better beware: the plastic goldbrickers will cheat her with an imitation it would take an expert eye to detect.

The only traffic on these trading treks we can surmise is of the Pinson women with their burden baskets going to Eva to fetch home the rounded limestone boulders the size of basketballs down to baseballs from the torn and

Mound Bottom on the Harpeth River, as viewed from the summit of the Great Harpeth Mound, on Highway 70 west of Nashville. A thousand years ago this fertile land was in Indian corn and was the gathering place of Mound Builders who occupied the locality from the time of Christ. (Tenn. Conservation Dept. Photo)

Central Mound in the mound group at the Fortified City near Shiloh National Park, Shiloh, Tenn. (Photo National Park Service, 1961)

turgid streams pouring their swills from the tall hills into the Tennessee, and rolling the balls for miles until they were symmetrical. The squaws would use these stones to heat in the cook-fires outside the houses and place in the boiling beans, corn, hominy, and wild duck pies.

The burden men would tote the salt. Eva squaws would have the finest clays for pottery, and the lazying warriors in this era of peace would inhale Pinson tobacco.

Not, of course, that Pinson tobacco was any final brand on primitive smokes and chews. Rivals were far and near —in distant Virginia and Maryland; the nearer land of Arkansas. We use modern names for a weed that goes back into the misty dawn of antiquity. The first written record by the hand of white man was done by Christopher

Columbus, under date of November 20, 1492. The word itself comes from Tobaco, a province of Yucatan, New Spain—we are told by Professor John Fiske. Mound Builders—Indians—esteemed tobacco as sacred, and the cigarette companies go on cherishing the myth by the outlay of millions of dollars in advertising. Columbus beat the coffin-nail rollers to the cigarette when he found the Indians in San Salvador puffing smoke from tobacco leaves rolled in corn-shucks, with a blend of long green and dried sumach leaves. The sumach leaf was a milding agent long secret with the Pinson folk. Spanish gentlemen in 1502 found the South American savages chewing tobacco, and the French navigator, Jacques Cartier, said, "I found the savages along the St. Lawrence sucking themselves so full of smoke that it oozed out of their mouths like smoke from a chimney." Migrations of the weed accompanied the great men who took up the habit in America—Francisco Fernandez took plants from Mexico to Europe in 1538, and Sir Walter Raleigh toted a bag of tobacco seed to Ireland, in 1587; and Sir John Hawkins introduced it into England in 1686. "The seventeenth century saw the use of it increase to include all Europe, until millions of tons of it went up in poisonous fumes, and cesspools of tobacco spittle were squirted over the face of creation every year." Controversy raged from the beginning. Spenser called tobacco divine. Lyly said it was an unholy nicotian herb, "whose fumes were no more natural to swallow than to absorb lightning and no more sweet to inhale than asafetida." But the Indians said it was in the world from the beginning, and was always used by man. We find little difficulty in believing it will go on being used till the end of time. The Indian must get an ironic chuckle when he reflects that in revenge on the white man for dispossessing him of his land he is killing the white brother off with lung cancer.

Some 60 miles north of Pinson Town was a port of

Burial Mound excavation in East Tennessee. When the dam system was built on Clinch and other rivers, the remains of prehistoric civilization were inundated. This photograph, made in 1934, shows such a burial mound.

Early Settlers: the pioneer family of George Obadiah Harris, who came to West Tennessee by way of the Iron Banks route (Hickman, Ky.) and located in Mound Builder country that later became Obion County—Reelfoot Lake region. (Photo from original—courtesy Mary Hamilton Davies)

Mounds in the Mist 250

call of some importance for culture mongers, traders, and itinerant Mound Builders looking for better bricks: Obion River Temple Mound Site on Kneberg's map; Paris, Tennessee, to today's travelers, mostly on US 70. A thousand years ago it apparently was more of a ceremonial and religious center than a fortified city, as was Pinson, Harpeth, and Shiloh far to the south. At the headwaters of the north fork of the Obion, which today is little more than a muddy creek though in prehistoric times must

LOCATION: Spencer County, Indiana. Approximately one mile north of Owensboro, Kentucky—two miles west off U.S. Highway 431. Farmers in Southern Indiana river bottom area build homes and barns atop mounds due to backwater problems from overflow of Ohio River in spring season.
CIVILIZATION: Archaic

Henderson County, Kentucky. Approximately one mile northwest of Spottsville, Kentucky on slight rise over north bank of Green River.

CIVILIZATION: HOPEWELL (Woodland Period)

University of Kentucky made carbon 14 analysis and found that the pottery is BAUMER and the arrowheads are definitely HOPEWELL.

Decapitated bodies have been found in this mound over last five years indicating a warlike period in Hopewell civilization.

have been a waterway of importance, the mound is one of the most impressive of the West Tennessee monuments. "Its spacious plaza, a thousand feet long and five hundred feet wide, is flanked by five mounds. The largest is an immense pyramidal earthwork approached by a broad ramp leading to its summit. Including the ramp, it is nearly five hundred feet long and one hundred and seventy feet broad." The mound itself is but thirty feet high. But its situation on one of the blufflike banks of the Obion, on a level plateau, has the illusion of being of much greater

Mounds in the Mist 252

Arrow head found on living area mound of Hopewell tribe adjacent to burial mound #A.

height, especially when viewed from the flood plane of the river bends, over which it dominates. "Its great bulk represented six stages of construction, each succeeding addition increasing its dimensions." Archaeologists have been here. Their diggings and siftings establish the age as early in temple mound activity.

The lack of surviving outer defenses, such as earth walls and log palisades, moats, and other devices in use by Mound Builders would suggest, therefore, that here in the long ago Indians came in pilgrimages from Pinson, Eva, Reelfoot, and villages in Kentucky for great dances, feasts, religious ceremonials, sex orgies, fertility rites, and those social activities primitive man adored.

"People of the Flints" 253

As a part of this complex the Eva towns, and the mound villages at Big Sandy, on the Tennessee River, must have had close association.

Our Pinson trader and trafficker moved out southward some half day's jog to another town where business must have been more active, and the citizens perhaps a shade more hostile. He followed the Cisco-Savannah Trail, roughly today Highway 45 from Jackson to Corinth, Mis-

LOCATION: Henderson County, Kentucky. Approximately one mile northwest of Spottsville, Kentucky on slight rise over north bank of Green River adjacent to burial mound in #A. Approximately two years ago 21 heads were found in one hole on this mound.

Mound consisted supposedly of living area for Hopewell tribe.

Findings taken from site on Green River on January 25, 1967.
NOTE: A. five fish hooks in center
       B. rubbing stone—sand stone
       C. Deer antler—punching tool
       D. implements for making fish hooks—flint
       E. worked bone—deer bone
       F. fish scaler—flint

sissippi. A few miles from Savannah, where the Battle of Shiloh was fought during the Civil War, this other remarkable prehistoric city may be seen away from the battleground on a 60-foot bluff of the Tennessee River. We can give you the mathematics of its walls and bastions and embankments. But they seem so pallid compared to that early spring day when we quit the nostalgic twists of a great bloody struggle between modern men who should have known better than to butcher themselves with the same lust of savages thousands of years earlier, and took the quiet sunny road toward the river, following the pointer "To Indian Mounds." We moved through the ghosts of things past, under the gentle flecked sunshine through the virgin leaves, tasting the honey of sweet winds, and came to the two great central mounds that we remember as the heart of the old town. They looked like two big flat topped hills set down in a spinney of yearling oaks, their slopes beautifully tended and tamped, ancient erosions filled with dental precision, the gay glitter of sea

An ancient civilization thrived a thousand years ago near the now-modern town of Wycliffe, Kentucky. Then, these ancient inhabitants, known as Mound Builders vanished—leaving only mysteries in their buried city. But these mysteries entice investigators and intrigue visitors to this community in Western Kentucky. (Photo courtesy of Kentucky Department of Public Information)

Mounds in the Mist 256

More than 8,000 visitors came to Caddo last year. The intense interest of these visitors to the Caddo Indian Mound site shows the value of this type of tourist attraction. In another few years, unless restrained from the hand of "progress" little of this ancient civilization and culture will remain. (Photo Harold Phelps, Ark. P&P Commission)

shells in the limestone shale and clay—the work of the park caretakers—and the foothill dirt swept about as neatly as one's wife would do it. The size? Who can remember? Immense—in a way. But the sunshine and shadows and the wind and the loneliness, and that strange medicine the heart pumps through the arteries in the misty presence of spectres touching cool fingers to one's lips dismiss exact measurements. We don't recollect. We can quote the statistics.

"Two lines of fortifications enclose it, except on the river side. The outer wall, nearly a mile and a quarter long, has bastions projecting outward for forty feet and spaced two hundred and fifty feet apart. The inner wall parallels the outer at a distance of one hundred and fifty feet, and also has bastions that are staggered with those of the outer wall. These fortifications which remain today as earthen embankments were once topped with log

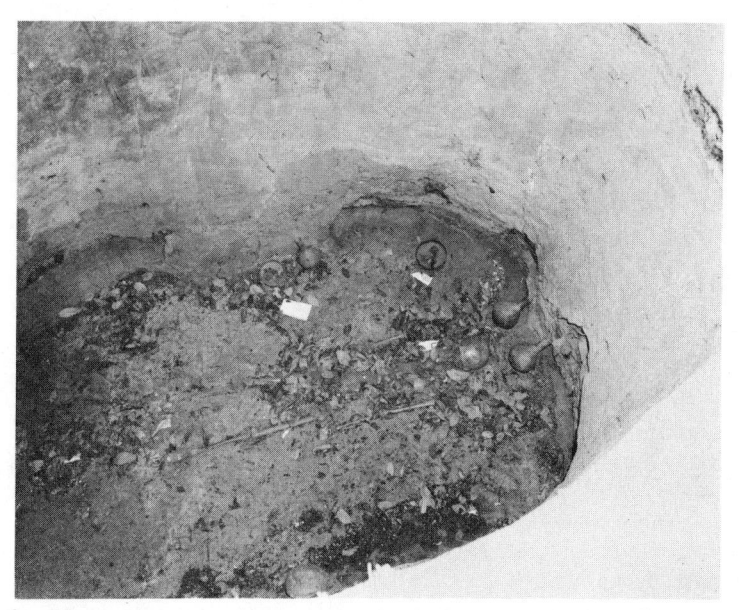

Caddo Indian Burial #2, on bank of old channel of Little Missouri River. The Caddo site is the best developed of the ancient Mound Builder villages. Arkansas seems to loiter behind most other states in excavating prehistoric spots. In ages past the region had a heavy Mound Builder population, but the ravages of time, erosion, bulldozers, and farming have almost obliterated the relics of a past civilization. (Photo Ark. Publicity & Parks Commission)

Mounds in the Mist 258

The Caddo Indian Burial Grounds, 1½ miles west of Murfreesboro, Arkansas, are kept in a very orderly manner with good protection from the weather. There are 7 mounds in the group, of which this temple mound covered by a 90-foot shed is the largest. The mound site was occupied by an estimated hundreds of Indians from A.D. 500 until about A.D. 1500. The Caddo Indians were expert workers in flint, human-effigy pottery and papers—a specialty of the Mound Builders of Arkansas; shell-beads, earspools, arrowheads. This prehistoric village was lost until rediscovered in the spring of 1964. (Photo Ark. Parks and Publicity Division)

palisades. A large temple mound occupies the center of the enclosure, with fifteen smaller earthworks distributed on either side."

Odd that we should remember two. Perhaps it was the ghosts and spring and the song of birds.

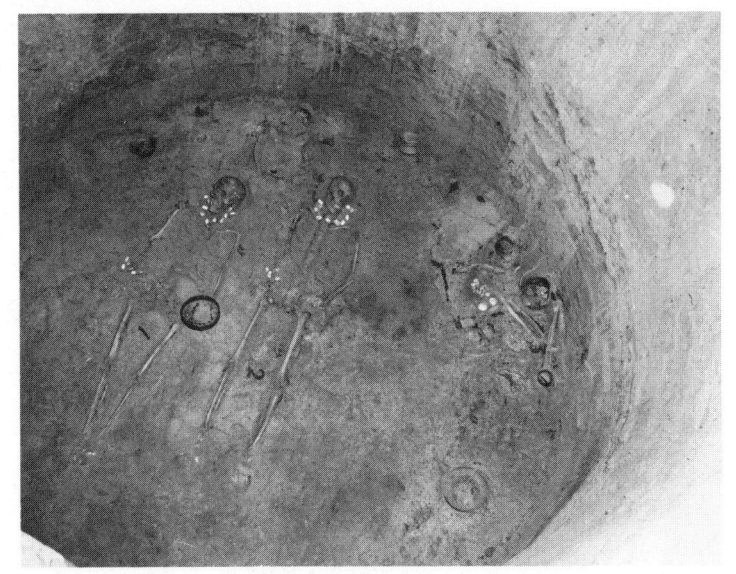

Careful excavation, not disturbing any remains, insure visitors of seeing the contents of these historical mounds just as the Indians left them. Skeletons are all of males—presumably of tribal chiefs, deep buried with all their earthly possessions—rare pottery, pipes, beads, artifacts.

The Toltec Mounds, from an old print. The Toltec site was 85 acres in extent with 17 flat-topped mounds and an enclosing earthwork and outside moat. Neglect, erosion, farming—these have all combined to destroy one of the finest mound groups in the country. (Photo by Kroll)

Among all the strange survivals of legend of the Mound Builders perhaps the strangest is of a former race of white men which the conquering Cherokee of the land now known as Arkansas found and drove away and who, they said, had built the mounds. Archaeologists have debated the mystery. Haywood, in 1823, said the invading Cherokee found "white people" near the head of the Little Tennessee, with forts extending as far down as Chickamauga creek. They were "moon-eyed" and unable to see in the daytime. Whether albinos or no, the invaders expelled them and occupied their circular houses, made of upright logs, covered with earth dug from the inside. Fred W. Allsopp, noted folklorist of Arkansas, comments, "Whether this race ever existed, and whether it was white or colored, or moon-eyed, cannot be proved." He does cite Mooney's reference, quoted by Barton in 1797, that such a prehistoric folk known as Mound Builders, apart from Indians generally credited as the builders, actually preceded the Indians in our Mound Builder land. What these references are worth is another question.

We can be sure of these things: The awe-inspiring mounds of Toltec, sixteen miles east of Little Rock in the Richwoods district of Lonoke County, in the ring-like hills in Crawford County, and similar rises in Sebastian County, prove beyond doubt that a prehistoric people erected these mysterious monuments to their culture some thousand or more years ago. "The Toltec mounds were among the loftiest in America. Some were as high as 150 feet when first discovered, but the washing rains of centuries have reduced them." General Jackson, drawn by reports of the strange hills, visited the mound region, though we have no word what he thought of them. A scientist estimated a huge tree growing on one of the mounds as more than 400 years old. "The excavation from which the earth was taken to construct the mounds formed a great lake in the vicinity."

"People of the Flints" 261

We have a catalog of motives, though nothing new to us: burials for noted chiefs; for fortifications; for refuges from flood waters; for ceremonial purposes. We are reminded the toil was done by women. Archaeologists digging in the mounds found tiles and bricks unlike any used in prehistoric times; skulls without skeletons and skeletons without skulls; in one locality acres of skulls were uncovered by Irishmen building a levee, and the devout Catholic toilers refused to finish the work. A family by the name of Aikman bought the land on which the mounds are located, in 1856. The two great mounds are known as Aikman Mounds Nos. 1 and 2. The flood waters of 1927 washed great gullies in the mounds, and an estimated $10,000 worth of relics have been recovered from the mound neighborhood. These artifacts ranged from skeletons of human beings, dogs, horses, deer, beaver; to bracelets, finger rings, and helmets, all of priceless worth, which repose in private collections or in some cases have drifted into museums. A legend survives that De Soto on his way to Hot Springs lingered to pow-wow with the Indians still occupying the mound area, and the romancers would have their little fling and say the great man had for a time as his mistress the beautiful princess Ulelah, who bore him a child and languished and died when her paleface lover took off in quest of healing waters and the fountain of youth.

At any rate Mounds 1 and 2 are both 60 feet high, and each covers half an acre of ground. Today the mounds stand lonely and forgotten and ravished, as Pinson has until recently.

That Pinson travelers visited and traded with this remote and populous gathering of Builders is not to be questioned. Among the articles for which they bartered were beautifully carved and etched tobacco pipes. The Toltec pipe makers had both strange skill and secret curing of the clays, to make their smoke tools the most coveted of pipes.

Their crafts were known far and wide, as distant as Etowah, whose traders came here with Pinson men. "Etowah maintained close contact with other areas of the Southeast. Marine shells from Florida, flint from Tennessee, copper from North Georgia, and pottery made in the Mississippi Valley all found their way to Etowah. Art styles found on pottery and in religious objects are typical of a wide area of the Southeast." Again we are reminded of how small a world it was thousands of years ago when men had only their legs to cross the lands, and their long arms to handle the oars of the canoes on the waterways. Where time meant nothing, distance vanished.

Despite the fact the Mound Builders were Stone Age men, with basic tools nothing but hand-fashioned rock, a thousand years ago they had achieved amazing skills. Pinson folk had developed crafts in clay—pottery, one of their fundamental arts—in wood, bone, shell, flint, copper and more rarely in gold. Copper and the softer gold were not smelted, but were taken in their raw states and hammered with stone tools into thin sheets, out of which were cut their ornaments. Hundreds of thousands of shell beads were made. Baskets and matting were woven from cane —it grew riotously along the Forked Deer and creeks and spring branches—and clothes were woven from plant fibers, from the hair of slaughtered beasts, from the feathers of many birds. There were wooden masks, rattles of gourds, ornaments carved from wood. From stone they manufactured spear and arrowpoints—an activity second only to pottery; and knives. They fashioned sewing implements, weaving tools, fishhooks, hairpins and combs of bone. We have so long imagined they cultivated their huge corn patches with crooked sticks that it comes as a surprise to discover that they made the most serviceable of one-shovel plows and flat and grubbing hoes of the wide bones of the buffalo. It was inevitable that a host of these small skills should fall to the women. But it would be a mistake to suppose the larger skills, and many of the more intricate and demanding skills, such as engraving shell and copper gorgets, and especially the war-and-hunting implements, should be done by chosen men, who were artisans in their fields. All able-bodied men were by no means warriors. The craftsmen with a sure pair of eyes and a feeling for the beauty and accuracy of such things as arrowpoints and the magnificent flint blades of Duck River flint became the dedicated artists. Indians generally, Mound Builders—Pinson men—were born with a special genius in their powerful hands; and the truly great ones whom we wish had left names as part of their legacy of memories were born potentially great as a Mozart or Beethoven was born a musical genius. This stone craft probably reached its zenith in the craft of the Duck River Indians.

Archaeologists today dispute whether the Duck River folk were true Mound Builders. They do not dispute about their extraordinary flint blades. Duck River empties its placid limestone waters into the Tennessee a short canoe ride upriver from Eva. Back to Pinson might stretch seventy-five miles. It was highly accessible by water and overland trails. The flint chippers had the highest standards of craftsmanship. "The Duck River Indians did not keep all their handiwork at home, for it was in great demand by surrounding tribes. The long swords and other ceremonial flints circulated . . . widely. Many pieces have been found in the great ceremonial centers throughout the South, including eastern Tennessee. The Duck River Indians were located about thirty miles south of two large flint quarries, one of which provided the enormous boulders necessary to make the long sword blades. Even today, partly undermined boulders can be seen just as they were left by the Indians during their last quarrying work. Incredible skill was required to break up the large boulders and secure slabs thin enough to be worked into

Sterling Shelton of Normandy, ranger at the new Old Stone Fort State Park, points pensively to rocks just as a team of archaeologists from The University of Tennessee found them. Wall was constructed of rock and earth and averages slightly more than five feet in height.

the long swords. The flint from these quarries can be easily recognized by its peculiar grain and color, and the finished objects always exhibit similarities in workmanship. Regardless where such pieces are found they can be identified as having been made by the Duck River Indians."

"The greatest of their masterpieces were buried long ago beneath the grave of a dead warrior. These included forty-six symbolic flint objects, exquisitely chipped to represent eagle claws, turtles, sun discs, axes, maces, and swords. Among the eleven swordlike blades, one is nearly twenty-eight inches long and none is less than seventeen inches."

Two pictures of the Fort Wall at the Gate. Originally, there were two walls, but one is almost worn away. They served as fortifications, constructed as they were on a natural plateau. The gate was at the point where the land between the forks of the Duck River is narrowest. The Parallel walls formed a *cul de sac or* "booby trap" which allowed those defenders to attack invaders from two sides and the front, holding them inside the corridor.

This cut is in the South Wall. Just below the south end of the fort and above the natural junction of the two streams that converge to form Duck River proper, there is an artificial channel or "moat" which connected the streams and would have served for defense purposes.

This is part of the South Wall. Most of the walls now look like low mounds. Inside the Fort Walls and the River Walls there are approximately 50 acres of land. These walls were constructed only in areas where the river bluffs did not offer natural protection, but if continuous, the walls would be more than a mile long.

University of Tennessee archaeologists are satisfied that a prehistoric group of American Indians built this enclosure some 1500 years or so ago and that the walls were probably under six feet high. They conclude that the area within the walls was probably used for temporary protection or for Indian ceremonial purposes since household implements and other artifacts which normally are found in an area that has been inhabited are almost completely missing in the Old Stone Fort. (Courtesy *Manchester Times*, "Tempo" January 1967)

The human form either did not often suggest itself to the stone carver as worthy material, or else it was too difficult to chisel. But sculptured images of a man and woman were uncovered in the quest, and were reasonable facsimiles of male and female. The highest projection of the Mound Builder's aesthetic and artistic expression was perhaps in his pottery. Here, gradually over the ages, he learned how to create with his hands, without benefit of the potter's wheel, some of the most exquisite objects made by primitive man. Large basins, jars, ladles, colanders, bottles, bowls of all imaginable shapes, pipes, cups, and vanity ornaments. Some of the vessels were modeled after animals and human figures.

The finest pottery was done in two ways—crafting with skilled handwork, such as rim-notching, figure moulding, pinch-clay overlay, ornate handle shaping, and other artistic vanities. Surfaces might be silken smooth, or pockmarked and freckled and paddle-grained, with scrolls of fabric weaving of the finishing paddle-stone. Pinson clays burnt beautifully, clean and pure of light to almost white shades. The second technique was painting. In earlier times the colors were laid on the raw surfaces, and eventually cured in with ovenbaking. But as time passed the artists pranked with what has become known as "negative painting." It was a fairly delicate technique. First the design—scroll, conventionalized pattern, freehand—was painted carefully. Wax then was put over the design. Suitable waxes were difficult for the Pinson craftsman to find. The best was the rare bumblebee wax. We remember that the honeybee was an importation of the white man. The fierce but beautiful bumblebee was native to America. He nested in hollows of dead snags, making it difficult to rob his food reserve; or often he might nest in hollow deadwood lying on the ground in the forest. The job was to dispossess him. A bee hunter would locate his nest, and then smoke him out, and make off with the parsimonious honeycomb before the mumbler came to. Where possible, the nest was left otherwise intact so he would hustle up some more sweets. The honey was dark, rank, deadly sweet, flavored according to source. This was so highly esteemed by Indians that if the big chief didn't get the delicacy, the hunter's beloved wench did. And the craftsman got the wax for his painting. After the wax was applied to the design, the untouched portion of the vessel was painted another color. When the vessel was fired, the wax burnt off and the outer paint was burnt in. This type eventually became widespread, and archaeologists have found specimens in Georgia, Alabama, sections of Tennessee, and the Mound Builders in Arkansas. Some authorities believe the technique was learned in some unexplained manner from the ancient Mexican and South American cultures. We might dare assume that the Mound Builders worked the method out for themselves. We do know that in the trading and bartering of the Mound Builders the artifacts spread afar.

The working of copper changed little in four thousand years, and such gold ornaments as were fabricated followed about the same pattern. "Nuggets of pure metal were beaten into thin sheets and, in the case of thick objects, like axe blades, several layers of the sheets were hammered together till they formed a solid mass. The final shaping and finishing was done by grinding with an abrading stone." It was to headdresses, breastplates, and other body ornaments that the craftsman spent his pains and genius. Such gold as the Mound Builders worked came by a long and devious route from the heads of rivers high up in what are North Carolina mountains. Only a maid of fine blood and great beauty merited the cupped breast plate over her brown breasts. Oddly enough the Indian did not greatly celebrate his beloved's breasts, as so often engaged the inspiration of Egyptian and related cultures. Perhaps our Mound Builder esteemed them mostly for their food producing qualities. Gorgets of shell and metal therefore were worn mostly by chains around the neck. Many of these were incised by painstaking etching in conventional designs of circles, animal motifs, birds, eagles, turtles, and conventionalized human figures, which bore scant resemblance to reality.

And the beads—thousands and millions of beads, beads, beads, of bone, of shell, of snake teeth, of the beautiful freshwater pearls that the early white traders made off with—the host of beautiful trinkets by which the Builder of the Mounds, the People of the Flints, sought to achieve some kind of immortality of the spirit by adorning the body of himself and his wench—and in the end even his own bones are unremembered.

16
Footprints of the Archaeologists

When it became reasonably certain that the Pinson locality would be established as a state park, the experts moved in with picks, shovels, and a bagful of technical archaeological jargon. Dan F. Morse, assisted by James Polhemus III and J. B. Graham, worked as field supervisor. Dr. Alfred K. Guthe, head of the Department of Anthropology, and Frank M. McClung Museum, of The University of Tennessee, Knoxville, was chief supervisor of the project of making an up-to-date map of the region and making a dry run on the archaeological possibilities of the 1012 acres of the Mounds site. The wheelhorses of the Jackson group dedicated to preserving Pinson as a shrine of ancient Indian cultures put their shoulders to the wheel—Dr. John Nuckolls, Seale Johnson, Ben Hazelwood, superintendent and Assistant Professor of the West Tennessee Agricultural Experiment Station; Robert M. Lancaster, of the Tennessee Highways Department, James West, and others—and all heaved together.

The initial investigation lasted for three weeks, from March 21 to April 13, 1963. There was no pretense of an exhaustive study. The best these men could do was scratch around in the primitive dirt, and report their meager findings. At this late date they expected no dramatic discoveries. Relics hunters had long since exhausted the surface artifacts—arrowheads, spear points, stone tools, sherds—pottery fragments—building sites; and if the fates were willing, some burials. Some of the landmarks Cisco and Meyer reported had disappeared, such as a few very low mounds and the embankment which upheld the palisades.

Mounds in the Mist 272

They found clays adapted beautifully to the making of pottery—gray, dove-gray black in color, with quartz, mica, glauconite, colored red, white, brown, yellow and pink; and this clay even today is shipped to all the principal pottery centers in the United States. It can readily be deduced that the Mound Builder discovered clays and colors some three thousand years earlier, before professors with high sounding degrees belatedly arrived. They noted that West Tennessee soils were yellowish or brownish loam; that the climate is generally mild, with abundant rainfall through winter and spring, followed in autumn by droughts lasting from two weeks to a month. The palefaces in the region grew cotton mostly; but soybeans and corn have pushed in ahead of cotton in the later years. Crop seasons usually lasted from early April to late October. All this the Mound Builders discovered aeons ago, beguiling them to settle widely in Pinson country.

They found no surface indication of a palisade around the "Inner Citadel." Although they admitted such a levee might have eroded away, or been long since levelled by the plough. But sherds and flint chips were collected almost everywhere, though sparingly. By excavating they discovered at the so-called Duck's Nest remains of well-trenched rectangular Mississippi house, superimposed upon a number of woodland features, including hearths, refuse pits, and circular patterns of post molds. At a very low mound (15) a test pit potsherds and flecks of charcoal. At another spot they could not decide whether the slight rise of dirt was a fragment of the palisades or a turn row where paleface farmers paused to turn their mule teams around, or a fence row. Here and there they made minor excavations—ditches, cuts in embankments, holes. They uncovered an important ceremonial area, with two Woodland village sites superimposed on one they presumed was a Mississippi village. "Soil for earthwork construction was skimmed from the surrounding surface and there may have been barrow pits at the bluff edge" of the Forked Deer.

The Twin Mounds engaged their interest, where in the village area around the singularly shaped mounds they made eight excavations. In addition five 2x2 foot holes were excavated in a line down the slope from the main village area to test the soil variation. "No artifacts were collected from these soil tests. The erosion which caused the major part of terracing dividing the village in two sections took place before the Woodland occupation since Woodland features were found on the slope."

Test Pit I ranged from five to ten feet wide and was 20 feet long. The spot covered 163 square feet. They augured almost five feet into the ground, but "artifacts and features were extremely rare." But they did find two post holes well beneath the ground surface. At Test Pit 2 they discovered a fire hearth. They isolated a series of post molds—holes to support timbers for houses or temples—from one foot 2 inches to one foot 7 inches approximately. A pattern yielded the supposition that a house stood here some 15x18 feet, perhaps oval in contour. They discovered a very ancient refuse pit containing flecks of charcoal and red ochre. Further, a basin-shaped hearth filled with burnt soil, but not lined with clay. There were other pits, and one yielded up well preserved bone and shell. "These clusters of refuse pits seem to be characteristic of the village area . . . and were consistently separated from the house sites."

"These three pits produced stone and pottery, bone and mussel shell. Turtle, deer, and possibly others are represented." But nowhere did they find identifiable bone and shell samples with the exception of the skull in a nearby mound. They regarded this relic as a freak preservation due to a hard clay barrier diverting drainage water away from the pit. "Finding bone and shell preserved is very unusual." The discovery of an infant skeleton seems to have been another such freak. "It was on its back with trunk extended, arms straight along the sides, and legs flexed toward the chest. The skull was oriented to slightly east of south. The bones are in poor to fair preservation. The infant had died at birth or soon afterward." One other spot revealed a relatively large quantity of burned hickory nuts.

They were disappointed to find so poor a break between sand-tempered and clay pottery. Eroded surfaced sherds were mostly small. Cord impressions were deep enough even after minor eroding. They found only three sherds of a type called Withers fabric-impressed. "The absence of fabric-impressed sherds at the Twin Mounds section indicate that Early Woodland is not a major component in this part of the site." They found about one-third of the sherds to be Baytown Plain. Two sherds exhibit a red highly polished exterior surface . . . a third sherd is a fragment of a flat vessel base . . . three Baytown Plain rim sherds are represented . . . one is only 3 mm. thick and was part of a small bowl or jar . . . one polished rim sherd has a thickened upper rim with plain rounded lip . . . another rim has a plain rounded lip . . . three eroded-surface, clay-tempered rim sherds were also found . . . one is from a small jar with the lip flattened so that it extends sharply outward from the upper rim. Of Mulberry Creek Cord-marked: One rim sherd exhibits a lip flattened by cord-wrapped paddle edge; another has a folded rim with plain rounded lip. Of Marksville: Most of the Marksville incised sherds appear to be parts of stylized bird designs, and are of a very fine and compact paste with polished surfaces. "Sand is never present in these sherds." There are Thomas Plain, Larto Red-filmed body sherds and Blue Lakes Cord-marked. A total of 43 sherds were found and catalogued.

Other pottery artifacts include Poverty Point objects which are irregularly shaped, fired balls of usually sand-tempered as well as probable weathered puddled clay

Air view of Poverty Point made by Dr. Junius Bird. Concentric light soil bands are tops of low ridges marking location of houses. Just left of center of the photo is large artificial mound. At right, the wooded area is the section destroyed by meandering stream action. Bayou Macon now bounds the eastern side. For full particulars, map, scale, and description see "POVERTY POINT, a late archaic site in Louisiana" by James A. Ford and Clarence H. Webb, Anthropological Papers, vol. 46, pt. 1, 1956. (Courtesy of The American Museum of Natural History)

hearth fragments. One object is a fired irregular ball tempered with clay(?) and mica. Two clay-tempered pipe fragments were found which may be from the same pipe. The stem fragment is circular in cross-section, measuring 1.3 cm in diameter. Inside diameter at the stem end is 1 mm and this quickly enlarges to 3 mm. The pipe could have been shaped like one from Greenhouse or from Poverty Point. Next to flint, ironstone was the chief stone worked. Sandstone occurs in the Pinson area and is used mainly in hearths. There is a great variety of color and texture in the flint present. Fragments surviving are flakes from scrapers and knives. Of blade flakes, some true Hopewell-type were collected. Of projectile points some expanded-stemmed and crudely side-notched points were discovered. These were similar to Late Hopewell forms in central Illinois. Two Gary points, a bifaced knife, celts, axes, and choppers were collected. Other relics were hammerstones, quartz pebbles, quartz crystals, and bone fragments pretty much completed the gatherings. There was one turtle-shell fragment, and a fragment of bone awl.

Mound 31 is located just east of the Twin Mounds. An excavation unit was placed some ten feet east of center. The mound itself is about 50 feet in diameter, two feet high and badly eroded. It might have been square shaped at one time. Construction seems as follows: first the humus zone was cleared off. Next an area slightly over two feet in diameter was fired causing the underlying sterile clay to be burned red to the depth of about four inches. Two small circular holes were contemporary with the fired area. These were situated just outside the edge of an area of burned dirt which was highly mottled with charcoal and debris. This was immediately over the fired clay area. The test plot generally contained charcoal and ash. There were basins evidently associated with ceremonies from the beginning of mound construction, and suggest the probability of a central tomb and/or charnel house existing in this mound. In another stage of mound construction a test pit indicated a primary mound in the center of the mound. This is composed of ash and light brown clayey loam. Three other levels of dark brown clayey loam over ash and burned floor. The pit was excavated no deeper except to remove a disarticulated skull with the mandible in place from the base of the pit in the south profile.

The skull was oriented so that the foramen magnum

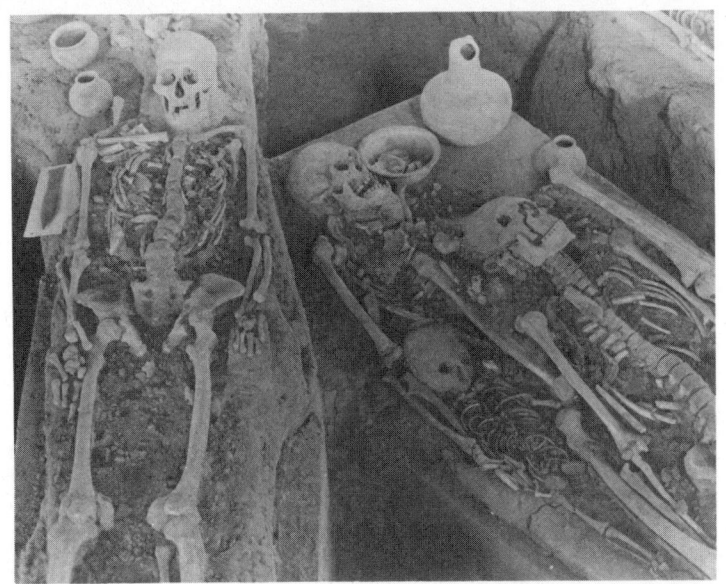

Two views from the burial mound. This mound is in two distinct layers and contains 153 skeletons. Bodies were laid out rather than within. Some remains were fully extended while others were bundled in a curled position. A few were cremated. Artifacts found with the skeletons indicate a highly developed culture and a belief in a life after death where items used and loved in this world would be needed and used again. (Photo courtesy of Kentucky Dept. of Information)

pointed to the north and the face to the west. The skull is in an extremely bad condition of preservation. It appears to be a male since the bone is relatively thick and heavy; on the basis of tooth wear it may be around thirty years of age. "A peculiar green stain was found on the dirt at the back of the head near the base of the skull. However, no copper artifacts were found and this stain may be natural, due perhaps to the presence of copper in the ground water." While removing the skull, a rim sherd was found in the fill near the base of the pit. The sherd is from a jar with a slightly curving rim. It is clay tempered with a polished plain exterior surface and flat lip—a Baytown Plain. The thickness is from .4 to .5 cm. Other trophies are a black flint chunk and two eroded sand-tempered body sherds, and one polished-surface Baytown Plain body sherd; one ironstone chip, one badly eroded fragment of an irregularly shaped pottery object with a sandy paste; one eroded surface clay-tempered body sherd with sand inclusions; and one Blue Lakes Cord-marked body sherd.

A complete catalogue of other artifacts would name the following categories: Twin-Lakes Fabric-impressed; Baytown Plain and Mulberry Creek Cord-marked; Larto Red-filmed; Thomas Plain and Blue Lakes Cord-marked; Sand-tempered Incised; Poverty Point; various projectile points, a triangular knife; blades, scrapers, celts and choppers; hammerstones, sandstones and other artifacts.

The Great Central Mound, because of its enormous size and commanding position in the Pinson Complex, led the archaeological expedition to excavation by no means exhaustive. "The flat summit measures 50 and 60 feet square. Because of erosion and relatively modern disturbances, the flat summit varies as much as five feet in absolute elevation." The four corners, and ramp, are readily identifiable from the summit. An erosion 30 feet wide has gnawed 20 feet into the southeastern side. A couple of feet separate the gully from a deep hole 17x23 feet dug by vandals. In a few years, at the present rate of erosion, half the summit will be washed away. "Our test excavation was placed in the southwestern corner of the old excavation," exposing an area 11 feet by over 8 feet. "A total of four levels were found beneath the spoil overburden." A hard whitish clay was found, mottled with charcoal. The next highest level is composed of mottled brown and yellow clayey loam deposited as basket loads. On top of this level was mottled brown and yellow clay. The uppermost level is brown to light brown silty loams. Besides several fragments of native sandstone, the only objects found during the excavation was a Baytown Plain body sherd with a high mica content in the paste. The sherd probably is an accidental inclusion in soil brought to the area for mound construction (by the squaws). That the soil is not all substratum in nature indicates that even at this late stage, at least some fill dirt was being skimmed from the ground surface rather than obtained deep in burrow pit.

Mound 29—Ozier Mound—suffered two test pits. "This mound is square topped, 130–160 feet on a side at the base and 95–113 feet on a side at the summit. It is 12 feet high and its sides are oriented essentially with the cardinal points of the compass. One excavation exposed the mound profile and the other was made to test a possible house site. This test strip was 43 feet by 27 feet, to the depth of 65 feet. There had been a brick house here, with dirt basement, dating to the middle or late 19th to early 20th century and had burned down. A ten-foot-thick charcoal brick, and iron zone lay directly upon a one-foot-thick hard packed floor. Until recently the mound surface was under cultivation. The artifacts of modern occupation were about—china fragments, brick bats, iron nails of the square type, a shell cutton, cartridge shell, fragments of ironware. The second pit was dug on the north edge so as to obtain a relatively undisturbed soil profile. The augur boring disclosed a surface of yellow clay about a foot thick beneath the present ground surface. It was presumed to have been the base of an earlier mound. Present were sandstone fragments, clayey loam, and some sherds. The rest of the mound is made up of a "loaded" fill, mostly light brown to brown clayey loam. The zone of loading appears to be top soil, probably skimmed from the surface within the embankment area.

"The Pinson Mounds Site is a 1012 acre area consisting of mounds, village and camp sites, an earthen embankment." The general region is productive agriculturally. It was once in steamboat and keelboat times the main water avenue to the Mississippi River. "Our assignment was requested for the main object of conducting test excavations. The time allotted was limited and the area to be tested large . . . a sort of cultural inventory." Six mounds, two villages, and an embankment were investigated. Evidence of Archaic, Woodland, Mississippian, and historic cultures was recovered.

These evidences consisted of Early, Middle and Late Archaic artifacts, broken points, flint tools, rounded stemmed points, and remains of hearths. Early Woodland relics, such as fabric-impressed sherds, were found everywhere. "It was very apparent from our test excavations that Marksville-Hopewell was responsible for the construction of the earthworks." This is the most northern extent of Marksville and is of much help toward filling the previously existing gap between Marksville and Illinois Hopewell, two of the four recognized aspects in the Hopewell Phase. There probably are at least two Hopewell components at the Pinson Mounds. The surface collection made on Mound 14 is significantly different from samples collected at the Twin Mounds section, in that there is a higher percentage of Mulberry Creek Cord-marked at Mound 14. During the latter part of Hopewell in this area there may have been a shift from sand-tempering to clay-tempering. . . . Of most interest to us here are the Marksville-like sherds. . . . These include Marksville Incised, Marksville Zoned Dentate Stamped, and Cord-marked Stamped. Pinson Marksville village features consist of circular houses with a central hearth and a nearby cluster of refuse pits and deep hearths. In some cases mound construction is exceedingly complex but in others less so. Mounds are similar to the Hopewell Site in Ohio, and Troyville, being both conical and flat-topped, and square shaped with sharp corners and no ramp. The construction involved sand floors, hearths, charcoal "cache" pits, superimposed flat-topped and conical mounds, and ash lenses.

The Ozier Mound and the Great Central Mound are typical Middle Mississippi temple mounds. Their tops are flat, square outline and pronounced rounded corners, and a single ramp oriented toward the northeast. The large size of these mounds suggests that other Mississippi mounds should be present. Burial spots should also be nearby. One mound was superimposed upon a Woodland village. Further evidence of Mississippi construction is the presence of Baytown sherds. A Mississippi projectile point was found. For definite proof we should have a large sample of shell-tempered pottery. Two other sites are known in West Tennessee—the Ames plantation complex on Wolf River, and the Obion site located near Paris, Tennessee, on the north fork of the Obion River, this latter being a temple mound with a ramp 200 feet long. Pottery found at Obion by Douglas Osborne was 84 per cent clay-tempered and 16 per cent shell-tempered. This is comparable to Pinson. Another parallel is the Emerald and Anna Mounds near Natchez, Mississippi. Here again large temple mounds produced a large proportion of Clay Grit Plain and a very small percentage of shell-tempered plain sherds. Obion overlaps with Troyville, and Etowah barely overlaps with Obion. Moundville is placed so as to over-

Mounds in the Mist 282

Emerald Mound, near Natchez, Miss.
"Emerald Mound is the third largest temple mound in the United States, surpassed only in size by Monk's Mound in Illinois and Poverty Point Mound in Louisiana. It covers nearly 8 acres and measures 770 by 435 feet at its base. The secondary mound, which seems dwarfed atop its huge platform, is in its own right a large mound when compared with others in the Southeast." The builders of Emerald have been dead for centuries and wind and rain have softened its contours, but its massive bulk makes it a majestic earthwork. Most Mississippian mounds were built between A.D. 1000 and 1600. Emerald spans an era between 1300–1600. Its basic purpose was ceremonial; centuries ago a great temple stood on its flat top. The surrounding folk grew corn, beans and pumpkins, and with fish and game victualed a dense population. (Photo National Park Service, Tupelo, Miss.)

Bynum Mounds excavation. Note the care of this scientific work. Every ounce of earth is sifted. All artifactual material is abstracted, marked and stored. Upon completion of the excavation, the dirt is returned to its place in the restored mound, which, before excavating, has been charted, thus making the restored mound an exact replica of the original. (Photo courtesy Natchez Trace Parkway Dept. of Interior)

lap both Etowah and Lamar, and the Emerald and Anna Mounds are situated so that they are roughly contemporaneous with Lamar. Obion and the large Pinson Mounds seem parallel with Emerald and Anna. In the village deposit beneath the Emerald Mound there were wall trenches belonging to rectangular structures. A straight wall trench was found also in the large Obion Mound. In addition, at the Obion there were clay-tempered, footed elbow pipes, pottery discs, and pottery trowels. Also collected were salt pan sherds plus rare examples

Deep fire pit in shallow pit floor located at Bynum Site. (Photo National Park Service)

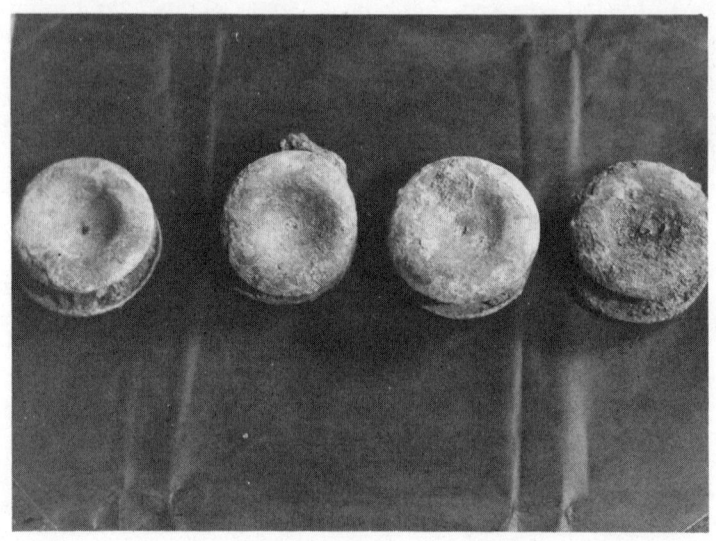

Copper earspools, usually found near wrists, from Bynum Mounds. (Photo National Park Service, Tupelo, Miss.)

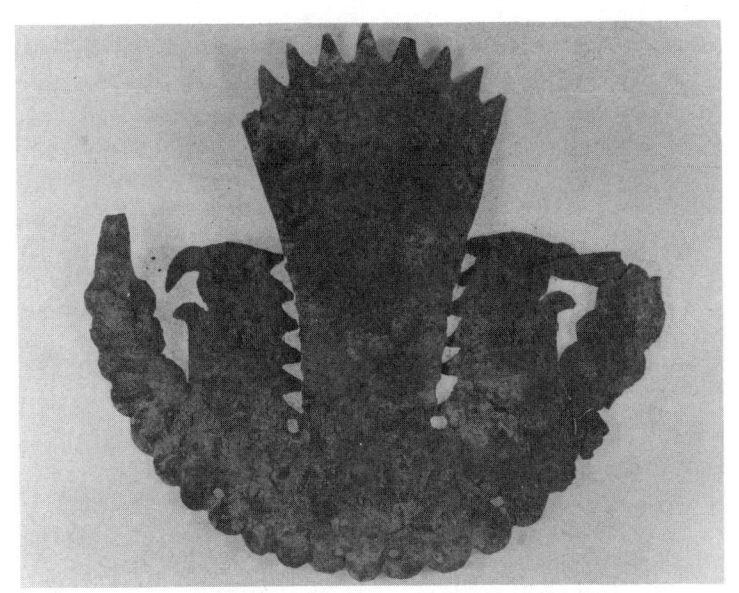

Mangum plate, hammered copper sheeting, formed of separate parts overlapped and pounded together, found at Mangum Mound site, Mississippi. (National Park Service, Tupelo, Miss. photo)

of polychrome sherds, plate rims, bottle fragments, and loop and strap handles. Also present in the Obion assemblage are small plain and side-notched triangular flint projectile points, large oval and pear-shaped polished flint hoes, and a stone, sharp-lipped discoidal. If the Obion site is truly "early" Mississippi, then a considerable amount of cultural change, not to mention a lot of mound construction, took place in an exceedingly short period of time. Questions growing out of this inquiry are: How available is mussel shell in these rivers? Where are the "Middle" Mississippi sites if Obion and Pinson are "Early"

Mounds in the Mist 286

Crowned skeleton buried in refuse pit at Bynum Site. The Bynum group of mounds is about 30 miles from Tupelo, Miss., and consists of 6 mounds. Though not spectacular in size, the group is notable for dating about 700 A.D., making them some 600 years older than Emerald. Indian food consisted of native plants, fish, shellfish, game, and maize. They built circular houses of willow and reed and clay; they made plain but durable pottery; wove textiles. They borrowed cultural ideas from other Mound Builders; established burial mounds, developed a complex social and religious organization. Reverence for the dead was an important element in their culture. They practiced mound burial as well as cremation. Eventually they worked in copper brought probably from Lake Superior. How long were they building these mounds? "We can only say that at some time, one generation, ten generations, after completing the last mound they departed from the area and never returned." (Natchez Trace Parkway photo)

Base of a Mound Builder temple, Obion Temple Site. (Photo courtesy U. T. Dept. Anthropology, University of Tennessee)

Elaborate temple base, Obion Temple Mound Site. (Photo 1940 UT Dept. Anthropology, University of Tennessee)

Another temple base, with firepot. Obion Temple Site. 1940. (Photo courtesy University of Tennessee, Dept. Anthropology)

The great Obion Temple Mound in 1940, at the time the Dept. of Anthropology, University of Tennessee, was making extensive excavations. Note the road leading to the mound summit. In this period Harvard University sent a crew of archaeologists to dig, and local citizens still report that 4 boxcar loads of artifacts and pay dirt were removed to various museums. (Photo courtesy U.T. Dept. Anthropology, University of Tennessee)

The only burial recovered from the Obion Site. Only one burial, so far, has been recovered at the Pinson site. At the Ancient Buried City hundreds of burials have been uncovered. Why this is so we can only surmise. The populations at both Obion and Pinson exceeded those of the Ancient Buried City. Some account for it by the manner of burials, either cremation or preservation. (Courtesy the Department of Anthropology, The University of Tennessee)

Mississippi? Are there any discernible differences between clay-tempered Mississippi and Woodland sherds? Once these questions are answered, we may have an intriguing archaeological and even culturological problem as well as a firmer basis from which to investigate.

The whole Pinson site should be sectioned off, a contour map made of the area, and extended field seasons devoted to the archaeological investigation. There are no active amateurs in the Pinson country, and the region thus

A photograph of this type for the layman is almost meaningless. To the archaeologist it is an historical record of 300–600 years of Indian Mound Builder culture. "The earlier digs are not recorded in so far as the people actually excavating anything is concerned. The emphasis was rather on the stratigraphy, the floor plan and the burials." (Dr. A. K. Guthe, Head of the Department of Anthropology at The University of Tennessee). This picture was made in 1940 at the Obion or Work Farm Site. Notice the different layers of earth. (Courtesy the Department of Anthropology, The University of Tennessee)

A strangely beautiful cone of earth—grim and symmetrical. The Great Central Mound at the Obion Temple Mound. (Courtesy the Department of Anthropology, The University of Tennessee)

Examining a crater left by archaeologists from Harvard University and University of Tennessee. (Photo by Kroll)

Looking across a sunny valley at Ponder's Hill. Turley Stewart: "I have always heard it said it's an Indian burial ground." While no excavating has ever been done to confirm or refute the legend, it is entirely possible the spot is one of the unnumbered and forgotten graveyards of prehistoric people. (Photo by Kroll)

Dr. W. O. Inman and Turley Stewart, two Paris historian-archaeologists, pose in front of the abandoned Work farmhouse, on the farm of which the 25-acre temple mound site is located. The farm for the past seven years has been in the soil bank, rough hay being cut from the mounds. (Photo by Kroll)

View across the flood plain of the north fork of the Obion River, from the summit of the large temple mound. In prehistoric times the bottom was covered with free flowing springs which furnished the Indians with water. The narrow channel flows in the line of timber. (Photo by Kroll)

The large mound was once flanked by five smaller ones, of which only this rise of ground, and the secondary mound, remain. Dr. Inman looks toward the south in the area where the densest population lived a thousand years ago. (Photo by Kroll)

From the smaller plaza area of the second largest mound Turley Stewart points toward the great temple mound to the west. In the level ground behind them the dwellings of the village stretched. (Photo by Kroll)

Turley Stewart pushes through brambles and rank grass across the spacious plaza, 1000 feet long and 500 feet wide, that once faced the immense mound, itself 500 feet long and almost 200 feet wide. The large temple which surmounted the mound accommodated the estimated population of three to four thousand Mound Builders. (Photo by Kroll)

is unknown archaeologically, as is most of West Tennessee. Erosion of the Great Central Mound must be halted, and cultivation of area ceased, save for a protective cover crop. Excavation of the Pinson Mound Site will shed much light on northern facet of the Southeastern Hopewell aspect, help resolve the Mississippi clay-tempered pottery problem, and also initiate a sorely needed detailed study of West Tennessee prehistory.

17
The Mystery in the Mists

And yet, after all this has been said and done, the mystery of how, when, and where the Pinson Mound Builders disappeared remains as impenetrable as in the beginning of our study. Whether the archaeologists, now that the Mounds are to be converted into a state park and excavated authoritatively, will come up with the answer remains for time to tell. Until then, we can only depend on plausible speculation.

Meyer suggested that great hordes of conquering Indians fell upon the Pinson Mound Builders and either massacred them or drove them into exile, or enslaved and even absorbed the survivors. The six-mile embankment and heavy palisades imply that Mound Builder towns may have lived under fear of such attack. Meyer's theory, upon close examination, reveals flaws. It *could* have happened, of course. But one thinks first of the strong fortifications of the City of Cisco, the possible force of the warriors, the ferocity of the defense, and the final disposition of the casualties. What went with all those dead Mound Builders? No burials have been found thus far in the Pinson locality—not certainly to the number of hundreds of thousands. You can't have a battle without some dead men, and you do have to do something with them. It's unlikely the acid soil dissolved their bones. About the same time—we'll arbitrarily set the date as 1500 A.D.—in Georgia the Etowah Builders disappeared or were dispersed or conquered; 250 miles to the north the Cahokia Builders seem to have met with a similar fate. To believe there were vanquishing hosts attacking all three of these strongholds of Mound Builders and subjugating all of them somehow seems absurd. Besides, there would likely have remained legends among the Indians of the great wars which they would recite to the early white settlers coming into North America.

Another more tenable theory was the visitation of a great devastating plague that carried our Mound Builders off in great numbers. Yet, what disease would have swept away three Mound Builder populations at the same time without annihilating the entire Indian people? Iberville, writing in 1700, tells of the wholesale hazard of "a flux of which the savages almost always die." Had the white man not brought smallpox and measles to the Indians, against which they had no racial resistance, we could accuse those diseases. But our Mound Builders had dispersed before the white man arrived. De Soto must have passed near Pinson in 1540, but there is no record of his visiting a populous center like the Mounds. It seems unlikely in any case that his men would have transmitted ailments deadly enough to carry off the Pinson folk. And again, we have the unanswered question of the other great Mound Builder centers.

Indians were exceedingly superstitious, and this suggests another possibility. All of West Tennessee—much of Mound Builder land—was in an earthquake area that erupted historically in the New Madrid earthquake which tore up the region, most notably around Reelfoot. Indian legend relates that great quakes had shaken the lands beyond human memories. It just could be such an upheaval upset the Pinson Great Chief so that he had a dream—a nightmare—in which he was warned of impending doom and commanded to lead his people from this accursed land. We know the Indian's philosophy concerning dreams; if the Great Spirit warned their leader, the folk would follow him in terror, leaving their fair city rather than encounter the wrath of the Great Spirit. Here again, is absurdity. For the Mound Builders were not about to pull up stakes and leave all those splendid corn fields, those patches of pumpkins and squash, most of all those sacred piles of earth their women had toted over the centuries, just to follow a chief's crazy notion, due probably to his devouring too much buffalo ham. They'd dose him with blackroot to settle his stomach and take him to the temple atop Great Central Mound, leaving him there under guard till he could dream a sweeter dream.

There was, of course, syphilis. It was an Indian disease. Their free-love living spread it generally, and it likely was as widespread as the Indian himself. Many skeletons from the ancient ruins show bone malformation from the deep disease. Like corn, the origin of this infirmity is lost in the mists of time. It appears in medical lore very early, and whether it was known in Europe before 1493—the year after Columbus's visit—has been debated. There seemed no evidence of pre-Columbian syphilis in the Eastern hemisphere before the return of the Spanish sailors from Hayti from whom it spread among the inhabitants of Barcelona. "In 1493 it reached Italy with the army of Charles III. His soldiers syphilated Naples; the disease spread throughout Italy, and in a few years Europe was aflame." On the other hand, writers for the antiquity of the disease in Asia and Europe rely on certain old Chinese records, on Biblical references to it—or a disease like it— and on ancient medical studies of diseases resembling it, and on suggestive bone lesions in very old skeletons. As we know the disease, it may be of American origin, but there is no actual proof.

It is safe to assume that the Indian had gradually built up a fair degree of racial resistance, though doubtless the disease plagued him through the centuries. But it would not have destroyed his populations—not all at once. There remain the fevers always prevalent in the southern lowlands—swamp fever, black water fever, and just plain malaria fever. There again our Mound Builder had a certain immunity; that is, his system had built up a type of protection, and he had learned the use of herbs, roots, and barks to control it.

"In North America the angel of death seems to have preceded rather than followed the white man." Swanson's statement seems to clear the white man of exterminating his red brother, though eventually he did his best to that end. If we can come finally to a real and plausible explanation of the mysterious disappearance of the Pinson Mound Builders, it must be deduced through the history of what happened to the Natchez within the historical period. The French De la Vente wrote, in part:

"Touching these savages . . . it appears visibly that God wishes that they yield their place to new peoples. One can learn from the most aged that they were incomparably more numerous than now . . . they came here to the number of more than 5,000," but were reduced to something like half that number. "The other nations say that many centuries ago they were, some 3,000; others 2,000; others a thousand, and all that is reduced now to a very moderate number. What is certain is that our people in the six years in which they have been descending the river [Mississippi] know certainly that the number has diminished a third, so true it is that God wishes to make them give place to others. . . . The reason for it is very clear. It is that, for I do not know how many years, they have placed all their glory in carrying away scalps of their enemies." He adds sorrowfully, being a man of God, that the English have encouraged them in this slow process of extermination.

"These causes," Swanson added, "were however of less importance than diseases, neglect of childen, and immorality."

The Luxembourg memoir states: "The women of Mississippi are fecund, although the country is not extremely well peopled with savages. The severe way in which they rear their children makes a large part of them die; and diseases like fever and smallpox, for which they know no other remedy than to bathe however cold it be, take off a great number of them." The record adds the interesting note we have previously quoted, ". . . the girls, although given as they are to their pleasures, have means of guarding against pregnancy."

Out of all this emerges one fact: in long ago prehistoric times the Mound Builders, and Indians generally, were far more numerous than when the white man came, and their numbers had been steadily diminishing for several centuries before the Columbus era. Why around the year 1000 the Pinson folk seemed most populous we can only conjecture. But that period was their halcyon time. Tribes were at peace, the cornfields were prosperous and the Forked Deer forests were abundant with game and wild food. The runs and ranges were heavy with trampling buffalo, elk, and deer; small game was plentiful. The river gave up its fish. The skies were dark with bird life, and the Pinson folk ate them to their bones and wove the feathers into beautiful garments. There were good neighbors on all four winds—Cahokia, Moundville, Etowah, Emerald, a dozen other populous centers.

Thus we have a period of time during which Pinson flourished and spread as far as twelve miles down the river, and miles back in the bottoms, with the "citadel" town-place as refuge in the event of war. It was during this tranquil time that the people erected the vast number of lesser mounds in the complex. How long this period was we can rely only on conjecture. An examination of the life cycle of other centers suggests that 500 years was a long while for a great town to survive. Etowah, A.D. 1000 to A.D. 1500; Moundville, 1200 A.D. to 1400 A.D.; Ocmulgee, A.D. 900 to A.D. 1100; Kolomoki, A.D. 1200 to A.D. 1300; Emerald, A.D. 1300 to A.D. 1600—to check a random list. There seems to be some evidence that Pinson was not depopulated until some time in A.D. 1400, since the oldest tree growing on Ozier or the Great Central Mound was estimated at 400 years; the Pinson party found the timber in the old fields fairly small; and the very earliest settlers who noted the six-mile embankment found time-charred remains of the posts forming the palisades. Most of the erosion of the mounds has been within the historical period, and it would seem probable that over as long as a thousand years weather and time would have worn them down. None of these clues is conclusive, though it does seem improbable the Pinson folk would have built immense mounds only to abandon them. Unless something drove them away they would have lived there for some centuries.

We can safely discount Meyer's conquering-hordes theory, or even any sudden catastrophe. It was not an earthquake, a pestilence or an insane chief leading his people into the wilderness. What was true of Moundville would be equally true of Pinson. "We have seen that Moundville declined rather rapidly after a florescence in the fourteenth and fifteenth centuries." (McKenzie, *Journal of Alabama Archaeology*). "This decline was not catastrophic, for there is no reason to suppose that the culture and population disappeared without a trace. In fact, there is good reason to believe that aspects of the culture and the remainder of the population spread widely through the Southeast after 1500. The decline . . . seems not to have been an extinction but rather a dissolution of cultural configuration with replacement or recombination of traits."

McKenzie's conclusion is probably supported by what is known of simple societies today: the land can support a hunting-gathering-farming people just so long before the local food resources become exhausted. (David L. DeJarnette, Anthropology, Moundville State Monument). The large populations of great villages such as Pinson, Moundville, Cahokia, Etowah, must have eventually created a heavy strain on the available plant and animal foods. The autumn migrations of brutes may have been diverted by wider hunting through the localities; certainly the fields after years, centuries, of cropping would become exhausted. Under such circumstances the people tend to move and relocate. This is supported by the spreading of the Pinson villages, the erection of more and more mounds, though the Great Central Mound and Ozier remained the seat of city-state government and religious activity. The walled-in town was the temple area, a place of refuge in time of wars. The people spread out, and fragments broke away, to drift most likely to the south, where they identified with the tribes that later became historic.

"We know that these Indians were the ancestors of the historic tribes—Natchez, Creek, Choctaw, and others." When the Europeans found them, these three tribes seemed to have preserved the most important of the Mound Builder folkways, though some of the distinguishing characteristics of Mound Builders, such as skills in pottery, weaving, basketry, engraving, government, religion and social patterns, had degenerated into grosser substitutions. Though still hunters and farmers, they were more and more given to wars; and as scalps increased a man's stature, his corn ears declined in honor, and his women inherited the farm chores as well as the household tasks.

This decline and dispersion of Pinson and other cultural centers did occur rather suddenly just before and during the period of European arrivals. If God, as our good priest declared, had already sounded the doom of the red man, the white man was a good co-laborer with God. Partisan wars hastened the depletion of the able-bodied male population. By inference this increased the promiscuity of the young female population, already remarked for their "immorality." There was no sanitation in the towns against ailments that killed something like half the young while still children. The custom of head-flattening and the sacrifice of the first-born male baby were still in use when the Europeans appeared. Smallpox, measles, and influenza swept away great segments of people. Fruitful centuries when squaws produced an average of ten young during years of fecundity, allowing for death in childhood and in battle—in time of peace at a minimum—with still a surplus for population explosions, were closed for good. Five hundred years of this and so few of them would remain they could no longer keep up the old temples and tabernacles and fields. Perhaps they dispersed to join other tribes— the Natchez to the deeper South, who themselves were diminishing rapidly; the Choctaws, whose folkways so closely resemble the habits of the Mound Builders we can suppose they were Mound Builders; the Chickasaws, the Creeks, the Cherokees far up the higher rivers. Where the Cahokia folk went we can only surmise the same way, but likely they amalgamated with the northern and western Indian tribes and lost any identity they may have had in the beginning. Certainly the Mound Builder culture, as Paul Radin wrote, salted the surviving Indian cultures down to the present time: "All aboriginal culture east of the Mississippi represents what has been salvaged from the great mound-builders."

We are confused as to the possible date the mounds were abandoned. Dr. Charles Nash suggests A.D. 800. Consensus of other expert opinion places it much later— perhaps A.D. 1400. We simply do not know. We only know our builders of the mounds vanished in the mists.

18
Through Mists to Reality

When asked how he, together with a group of dedicated citizens of Jackson, Tennessee, began the movement that would result in the establishment of the Pinson Mound area as a state park and registered national historical landmark, Dr. John B. Nuckolls quoted a familiar verse of Scripture, "Ask, and it shall be given unto you; seek, and ye shall find; knock, and it shall be opened unto you" (Matthew 7:7). Then he continued, "At the very moment Christ was teaching this philosophy the Woodland Indians were using what we now call the Pinson Mounds as a religious and ceremonial center. The Woodland Indians occupied all of West Tennessee, and the mounds were monuments to the age-old, worldwide search for God." He added wryly, "It would be a long time before their descendants would have Jesus preached to them and the Prince of Peace presented along with fire-water, guns, powder and lead, and pestilence. Yes, a long time before they would become involved with the white man's wars and eventually find themselves pretty well annihilated by this Christian white man."

But the massive mounds remained, and this enthusiastic group of citizens addressed their energies to asking, seeking and knocking in an effort to preserve them. Back in the 1880s Jay Guy Cisco had this vision, though he got nowhere with it. The contemporary visioneers included Judge Tip Taylor, a member of the Tennessee Conservation Commission, County Judge Leroy Pope, Robert P. Mahon, editor of *The Jackson Sun*, Seale Johnson of the Tennessee Historical Commission, attorney Keith Short of the state senate, Dr. Charles Nash who heads the Department of Anthropology at Memphis State University, Tom and Madeline Kneberg Lewis, archaeologists at The University of Tennessee, who co-authored *Tribes That Slumber* and have written other more professional archaeological books, Judge Brooks McLemore, E. L. Morgan, Glenn Rainey, lawyers Walter B. Harris and Tom Rainey, state legislators Lowell Thomas and Thomas McKnight, Dr. G. H. Berryhill, County Judge Hugh Harvey, Jackson Mayor George Smith, Jackson City Commissioners Ben Langford and Tobe Bailey. These add up to a formidable list of askers, seekers, and knockers. And they were encouraged by the support of Commissioners Donald McSween and Boyd Garrett of the State Department of Conservation, Colonel William Slayden and Walter Criley, Deputy Commissioner of the Conservation Department and Chief Planner of State Parks, respectively.

Now it is not to be supposed there was any active opposition to the state park idea; there was simply a wall of indifference—local indifference, apathy in high places, a curious lack of prehistory consciousness, lingering enmity toward the Indian, and the tradition of land-lust among rural people everywhere. True, people who stared at the mounds always felt a sense of awe, but "well, well," was usually the extent of their reactions. They simply got into their cars and drove away. Any thought of doing something about these piles of dirt never occurred to them. What could be done about them, anyway? Besides, who cared?

The "inner circle," as Dr. Nuckolls speaks fondly of his friends and associates in the enterprise, was made of people who really cared and believed much might be done. Dr. Nuckolls himself is a published archaeologist, though of amateur status. Robert Mahon, whose untimely death impaired the advancement of the project for some time, lent his editorial mind and news columns to advancing the Pinson Park scheme. Seale Johnson's book publishing increased his stature and he succeeded in getting members of the Historical Commission to visit the Pinson area—inclement weather necessitated several trips before the whole group could view the area in its entirety. However, they were sufficiently impressed to donate $1,000.00 toward expenses incidental to the purchase of land for the park. Dr. Nash, even before chosen as archaeological adviser, had studied the Pinson Mound group and repeatedly said, "This has the potential of becoming a park second to none in the nation." Judges Taylor and Pope stirred the political pot quite effectively and enjoyed crusading, leading, and presiding over groups interested in the establishment of the park.

Remoter stars in the firmament twinkled enthusiastically. Among these was Nell Nuckolls, the woman behind the men, the power behind the throne. Dr. Nuckolls said of her, "Her interest and encouragement behind the scenes was invaluable. She was always willing to open our home for meetings and entertainment when it seemed desirable to do so. I feel she deserves great praise and that she stands tall among the others."

"It would be misleading indeed," he added, "if I left the impression that officials in Nashville had to be pressured all the way. There are so many worthy projects in Tennessee that those in charge must be discriminatory in distributing funds. There were those in the Department of Conservation who, from the outset, labored arduously for the establishing of a Pinson Mound State Park."

After the Inner Circle was formed, they enlisted the support of various organizations that were to become vitally helpful. Perhaps the first of these whose moral and financial support was essential was The Jackson Chamber of Commerce, through which the popular mind was reached. Naturally, the active West Tennessee Historical Society was sympathetic toward the movement as evidenced by its generous contribution. The year Dr. Nuckolls was president of the Tennessee Archaeological

Society, the group met in Jackson. Here, where it really counted, the park scheme was widely publicized and *The Tennessee Archaeologist* published Dr. Nuckolls' article on the Pinson Mounds, relating the known facts and current opinions.

"Though subsequent knowledge has now outdated this article," Dr. Nuckolls stated, "it was useful in awakening interest in the Pinson Mounds among amateur archaeologists throughout the state."

Its influence spread beyond state lines. Matthew W. Stirling, then the director of the Smithsonian Institute, wrote a strong letter favoring the park; he remembered Meyers' being a member of the Smithsonian. James A. Ford, nationally known and widely respected archaeologist, added his voice of authority from the American Museum of History in behalf of the idea. And shortly thereafter, the National Park Service designated the Pinson Mounds as a Registered National Historic Landmark, a gratifying distinction to those promoting the state park plan. The Department of Anthropology of The University of Tennessee accepted a contract to make extensive tests of the area. Local and regional newspapers gave the movement full coverage. Truly, things were looking good.

Many worked diligently toward the happy conclusion they felt would soon be forthcoming. Again it was not so much a task of overcoming opposition as it was to marshal opinion, sell the plan to those in authority who had the final say-so of state monies in competition with all the other needy projects demanding funds.

Almost coincidentally Old Stone Fort was established as a state park. It is to be noted that Tennessee has long lagged in its celebration of ancient Indian life. Though by no means the most tardy of the states, it has been low on the list of the historically conscious. Illinois, Indiana, and Ohio have taken the lead in conserving their mounds—Cahokia, Angel, Serpent. Hardly a step behind, Georgia established Etowah, Kolomoki, and Ocmulgee—three of as splendid monuments to the Mound Builders as exist. At Moundville, Alabama established Moundville State Park in 1933; this spot today boasts beauty as well as antiquity. The Emerald Mound in Mississippi became a unit in Natchez Trace Parkway in 1938. The Caddo Mounds in Arkansas were developed in 1965, the first in the state, though the great Toltec Mounds remain neglected. Glen Kizzia, speaking of the Caddo Mounds, said, "Since so many of our archaeological sites are being destroyed by highways, reservoirs, etc., I felt these should be preserved. This we began doing in the spring of 1965."

Somewhat belatedly, Tennessee—as well as Arkansas—is seeking to save whatever can still be salvaged from the remote past and to convert it into parks for people's pleasure and information. Much is yet to be done. But it will be done! Devoted to the cause, the Jackson group has persevered to partial achievement: recently, the sovereign state of Tennessee has placed the Pinson Mound area under supervision of the Department of Conservation which has jurisdiction over state parks. Thus, ere long, perchance, Dr. Nash may supervise excavations at the Pinson site; at least, those who care can now visualize their dream as near fulfillment. Those who are concerned believe their faith will be justified. Somehow they know that out of the mystic past some of the mystery and mist will dissolve, and artifacts from Pinson Mounds will reveal folkways of those ancient Mound Builders that lived and laughed and loved in Tennessee.

Index

General Index

Aboriginals, 173
American Museum of History, 307
Ames Plantation Complex, 281
Ancient Buried City, 187, 189, 289
Angel Mounds, 307
Anna Mounds, 281, 283
Archaic Civilization, 176, 241, 280
Artifacts, 107, ff.
Aztec Civilization, 143, 254

Bailey, Tobe, 305
Baptist, 62, 96
Barrow Pits, 148, 227
Basket making, 209, ff.
Baytown Plain body sherd, 279, 281
Bennett, John W., 152
Berryhill, G. H., 305
Bolivar, 99, 177
Bradbury, 13
Brown, Jim, 13
Burial Mounds, 228, 231, 232, 249, 251, 277, 283–286
Bynum Mounds

Caddo Mound, 256, 257, 308
Cahokia Mound, 147, 148, 152, 162, 169, 296, 300, 301, 303, 307
Cairo, 177
Caldwell and Doherty Surveys, 66
Campbell, John W., 104, 115
Catholic, 67

Ceremonial pipe, 233
Cherokee, 36, 42, 43, 44, 66, 303
Chickasaws, 36, 40, 43, 44, 66, 303
Choctaws, 36, 44, 302, 303
Christianity, 67
Chucalissa Museum, 126, ff.
Cisca, 112
Cisco, Bertie, 108, ff.
Cisco, City of, 101, 131, 296
Cisco, John Guy, 101, 105, 113, ff., 304
City of the Dead, 195, ff.
Coahoma group, 183
Corn Crib Mound, 234, 242, 243
Creek tribes, 302, 303
Cremation, 105
Crowley's Ridge, 89

Dancing, 177, 178
De Jarnette, David L., 228, 232, 301
De Soto, 97, 112, 297
Doak, Bill, 13
Donelson, John, 60
Dwellings, 96

Elizabethtown, 99
Emerald Mound, 281, ff., 300
Erosion, 295
Etowah Mounds, 97, 162, 164, 169, 281–283, 295, 296, 300, 308

Eva Mound, 177, 189
Excavation, 295

Festivals, 215
Fitzhugh, Henrietta, 98 ff.
Folktales, 66
Folkways, 69 ff.
Ford, James A., 307
Forked Deer, 14, 16, 18, 50, 51, 55, 89
Franquelin map, 112
French traders, 41

Gibson County, 66
God, 61
Graham, J. B., 271
Great Central Mound, 121, 182 ff., 228, 281, 301, 302
Great Spirit, 63
Greenville, 99
Grinder's Trace, 91
Guthe, Alfred K., 271, 290

Hargrove, John, 13
Hariot, Thomas, 200
Harpeth Mound, 75, 108, 177
Harris, Edward, 42, 48, 56, 60, 71
Harris, Walter B., 305
Harvey, Hugh, 305
Hatchie River, 89, 246
Hazlewood, Ben, 271
Head flattening, 219
Henderson, Richard E., 60
Henderson, Tom, 14, 43
Henderson, town of, 98
Holden, John, 95
Hopewell civilization, 251
Hopewellian culture, 181, 183
Hopewell Mounds, 252, 253
Housebuilding, 179, 203
Howard, M. H., 13, 18, 19

Iberville, 297
ignis fatuus, 63

Illinois-Hopewell, 280
Inman, W. O., 292, 293

Jackson Purchase, 88
Jackson-Shelby treaty, 65
Jackson, Tennessee, 13, 16, 95, 115
Jacob's staff, 54
Jefferson, Thomas, 60
Jennings, Jesse D., 230
Johnson, Seale, 173, 271, 304, 305
Jones, Colonel Rick, 102
Journeybread, 43, 48

Key Corner, 55, 62, 65
King's Mountain, Battle of, 28
Kizzia, Glen, 308
Kneberg, 108, 201, 203
Kolomoki Mound, 163, 300, 308

La Crosse, 135
Lake County, 66
Lancaster, Robert M., 271
Langford, Ben, 305
Lewis, Madeline K., 305
Lewis, Tom, 305
Lewis, William Tyrell, 40
Lexington, town of, 98
Long Hunters, 28, 43
Luxembourg Memoir, 292

Madison County, 65, 104
Mahon, Robert, 304, 305
maize, 200 ff.
Malone, James, 63
Mangum Mound, 285
Mapmakers, 63
Marksville-Hopewell, 280
Master Farmer period, 166, 167
Mayas, 143
McCorkle, Samuel, 13, 14, 17, 18, 19
McIver, Dick and Duncan, 13
McKnight, Thomas, 305
McLemore, Brooks, 305

Index

Memphis, 91
Methodist, 62, 96
Meyer, William E., 24, 106, 111 ff., 117, 122, 178, 235, 296, 301, 307
Miller, Carl, 106
Mississippian Culture, 181, 183, 280

Reelfoot, Chief, 66–70
Reelfoot country, 75 ff.
Reelfoot Mound, 169, 244, 297
Reelfoot river, 65
Revolutionary War, 60
Reynoldsbourg, 91
Robertson, James, 41–49, 59, 60, 174
Rutherford, Henry, 42–68, 71
Rutherford, James, 41–49, 59, 60, 174

Sacrifice of firstborn, 220
Saul family, 114
Saul's Mound, 139, 166
Schools, 94
Selmer, 102
Serpent Mound, 245, 307
Shawnee, 74
Shiloh, 177, 247
Short, Keith, 304
Shroeder, Gail, 152
Smith, George, 305
Smudge smoke, 49–51
Stewart, Turley, 292–294
Stirling, Matthew W., 116, 307
Stone River, 74
Succotash, 47

Sycamore Shoals, 43, 61, 72

Table showing size of Pinson Mounds, 118, 119
Taffy, 71 ff.
Tatum, William, 64
Taylor, Judge Tip, 304, 306
Temple Mounds, 132, 133, 154, 250
Tennessee State Park Commission, 173
Thomas, Lowell, 305
Tobacco, 247 ff.
Toltec Mound, 259, 261, 308
Traders, 78, 245 ff.
Trail of Tears, 68
Transylvania Company, 43, 74
Tupelo, 286
Tuscumbia, 88
Twin Mounds, 20, 23, 155, 166, 273, 280
Two Horses, 56–68

Washington, George, 60, 88
Watlington, 114
Wautauga, 61
Weaponry, 170–179
West, James, 271
Western District, 27, 35, 40–41, 55, 60, 171
Woodland Culture, 178, 181–183, 280, 304
Wyandottes, 74
Wycliffe, 192, 255

Yuchis, 112

Mounds in the Mist

Index of Mound Views

Mound 6 (Twin Mounds), view to Northeast, 20
Mound 6 (Twin Mounds), view to East, 20
Mound 6, View to East, 21
Mound 6, View to Northeast, 22
T.P. 3-F 1 (Twin Mounds), view to North, 22
T.P. 2 (Twin Mounds), view to Southeast, 23
T.P. 1 (Twin Mounds), view to South, 23
Mound 5, View to South, 24
Mound 12, View to South, 25
Mound 9, View to East, 26
Mound 9, View to East, 26
Mound 9, View to South, 27
Mound 9, View to East, 28
Mound 9, View to Northeast, 29
Mound 31, T.P. 1, View to East, 29
(Duck's Nest—T.P. 1), View to Northeast, 30
(Duck's Nest—T.P. 1), View to Southeast, 30
(Duck's Nest—T.P. 1 and Ext.), View to Northeast, 31
(Twin Mounds—T.P. 3 & 4), View to Northeast, 32

Mound 14, T.P. 1, F-10, 11, 12, & 13, View to Northeast, 32
Mound 14, T.P. 1, View to Southeast, 33
Mound 14, T.P. 1, F 44, 45, 47, View to Northeast, 33
Mound 14, T.P. 1, View to Northwest, 34
Mound 14, T.P. 1, View to Northwest, 35
Mound 14, T.P. 1, View to Northwest, 36
Mound 14, T.P. 1, View to Northeast, 37
Mound 14, T.P. 1, View to Northeast, 37
Mound 29, View to Southwest-South, 38
Mound 29, View to Southwest-South, 38
Mound 29, T.P. 1-0-4.5', View to East, 39
Mound 30, T.P. 4, View to North, 39
Mound 29, T.P. 3, View to South, 40